CHRISTIAN ATHEISM

How to Be a Real Materialist

SLAVOJ ŽIŽEK

BLOOMSBURY ACADEMIC
LONDON · NEW YORK · OXFORD · NEW DELHI · SYDNEY

BLOOMSBURY ACADEMIC
Bloomsbury Publishing Plc
50 Bedford Square, London, WC1B 3DP, UK
1385 Broadway, New York, NY 10018, USA
29 Earlsfort Terrace, Dublin 2, Ireland

BLOOMSBURY, BLOOMSBURY ACADEMIC and the Diana logo are
trademarks of Bloomsbury Publishing Plc

First published in Great Britain 2024
This book is published in 2024, and it does not reflect the attitudes of its time.

Cover design: Ben Anslow

Bloomsbury Publishing Plc does not have any control over, or responsibility
for, any third-party websites referred to or in this book. All internet addresses
given in this book were correct at the time of going to press. The author and
publisher regret any inconvenience caused if addresses have changed or sites
have ceased to exist, but can accept no responsibility for any such changes.

A catalogue record for this book is available from the British Library.

A catalog record for this book is available from the Library of Congress.

ISBN: PB: 978-1-3504-0931-6
        ePDF: 978-1-3504-0932-3
        eBook: 978-1-3504-0933-0

Typeset by RefineCatch Limited, Bungay, Suffolk
Printed and bound in Great Britain

To find out more about our authors and books visit www.bloomsbury.com
and sign up for our newsletters.

It may sound boring, but it is again to Jela.

CONTENTS

INTRODUCTION: WHY TRUE ATHEISM HAS TO BE INDIRECT

I am not only politically active but often also perceived as politically radioactive. The idea that political theology necessarily underpins radical emancipatory politics will for certain add to this perception.

The basic premise of atheists today is that materialism is a view which can be consistently exposed and defended in itself, in a positive line of argumentation without references to its opposite (religious beliefs). But what if the exact opposite is true? What if, if we want to be true atheists, we have to begin with a religious edifice and undermine it from within? To say that god is deceiving, evil, stupid, undead . . . is much more radical than to directly claim that there is no god: if we just posit that god doesn't exist, we open up the way towards its *de facto* survival as an idea(l) that should regulate our lives. In short, we open up the way to the moral suspension of the religious. Here one should be very precise: what one should reject unconditionally is the Kantian view of religion as a mere narrativization (presentation in the terms of our ordinary sensual reality) of the purity of moral Law. In this view, religion is for the ordinary majority who are not able to grasp the suprasensible moral Law in its own terms. What one should insist on, against this view, is that religion can in no way be reduced to this dimension, not only in the sense that it contains an ontological vision of reality (as created by God(s), regulated by divine providence, etc.), or in the sense of intense religious and/or mystical experience which reaches well beyond morality, but also in the immanent sense. Just recall how often, in the Old Testament, God appears unjust, cruel, and even frivolous (from the book of Job to the scene of imposing circumcision).[1] Is Christianity itself not unique among religions due to the fact that it cannot be accessed directly but only through another religion (Judaism)? Its sacred writing – the Bible – has two parts, the Old and the New Testament, so that one has to go through the first one to arrive at the second one.

Back in 1965, Theodor Adorno and Arnold Gehlen held a big debate (*Streitgespraech*, as they call it) on German public TV[2]; while the topic circulated around the tension between institutions and freedom, the actual focus of the debate was: is truth in principle accessible to all or just to the selected? The interesting paradox was that, although Adorno's writings are almost unreadable for those non-versed in Hegelian dialectics, he advocated the universal accessibility of truth, while Gehlen (whose writings are much easier to follow) claims that truth is accessible only to the privileged few since it is too dangerous and disruptive for the crowd of ordinary people. If the problem is formulated in these general terms, I am on the side of Adorno: truth is in principle accessible to all, but it demands a great effort of which many are not able. However, I would like to advocate a much more precise thesis. In an abstract sense of scientific "objective knowledge" our knowledge is of course limited – for the large majority of us it is impossible to understand quantum physics and higher mathematics. But what is accessible to us all is the elementary move from our experience of lack (our imperfect universe, the limit of our knowledge) to redoubling this lack, i.e., locating it in to the Other itself which becomes a "barred" inconsistent Other. Hegel's notion of God provides the exemplary case of such a redoubling: the gap that separates us, finite and frail sinful humans, from God, is immanent to God himself, it separates God from himself, making him inconsistent and imperfect, inscribing an antagonism into his very heart. This redoubling of the lack, this "ontologization" of our epistemological limitation, is at the core of Hegel's absolute knowing, it signals the moment when Enlightenment is brought to its end.

All chapters are interventions in an ongoing debate. In (1) I propose my own solution to the dialogue between Lorenzo Chiesa and Adrian Johnston about psychoanalysis and atheism; in (2) I reply to my Buddhist critics who claim that I miss the proximity between Lacan and Buddhism; in (3) I deal with conflicting philosophical interpretations of quantum mechanics; in (4) I engage in a dialogue with Alenka Zupančič about Antigone, the sacred and the obscene, against the humanist reading of Antigone's act as a demand for inclusion of all marginalized minorities into the human universality; in (5) I try to dispel some misunderstandings that blur the actual social and subjective effects of Artificial Intelligence; last but not least, in (6), I promote my thesis on the need for theology in radical politics against the standard advocacy of materialist politics of emancipation. In spite of this dialogical character, the book follows a very precise line: from the basic determination of my Christian atheism, through outlining the difference between my atheism and Buddhist agnosticism, asserting the deep atheism of quantum physics, an exploration of the triangle of divine, sacred and obscene, and a materialist critique of the anti-Christian spiritual reading of Artificial Intelligence, up to an explanation of why emancipatory politics doesn't work without theological (or, more precisely, theosophical) dimension.[3]

So let me provide a clear and condensed description of this book's basic premises. I try to bring together three recurrent themes of my work which, that's my hypothesis, turn out to be three aspects of the same nucleus: the atheist core of Christianity; ontological implications of quantum mechanics; transcendental/ontology parallax.

- What makes Christianity unique is how it overcomes the gap that separates humans from god: not by way of humans elevating themselves to god through pious activity and meditation and thus leaving behind their sinful lives, but by way of transposing this gap that separates them from god into god himself. What dies on the cross is not an earthly representative or messenger of god but, as Hegel put it, the god of the beyond itself, so that the dead Christ returns as Holy Ghost which is nothing more than the egalitarian community of believers (as Paul put it, for Christians, there are no women and men, no Greeks and Jews, they are all united in Christ). This community is free in the radical sense of being abandoned to itself, with no transcendent higher power guaranteeing its fate. It is in this sense that god gives us freedom – by way of erasing itself out of the picture.

- The ontological implications of quantum mechanics point – not towards a deceiving god, as Einstein thought, but – towards a god who is himself deceived. "God" stands here for the big Other, (for Einstein) the harmonious order of laws of nature which are eternal and immutable, allowing no exception, part of objective reality that exists independently of us (human observers). The basic insight of quantum mechanics is, on the contrary, that there is a domain (whose status is disputed) of quantum waves where chance is irreducible, where things happen which can be retroactively annihilated, etc. – in short, a domain that escapes the control of the (divine) big Other (information travels faster than light, etc.). When this insight was combined with the idea that quantum oscillations collapse into our ordinary reality only when an observer perceives and/or measures them, this is usually read as an argument against materialism, against the view that reality exists out there independently of us – some even propose god as the ultimate observer which constitutes reality. My thesis is, however, that Einstein was right in designating the big Other of natural laws as "divine" – a truly radical materialism does not reduce reality to what we perceive as our everyday external world, it allows for a domain which violates natural laws.

- The biggest cut in the history of philosophy takes place with Kant's transcendental revolution. Till Kant, philosophy (no matter how sceptic) was dealing with the ontological dimension in the simple sense of the nature of reality: what counts as reality, can we know it, how is this reality structured, is it only material or also, even primarily, spiritual, etc. With Kant, reality is not simply given, waiting out there to be discovered by us, it is "transcendentally constituted" by the structure of categories through which we apprehend it. After Kant, this transcendental dimension is historicized: every epoch has its own way of perceiving reality and acting in it. For example, modern science emerged once reality was perceived as the space of external material existence regulated by its laws, and reality was thus strictly separated from our subjective feeling and projections of meaning. Parallax means here that the two approaches are irreducible to each other and simultaneously imply each other: we can investigate reality as an object and explain its evolution, up to the emergence of human life on earth, but in doing this, we already approach reality in a certain way (through evolutionary theory and its concepts) which cannot be deduced from its object but is always-already presupposed (we presuppose that nature is regulated by complex causal links, etc.).

The book brings together these three topics into a project of "Christian atheism": the space for the experience of the "divine" is the gap that forever separates the transcendental from the objective-realist approach, but this "divine" dimension refers to the experience of radical negativity (what mystics and Hegel called "night of the world") which precludes any theology focused on a positive figure of god, even if this figure of god is radically secularized in modern scientific naturalism. In Christianity, this gap registers the absence of god (its "death") which grounds the Holy Ghost. And, last but not least, the dimension of radical negativity also holds open the space for every emancipatory politics which takes itself seriously, i.e., which reaches beyond the continuity of historical progress and introduces a radical cut that changes the very measures of progress.

The Self-Destruction of the West

But, as we learned from Hegel, moments of a dialectical process can be counted as three or as four – and the fourth missing moment is here politics, of course. (The political dimension is not limited to the final chapter, it runs as an undercurrent through the entire book, popping up even in its most philosophical parts.) This brings us back to my political radioactivity – to resume it, let me begin by Jean-Claude Milner's claim[4] that what we call "the West" is today a confederation under the US hegemony; the US reigns over us also intellectually, but here "one has to accept a paradox: the US-American domination in the intellectual domain expresses itself in the discourses of dissent and protest and not in the discourses of order." Global university teaches us

to refuse the economic, political, and ideological functioning of the western order in part or entirely. Inequality plays the role of an axiom, from which all ultimate criticism derives. Depending on the various situations, one will privilege this or that specific form of general inequality: colonial oppression, cultural appropriation, the primacy of white culture, the patriarchy, the conflicts of gender and so on.

Remi Adekoya points out that research uncovered a strange fact: when the voters were asked which value they appreciate most, in the developed West the large majority chose equality, while in sub-Saharan Africa, the large majority largely ignored equality and put at the first place wealth (independently of how it was acquired, even if it was through corruption). This result makes sense: the developed West can afford to prioritize equality (at the level of ideological self-perception), while the main worry among the poor majority in sub-Saharan Africa is how to survive and leave devastating poverty behind.[5] There is a further paradox at work here: this struggle against inequality is self-destructive insofar as it undercuts its own foundation, and is thus unable to present itself as a project for positive global change:

> Precisely because the cultural heritage of the West cannot free itself from the inequalities that made its existence possible, past denouncers of inequality are themselves considered to benefit from one or another previously unrecognized inequality. . . . all the revolutionary movements and the notions of the revolution themselves are subject to suspicion now, simply because they belong to the long line of dead white males.

It is crucial to note that the new Right and the Woke Left share this self-destructive stance. In late May 2023, the Davis School District north of Salt Lake City removed the Bible from its elementary and middle schools while keeping it in high schools after a committee reviewed the scripture in response to the Utah Parents United complaint, dated December 11 2022, which said: "You'll no doubt find that the Bible (under state law) has 'no serious values for minors' because it's pornographic by our new definition."[6] Is this just a case of Mormons against Christians? No: on June 2 2023, a complaint was submitted about the signature scripture of the predominant faith in Utah, The Church of Jesus Christ of Latter-day Saints: district spokesperson Chris Williams confirmed that someone filed a review request for the Book of Mormon. Which political-ideological option is behind this demand? Is it the Woke Left (exercising an ironic revenge against the Rightists banning courses and books on US history, Black Lives Matter, LGBT+, etc.), or is it the radicalized Right itself which (quite consequently) applied their criteria of family values to their own founding texts? Ultimately it doesn't matter – what we should note is rather the fact that the same logic of prohibiting (or rewriting, at least) classic texts got hold of the new Right as well as on the Woke Left, confirming the justified suspicion that, in spite of their strong ideological animosity, they often formally proceed in the same way. While the Woke Left systematically destroys its own foundation (the European emancipatory tradition), the Right finally gathered the courage to question the obscenity of its own tradition. In an act of cruel irony, the Western democratic tradition which usually praises itself for including self-criticism (democracy has flaws, but also includes striving to overcome its flaws . . .), now brought this self-critical stance to extreme – "equality" is a mask of its opposite, etc., so that all that remains is the tendency towards self-destruction.

But there is a difference between the Western anti-Western discourse and the anti-Western discourse coming from outside: "while an anti-Western discourse is deployed within the West (and the West takes pride in this), another anti-western discourse is held outside of the West. Except that the first takes inequality for a fault, which one does not have the moral right to take advantage of; the second on the contrary sees in the inequality a virtue, on the condition that it is oriented in one's favor. Consequently, the proponents of the second anti-western discourse see the first as an indication of the enemy's decadence. They do not hide their contempt."

And their contempt is fully justified: the result of the Western anti-Western discourse is what one might expect: the more Western liberal Leftists probe their own guilt, the more they are accused by Muslim fundamentalists of being hypocrites who try to conceal their hatred of Islam. Such a paradigm perfectly reproduces the paradox of the superego: the more you obey what the pseudo-moral agency demands of you, the more guilty you are: it is as if the more you tolerate Islam, the stronger its pressure on you will be. One can be sure that the same holds true for the influx of refugees: the more Western Europe is open to them, the more it will be made to feel guilty that it failed to accept even more of them – by definition it can never accept enough of them. The more tolerance one displays towards the non-Western ways of life, the more one will be made to feel guilt for not practising enough tolerance.

The woke radical reply to this is: the non-Western critics are right, the Western self-humiliation is fake, the non-Western critics are right to insist that whatever the West concedes to them, "this is not that," we retain our superior frame and expect them to integrate – but why should they? The problem is, of course, that what the non-Western critics expect is, to put it brutally and directly, that the West renounces its way of life. The alternative here is: will, as the final result of the Western anti-Western critical stance, the West succeed in self-destroying itself (socially, economically) as a civilization, or will it succeed to combine self-defeating ideology with economic superiority?

Milner is right: there is no big paradox in the fact that the self-denigrating critical mode is the best ideological stance for making it sure there will be no revolutionary threat to the existing order. However, one should supplement his claim with a renewal of (fake, but nonetheless actual) revolutionary stance of the new populist Right: its entire rhetoric is based on the "revolutionary" claim that the new elites (big corporations, academic and cultural elites, government services) should be destroyed, with violence if needed. In Varoufakis's terms, they propose a class war against our new feudal masters – the worst nightmare is here the possibility of a pact between the Western populist Right and the anti-Western authoritarians.

In my critical remarks on MeToo as ideology, I refer to Tarana Burke, a black woman who created the MeToo campaign more than a decade ago; she observed in a recent critical note that in the years since the movement began, it deployed an unwavering obsession with the perpetrators – a cyclical circus of accusations, culpability and indiscretions: "We are working diligently so that the popular narrative about MeToo shifts from what it is. We have to shift the narrative that it's a gender war, that it's anti-male, that it's men against women, that it's only for a certain type of person – that it's for white, cisgender, heterosexual, famous women."[7] In short, one should struggle to re-focus MeToo onto the daily suffering of millions of ordinary working women and housewives . . .

At this point, some critics have accused me of advocating a simple move from harassment in our behaviour and language to "real" socio-economic problems, (correctly) pointing out that the thick texture of behaviour and ways of speaking is the very medium of the reproduction of ideology, plus that what counts as "real problems" is never a matter of direct insight but is always defined by the symbolic network, i.e., it is the result of a struggle for hegemony. I thus consider the above-mentioned reproach against me a bad joke: I all the time insist on the texture of unwritten rules as the medium in which racism and sexism reproduce themselves. To put it in more theoretical terms, the big implication of "structuralist" theories (from Levi-Strauss and Althusser up to Lacan) is that ideological superstructure has its own infrastructure, its own (unconscious) network of rules and practices which sustain its functioning. However, do such "problematic" (for some) positions of mine indicate that, in the course of the last decades, I changed my position? A critic of mine recently insisted on the "contrast between (my) writing at this point (1997 when he was in his late 40s) and (my) more recent transition into a post-left figure" – he begins with approvingly quoting a passage from my *Plague of Fantasies* and then adding his comment:

> If racist attitudes were to be rendered acceptable for the mainstream ideologico-political discourse, this would radically shift the balance of the entire ideological hegemony . . . Today, in the face of the emergence of new racism and sexism, the strategy should be to make such enunciations unutterable, so that anyone relying on them automatically disqualifies himself (like, in our universe, those who refer approvingly to Fascism). One should emphatically not discuss 'how many people really died in Auschwitz', what are 'the good aspects of slavery', 'the necessity of cutting down on workers' collective rights', and so on; the position here should be quite unashamedly 'dogmatic' and 'terrorist'; this is not a matter for 'open, rational, democratic discussion'.

> *Plague*, p. 38

Well said. Much as for example one shouldn't engage in conversations about whether trans women are "really" women. In fact Žižek in his late 40s holds that "the measure of ideologico-political 'regression' is the extent to which such propositions become acceptable in public discourse. Would he therefore see his older self as a symptom of such regression?"[8]

My counterpoint is here an obvious one: can we really put woke and trans demands into the series of progressive achievements, so that the changes in our daily language (the primacy of "they," etc.) are just the next step in the long struggle against sexism? My answer is a resounding NO: the changes advocated and enforced by trans- and woke-ideology are themselves largely "regressive," they are attempts of the reigning ideology to appropriate (and take the critical edge off) new protest movements. There is thus an element of truth in the well-known Rightist diagnosis that Europe today presents a unique case of deliberate self-destruction – it is obsessed with the fear to assert its identity, plagued by an infinite responsibility for most of the horrors in the world, fully enjoying its self-culpabilization, behaving as if it is its highest duty to accept all who want to emigrate to it, reacting to the hatred of Europe by many immigrants with the claim that it is Europe itself which is guilty of this hatred because it is not ready to fully integrate them . . . There is, of course, some truth in all this; however, the tendency to self-destruction is obviously the obverse of the fact that Europe is no longer able to remain faithful to its greatest achievement, the Leftist project of global emancipation – it is as if all that remained is self-criticism, with no positive project to ground it. So it is easy to see what awaits us at the end of this line of reasoning: a self-reflexive turn by means of which *emancipation itself will be denounced as a Euro-centric project.*[9]

With regard to slavery, one should note that it existed throughout "civilized" human history in Europe, Asia, Africa and Americas, and that it continues to exist in new forms – the white Western nations enslaving Blacks is not its most massive form. What one should add, however, is that the Western European nations (which are today viewed as the main agents of enslaving – when we hear the word "slavery," our first association is "yes, whites owning black slaves") were the only ones which gradually enforced the legal *prohibition* of slavery. To cut it short, slavery is universal, what characterizes the West is that it set in motion the movement to prohibit it – the exact opposite of the common perception.

The title of an essay on my work – "Pacifist Pluralism versus Militant Truth: Christianity at the Service of Revolution"[10] – renders perfectly my core of my anti-Woke Christian stance: in contrast to knowledge which relies on an impartial "objective" stance of its bearer, truth is never neutral, it is by definition militant, subjectively engaged. This in no way implies any kind of dogmatism – the true dogmatism is embodied in an "objective" balanced view, no matter how relativized and historically-conditioned this view claim to be. When I fight for emancipation, the Truth I am fighting for is absolute, although it is obviously the Truth of a specific historical situation. Here the true spirit of Christianity is to be opposed to wokenness: in spite of the appearance of promoting tolerant diversity, wokeness is in its mode of functioning extremely exclusionary, while the Christian engagement not only openly admits its subjective bias but makes it a condition of its Truth. And my wager is clear here: only the stance of what I refer to as Christian atheism can save the Western legacy from its self-destruction while maintaining its self-critical edge.

Anti-Semitism and Intersectionality

This brings us to another radioactive feature of mine: my critique of certain critiques of anti-Semitism which also mitigate the critical edge of emancipatory, universalism: they denigrate the universal dimension of Judaism precisely when they enjoin us to recognize its unique status of anti-Semitism. On May 14 2023 the European Jewish Association's (EJA) annual conference took place in Porto, Portugal. It adopted a motion

> calling for antisemitism to be separated from other forms of hate and urging other Jewish groups to reject 'intersectionality,' a theoretical framework that separates groups into 'oppressed' and 'privileged.' 'Antisemitism is unique and must be treated as such,' according to the motion, which notes that unlike other hatreds, it is 'state-sanctioned in many countries,' 'given cover by the United Nations' and denied to be racism by other groups targeted by hatred.[11]

The key to these claims is provided by the presumed link between three notions: the unique character of anti-Semitism, intersectionality, the opposition between the oppressed and the privileged. Why is intersectionality dismissed as "a theoretical framework that separates groups into 'oppressed' and 'privileged'," and why is this problematic from the Jewish standpoint? Intersectionality is a very useful notion in social theory and practical analysis: when dealing with an oppressed group, we discover that it can be oppressed (or privileged) at multiple intersection levels – let's shamelessly quote a Wikipedia definition (because, let's face it, it's the definition most people will be using!):

Intersectionality is an analytical framework for understanding how a person's various social and political identities combine to create different modes of discrimination and privilege. Intersectionality identifies multiple factors of advantage and disadvantage. Examples of these factors include gender, caste, sex, race, ethnicity, class, religion, education, wealth, disability, weight, age, and physical appearance. These intersecting and overlapping social identities may be both empowering and oppressing.[12]

Consider a low-income Black lesbian: she is at a triple disadvantage almost anywhere in the world. In addition, we are never dealing just with a mechanical combination of these factors of (dis)advantage. The anti-Semitic figure of the "Jew" combines features of religion, ethnicity, sexuality, education, wealth and physical appearance. To be stigmatized as a "Jew" entails the attribution of a series of other features (they know how to speculate with money, they dogmatically stick to their religious rules, they are lazy and like to exploit others, they don't wash enough . . .). The upshot of intersectional analysis is that all individuals experience unique forms of oppression or privilege by dint of the makeup of their identities. Why, then, do those who insist on the uniqueness of anti-Semitism reject intersectionality?

The oppression faced by Jews in developed Western countries nowadays is somewhat more ambiguous, because the perception is that Jews occupy positions of privilege (economically, culturally, politically), and the association of the Jews with wealth and culture ("Hollywood is Jewish") in the public imagination is itself a source of classic anti-Semitic tropes. The EJA worries that this combination of oppression and privileges makes anti-Semitism just another form of racial hatred, not only comparable to others but even less strong weighed alongside other modes of oppression. When we apply an intersectional lens, the hatred for "the Jew" becomes just another minor case in the broader taxonomy of hatreds. Is this fear justified?

The EJA is right in its insistence that there is something exceptional about anti-Semitism. It is not like other racisms: its aim is not to subordinate the Jews but to exterminate them because they are not perceived as lower foreigners but as our secret Masters. The Holocaust is not the same as the destruction of civilizations in the history of colonialism, it is a unique phenomenon of industrially-organized annihilation. But it is the very coupling of "oppressed" and "privileged" which provides the key to understanding anti-Semitism, at least in its modern form. Under Fascism, "the Jew" served as the external intruder who could be blamed for corruption, disorder and exploitation. Projecting the conflict between the "oppressed" and the "privileged" onto a scapegoat can distract people's attention from the fact that such struggles are, in fact, intrinsic to their own political and economic order. The fact that many Jews are "privileged" (in the sense of their wealth, education and political influence) is thus *the very resource* of anti-Semitism: being perceived as privileged makes them a target of social hatred.

Problems arise when one tries to use the exceptional status of anti-Semitism to support a double standard, or to prohibit any critical analysis of the privileges that Jews, on average, enjoy. The title of a dialogue on anti-Semitism and Boycott, Divestment, Sanctions (BDS) in *Der Spiegel* is: "Wer Antisemit ist, bestimmt der Jude und nicht der potenzielle Antisemit"[13] ("Who is an anti-Semite determines the Jew and not the potential anti-Semite"). OK, but should then not the same also hold for Palestinians on the West Bank who should determine who is stealing their land and depriving them of elementary rights? Isn't apartheid sanctioned also in Israel? This is what the motion of the European Jewish Association refuses to accomplish.

More than that, the EJA's stance relies on its own intersectional framework. Any analysis of the privileged positions held by some Jews is immediately denounced as anti-Semitic, and even critiques of capitalism are rejected on the same grounds, owing to the association between "Jewishness" and "rich capitalists." The good old Marxist thesis that anti-Semitism is a primitive distorted version of anti-capitalism is thus turned around: anti-capitalism is a mask of anti-Semitism. But if the implication is that Jewishness is both exceptional and inextricably bound up with capitalism, aren't we just left with an age-old anti-Semitic trope? Do we not directly provoke the poor and oppressed to blame the Jews for their misfortunes? One should thus reject the EJA stance not because of some obscene need for "balance" between different forms of racism but on behalf of the very struggle against anti-Semitism.

However, the terrible situation in Israel can also give us a reason to hope. Something drastically changed in Israel itself and abroad, even in the US, the most pro-Israel state: even the people who were till now ready to tolerate everything that Israel does are now openly attacking it, and an awareness is rising that things cannot go on as they were till now. Israel presented itself as the only liberal democracy surrounded by authoritarian and fundamentalist Arab regimes, but what it is doing now is getting more and more similar to the worst of hard Arab regimes. The next step is already on the horizon: what Israeli hard-liners want is to turn into second-class citizens their own reformist secularized Jews . . .

This is how one should understand the motto that only a catastrophe can save us: maybe the authoritarian turn in Israel will trigger a strong counter-wave that will defeat it. In the case of Israel, this means that only the publicly asserted solidarity of the three religions of the book (Judaism, Christianity, Islam) can save the emancipatory core of Judaism – at the spiritual level, the greatest victim of the aggressive Zionism will be Jews themselves. What Christian atheism renders possible here is not the overcoming of the existing religions – on the contrary, it opens up the space for a spiritual bond which enables each of them to flourish freely. Here atheism plays a key role: the common space in which different religions can thrive is not some vague general spirituality but atheism which renders meaningless the struggle between particular religions.

The Importance of Seeing All Six Feet

This brings us back to intersectionality, this time the intersectionality of religions themselves – there is a (not too) vulgar joke which perfectly renders its point. The joke begins with a wife and her lover in bed; suddenly, they hear her husband unexpectedly coming home and walking up the stairs, heavily drunk. The lover gets into a panic, but the wife calms him down: "My husband is so drunk, he will not even notice that there is another man in the bed, so just stay where you are!" And, as she predicts, the husband, barely able to walk, just falls onto the bed. An hour or so later, he opens the eyes and says to his wife: "Darling, am I so drunk that I can't even count what I see? It seems to me there are six legs at the bottom of our bed!" The wife says soothingly: "Don't worry! Just stand up, walk to the doors in front of the bed and take a clear look!" The husband does this and exclaims: "You are right, there are only four legs! So I can go back and fall asleep again calmly . . ."

This joke may be vulgar, but it nonetheless involves an interesting formal structure homologous to Jacques Lacan's joke "I have three brothers, Paul, Robert, and myself." When fully drunk, the husband included himself into the series, counting himself as one of his brothers; after he was able to adopt a minimally sober external glance, he saw the he has only two brothers (i.e., he excluded himself from the series). What we would expect is that one sees the whole situation clearly when one observes it from the outside, from a safe distance, while when one is immersed into a situation one gets blind for its key dimension, for its horizon that delimitates it; in our joke, however, it is the external position which makes you blind, while you see the truth when you are caught in it (incidentally, the same goes for psychoanalysis and Marxism).

More precisely, the husband doesn't just exclude himself: his exclusion (standing by the door out of the bed) leads to the wrong inclusion, it makes him confuse the lover's legs with his own legs: he counts the lover's legs in the bed as his own, so he returns satisfied to the bed, and the lesson he gets is a very cruel one: he condones his wife making love with another man as his own act . . . The irony is, of course, that, in his more sober state, the husband acts as an idiot by way of excluding himself from the series: an unexpected version of *in vino veritas*. The libidinal truth of such situations is that, even when only the sexual couple is in a bed, there are six legs (the additional two legs standing for the presence of a third agency) – the Lacanian function of the "plus-One" is always operative. Here we should evoke the impossible trident (also known as impossible fork or devil's tuning fork), the drawing of an impossible object (undecipherable figure), a kind of an optical illusion: it appears to have three cylindrical prongs at one end which then mysteriously transform into two rectangular prongs at the other end (see Fig. 1)[14]:

In our case of the drunk husband, when he is in the bed (blue domain) and looks down, he sees three pairs of legs, but when he steps out (into the green domain) and looks at the bed, he sees two pairs of legs . . .

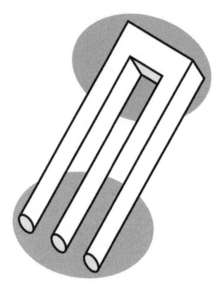

Figure I.1

We should not be afraid to go to the (obscene) end in this direction and imagine the same scene with "virgin" Mary and her husband Joseph. While Joseph is on a drinking binge, Mary has fun in their bed with (the person acting as) the Holy Spirit; Joseph returns home early and crawls to their bed; when he awakens a little bit later, he sees six feet at the bed's bottom, and then the same story as in our joke goes on – looking at the bed from the door, he sees only two pairs of feet and mistakes the Holy Spirit's pair for his own . . .

Does something like this not happen when we support Ukraine but ignore the struggle for justice in Ukraine itself? We turn a blind eye to how the Ukrainian struggle is monopolized by the predominant clique of oligarchs, so we shouldn't be surprised if the post-war Ukraine will be similar to the pre-war corrupted oligarchy colonized by big Western corporations controlling the best land and natural resources – in short, we suffer in the terrible war, but we are blind for the fact that our gains will be appropriated by our enemies, exactly like the drunk husband who condones his wife making love with another man as his own act. How to avoid falling into this trap? On 20–22 June 2023, there was a series of meetings in London coordinated by *"Europe, a Patient"* association, a pan-European, cross-partisan initiative, with the aim "to protect Ukrainian communities from exploitation after what they have already been through in this war." Rev. Rowan Williams, Rabbi Wittenberg and Ukrainian NGOs appealed for green, just and citizens-lead recovery:

> The challenge for Ukraine and all our international partners is to prevent creating the new breed of oligarchs in the process of post-war reconstruction. . . . Ukrainian people have suffered for too long at the hands of the fossil fuel industry, which are still financing the Russian war machine.[15]

Initiatives like this one are needed more than ever today because they unite support of Ukrainian defence with ecological concerns and struggle for social justice. Far from being megalomaniac, such combination of goals is the only realistic option: we can only support Ukraine if we fight a fossil fuel industry which relies on Russian oil, and if we simultaneously fight for social justice. The combination of different struggles is enforced by circumstances themselves. The destruction of the Kherson dam in early June (with flooded villages and mines floating in water) brought together war and ecological destruction: the destruction of the environment was consciously used as a military strategy. In itself, this was not something new: already in the Vietnam war, the US army sprayed large forest areas with poisonous gases that defoliated the trees (in order to prevent the Vietcong units hiding in the foliage). What makes the destruction of the Kherson dam worse is that it happened in an era when all sides pay lip service to the protection of environment – we are forced to do this because the threat to our environment is felt more and more in our daily lives. In the first week of June 2023, New York was caught in brown smoke (caused by forest fires in Canada), with people advised to stay indoors and to wear masks if they have to go outside – nothing new for large parts of the so-called Third World:

> India, Nigeria, Indonesia, the Philippines, Pakistan, Afghanistan, Papua New Guinea, Sudan, Niger, Burkina Faso, Mali and central America face extreme risk. Weather events such as massive floods and intensified cyclones and hurricanes will keep hammering

countries such as Mozambique, Zimbabwe, Haiti and Myanmar. Many people will have to move or die. As the impacts of our consumption kick in thousands of miles away, and people come to our borders desperate for refuge from a crisis they played almost no role in causing – a crisis that might involve real floods and real droughts – the same political forces announce, without a trace of irony, that we are being 'flooded' or 'sucked dry' by refugees, and millions rally to their call to seal our borders.[16]

So why do Western countries, while paying lip service to these problems, continue to cancel measures designed to limit climate breakdown? (Let's just mention two cases from the US: "legislators in Texas are waging war on renewable energy, while a proposed law in Ohio lists climate policies as a 'controversial belief or policy' in which universities are forbidden to 'inculcate' their students."[17]) To claim that "hard-right and far-right politics are the defensive wall erected by oligarchs to protect their economic interests"[18] is all too simple: ignoring the full scope of the threat to our environment is not limited just to the far Right and/or to big corporations, it includes Leftist conspiracy theories. Conspiracy theorists like to play with alternate history scenarios: what if . . . (the US were not to join the UK and attack Germany in the Second World War; the US were not to attack and occupy Iraq; the West were not to support Ukraine in its struggle against Russian aggression)? These scenarios are not emancipatory dreams about failed revolutions but, on the contrary, profoundly reactionary dreams of making a compromise with brutal authoritarian regimes and thus maintain peace.

To understand the "pacifist" opposition to the NATO military machine, we should return to the situation at the beginning of the Second World War when a similar Right-and-Left stance opposed the entry of the US into the war. The reasons listed were uncannily similar to the reason of today's "pacifists": why should the US get involved in a far-away war that doesn't concern it; Rightist discreet sympathy for Germany (no less discreetly supported by Germany); due to the Ribbentrop-Molotov pact, the Leftists opposed the war till the German attack on the USSR; the peace offer of Germany to the UK in the Summer of 1940 which was perceived by many as very generous; the worry that the entry of the US into the war would serve the vast industrial-military complex. This reasoning contains a grain of truth, as all good lies do: it is true that the US left the big depression behind only in the course of the Second World War; there are signs that Germany sincerely wanted peace with Great Britain in 1940 (recall the surprising flight of Rudolf Hess to England at that time to plea for the peace with Germany).

The most elaborated version of this line of thought was given in 2009 by Patrick J. Buchanan who argues that, if Churchill had accepted Hitler's peace offer of 1940, the severity of the Holocaust would have been greatly reduced. (The – often fully justified – critique of Churchill is also shared by the Left: the two recent radical critics of Churchill are David Irving, the Rightist with sympathies for the Nazi Germany, and Tariq Ali, a radical Leftist . . .) Endorsing the concept of Western betrayal, Buchanan accuses Churchill and Roosevelt of turning over Eastern Europe to the Soviet Union at the Tehran Conference and the Yalta Conference. Just as Churchill led the British Empire to ruin by causing unnecessary wars with Germany twice, Bush led the United States to ruin by following Churchill's example in involving the United States in an unnecessary war in Iraq, and he passed out guarantees to scores of nations in which the United States has no vital interests, which placed his country in a position with insufficient resources to fulfil its promises.[19] What we often hear today is a new variation on this Buchanan motif: the disintegration of the Soviet Union and the ensuing economic decay of post-Soviet states was experienced like a new Versailles treaty and gave birth to the easily predictable desire for revenge. Exactly like Hitler in 1940, Putin repeatedly offered peace to Ukraine; in the first years of his reign, he even proposed that Russia should join NATO . . . Seductive as this line of reasoning may sound (to some, at least), it should be rejected in exactly the same way Fascism has to be fought.

The problem is that today the hegemonic ideology not only prevents the urgently needed combination of struggles (seeing all six feet, in the terms of our joke); as we have just seen, it even imposes its own false combination in the guise of new conspiracy theories shared by the populist Right and parts of the Left. This new Right/Left alliance denounces eco-panic and "green politics" as a ruse of the big corporations to impose new limitations to the ordinary working people; it rejects helping Ukraine since the military aid serves the NATO industrial-military complex; it denounced anti-Covid measures as an instrument of disciplining the population . . . In a model case of denial, the biggest threat we are confronting today (including the reports of the traces of alien landings) are dismissed as a ploy of the big corporate capital in conjunction with state apparatuses. The message of such a denial is, of course, overtly optimistic, it gives us hope: the return to old normality is easy, we don't have to fight the new dangers, all we have to do is dismiss the threats, i.e., continue to act as if they don't exist. The proliferation of such denials is the main reason of the sad fact that we live in an era of "democratic recession":

> Authoritarianism is on the rise despite the liberal prediction that the spread of free markets would result in more democracy – that's because capitalism will always defend social hierarchies against the threat of economic equality.[20]

One has to complicate further this claim: the threat to democracy comes also from the false populist resistance to corporate capitalism. This is why the way out of this predicament resides not just in desperately clinging to multi-party liberal democracy – what is needed are new forms of building large social consensus and of establishing a more active link between political parties and civil society. The opposition of liberal democracy and new populists is not the true one; however, this in no way entails that the Trump–Putin camp is better than liberal democracy (in the same sense that it is wrong to have sympathy for Hitler because liberal democracy and fascism are not the true opposites). We should mobilize here the distance that separates tactic from strategy: strategically, liberal democracy is our ultimate enemy, but at the tactical level, we should fight with liberal democracy against new populists – in the same way that Communists fought with Western "imperialist" democracies against Fascism in the Second World War, knowing very well that imperialism is their ultimate enemy.

*

Did we not drift far away from our starting point, the notion of Christian atheism, and get lost in a mixture of political comments? No, because these comments demonstrate precisely how Christian atheism works as a political practice. Raffaele Nogaro (a priest from Rome who was 98 in 2022) claimed that Jesus is the "New Man" who loves everyone without distinction of person, whatever his culture, the colour of his skin, his religion or the depth of his atheism – everyone is asked by Jesus the same question: "Who do you say that I am?"[21] Note that for Nogaro, Christ is not a figure of authority telling people what they are: he is asking them about what they are saying that He is. And one should not take this as a cheap rhetorical trick in the sense of "I know who I am, the son of God, I just want to check if you know this." Christ is aware that, in some way, his very existence is at stake not only in what and how people are talking about him, but above all in how they act (or don't act) in society. Each of us has to give a reply to Jesus' question from one's existential depth, and then enact this reply.

1
LET A RELIGION DEPLETE ITSELF

Who Can't Handle the Truth?

Sometimes, even the lowest blockbuster trash purveys a useful lesson. Kevin Costner's *Postman* (otherwise a dismal failure) focuses on the structural necessity of an ideological Lie as the condition to reconstitute the social link – the film's premise is that the only way to recreate the Restored USA after the global catastrophe is by pretending that the Federal Government *still exists*, by acting AS IF it exists, so that people start to believe in it and behave accordingly, and the Lie becomes Truth (the hero sets in motion the reconstitution of the USA by starting to deliver mail as if he acts on behalf of the US postal system). This brings us to the paradoxical temporality of truth.

Most of us know well the culminating moment of *A Few Good Men* (Rob Reiner, 1992) when Tom Cruise addresses Jack Nicholson with "I want the truth!", and Nicholson shouts back: "You can't handle the truth!" This reply is more ambiguous than it may appear: it should not be taken as simply claiming that most of us are too weak to handle the brutal reality of things. We thus have to get rid of the metaphor of the Real as the hard core of reality (the way things "really are in themselves") accessible to us only through multiple lenses of how we symbolize reality, of how we construct it through our fantasies and cognitive biases. In the opposition between reality ("hard facts") and fantasies (illusions, symbolic constructs), the Real is on the side of illusions and fantasies: the Real, of course, by definition resists full symbolization, but it is at the same time an excess generated by the process of symbolization itself. Without symbolization, there is no Real, there is just a flat stupidity of what is there. Another (perhaps the ultimate) example: if someone were to ask a witness about the truth of the Holocaust, and the witness were to reply "You can't handle the truth!", this should not be understood as a simple claim that most of us are not able the process the horror of Holocaust. At a deeper level, those who were not able to handle the truth were the Nazi perpetrators themselves: they were not able to handle the truth that their society is traversed by an all-encompassing antagonism, and to avoid this insight they engaged in the murdering spray that targeted the Jews, as if killing the Jews would re-establish a harmonious social body. What nonetheless complicates the things even more is that the "truth" evoked by Nicholson is not simply the reality of how things stand but a more precise fact that our power (not just the military) has to follow illegal unwritten rules and practices (the "Code Red" in the film) to sustain its legal system – this is the truth soft liberals are not able to handle. Such a notion of truth involves a paradoxical temporal structure:

> Traditionally, truth seems to have posed as *a regulative idea of a state of direct accord*. However, this aspired directness was then compensated with the infinite postponement of achieving it. It is perhaps time to reverse this formula, hence, to conceive truth in the frame of indirectness, and then let it happen fully in the here and now. A mere change of perspective enables us to detect an entirely different 'life of truth.' Instead of conceptualizing 'truth' as perpetually *approximating* to a certain idealized state of full satisfaction, we will rather shift our attention to the instances of truth *emerging actually* within a particular historical reality, either inciting events of great magnitude and irreversible temporality, or producing incontrovertible and inextricable knots and excesses in everyday life, or producing unexpected surpluses in the flukes and flaws of speech. Truth seems impossible and is at the same time inevitable; it gives itself the veneer of eluding our grasp, but then crops up abruptly, even accidentally, and engages us in its discursive bindingness, its compulsory and inescapable effects, its political force and historical exigency, and perhaps its logical necessity.[1]

Truth is thus like *jouissance* (Jacques-Alain Miller once referred to truth as a younger sister of *jouissance*): impossible and inevitable at the same time. The worst thing one can do apropos truth is to conceive it as something – an unknown X – we gradually approach in an infinite process of approximation, without ever reaching it. There is no place for any type of the poetry of lack here, of how we ultimately always miss the final truth – this is not what Lacan means when he asserts, at the beginning of "Television," that truth can only be half-told: "I always speak the truth. Not the whole truth, because there's no way, to say it all. Saying it all is literally impossible: words fail. Yet it's through this very impossibility that the truth holds onto the real."[2] We repress truth, it eludes us, but it is always-already here in its effects, as half-said – say, as a symptom which undermines the hegemonic structure of our symbolic space. It is not only impossible to tell the whole truth, it is even more impossible to fully lie: truth always catches up with us in the cracks and displacements of our lies.[3]

According to Bertolt Brecht, if we directly strive for happiness, happiness escapes us, whereas it catches us as soon as we stop striving for it ("Yes, run for happiness/ But don't run too hard/ For all run after happiness/ Happiness is running after.") Is the same not also the case with truth? If we run after truth too hard, truth will stay behind, ignored. Can we say the same about God? Is God a lie, a product of our collective fantasizing, which gives birth not to his actual existence but to an actual social order based on his teachings and commands, an actual order in which institutions and habits are religiously grounded? It's not as simple as that: in the modern secular societies in which god is proclaimed dead, he returns as a disavowed ghost surviving his death – how?

God Is Undead[4], the definitive book on the ambiguous relationship between Lacanian psychoanalysis and atheism, is a substantial debate between Adrian Johnston (who advocates dialectical materialism) and Lorenzo Chiesa (who insists that agnostic scepticism is the only consistent stance of true atheism).[5] I agree with Chiesa that the direct assertion of indifferent ontological multiplicity, of not-One which precedes any identity, is insufficient – Johnston seems to move in this direction, which is why his "transcendental materialism" bypasses all too easily the transcendental dimension and comes dangerously close to simple materialist ontology. However, in contrast to Chiesa, I think that the oscillations that characterize the relationship between the One and the not-One leave no space open for a possible religious outcome:

what oscillations signal is an irreducible gap, crack, in the ontological edifice of reality itself. This crack is not the crack between our multiple symbolizations of reality and this reality "in itself," it is located into the very heart of reality itself. And the space of theosophy is located in the gap that makes the transcendental dimension irreducible to ontology – *vulgari eloquentia*, we cannot ever fully account for our transcendental horizon in the terms of universal ontology since every ontological vision of the whole of reality falls under the scope of the transcendental, and this is what makes all general ontologies from Spinoza's to Deleuze's ultimately untenable.

The oscillation on which Chiesa focuses can be reduced to the tension between the enunciated and the (process of its) enunciation: when we assert the irreducible non-One as the ultimate truth of being, our very position of enunciation functions as that of a One able to grasp all of reality in its truth, and vice versa, when we try to speak about the One as the supreme divine reality our position of enunciation necessarily gets inconsistent, caught in contradictions. In philosophy, this tension appears as the tension between the reality we confront and transcendental horizon through which we perceive reality – the supreme example: we can convincingly argue and demonstrate that there is no free will, that freedom is a "user's illusion," but our very practice of arguing implies that we act as free, trying to convince others to freely accept our arguments. So even if we know we are not free we act as if we are free. However, the reflexive shift from the enunciated content back to our process of its enunciation should not be taken as a step from illusion to truth: yes, we act and argue as if we are free, but cognitive science can explain how this illusion of freedom arose. It is a mega-achievement of modern science to suspend our subjective engagement and to focus on "objective reality": scientific results should not be judged by "whom they serve" or by reference to the subjective economy of those who elaborate them. When Lacan says that science forecloses the subject, this is not a negative judgement pointing out that science misses something but a gesture that sustains the very space of modern science. In short, scientific content cannot be "transcendentally deduced" from subjective activity (what Fichte tried to do), the oscillation between the two is irreducible. This is why what Chiesa calls irreducible oscillation is what I refer to as the irreducible ontological parallax.[6]

Subjectivity in Afropessimism

Where does theosophy enter here? It allows us to challenge the standard view according to which "objective reality" is out there, a transcendent object we are gradually approaching. What we experience as "objective reality" is always-already transcendentally constituted, so that we only touch the Real beyond or beneath reality when we experience "the night of the world," i.e., when reality dissolves and the only thing remaining is the abyss of subjectivity. It may appear that, when we talk about the ontological void of "inhuman" subjectivity, we are dealing with a transcendental-ontological category with no direct political implications: political projects and choices are ontic decisions and identifications which take place within an ontological horizon given in advance . . . However, there are moments of radical political action in which the ontological dimension as such is at stake; in theory, politics is raised at this level in so-called Afropessimism. Frank B. Wilderson III[7] elaborated the most convincing version of Afropessimism by way of posing questions that the predominant liberal Humanism avoids: "simply put, we abdicated the power to pose the question—and the power to pose the question is the greatest power of all"(ix). The question is: humanism presents itself as universal, all-encompassing, but this universality is already grounded in an exclusion. It is not just that humanism imposes a Western standard of being-human which reduces subaltern Others to a lower level of humanity; Humanism is based on the exclusion of a large group of humans (Blacks) as non-Human, outside the hierarchical sphere of Humanity, while Asians and Latinos are "lesser humans" who can demand full Humanity. (The young Gandhi played this game: when he protested against apartheid in South Africa, he didn't demand legal equality of Whites and Blacks, he just wanted the large Indian minority to get the same rights as the Whites.) Plus one should raise here another question which is very relevant in our multicentric world with the stronger position of Asia: are Blacks non-Human just from the standpoint of European Whites? What about Asians – what are Blacks for them? Also non-human?

One should acknowledge "the ontological claim of the Afropessimists that Blackness is that outside which makes it possible for White and non-White (i.e., Asians and Latinos) positions to exist and, simultaneously, contest existence. As such, not only is Blackness (Slaveness) outside the terrain of the White (the Master), it is outside the terrain of the subaltern."[8] This is why Blackness (Slaveness) in its basic ontological dimension remains untouched by the liberal Humanist discourses which praise and fight for "access to institutionality," "meritocracy," "multiculturalism," and "diversity" – discourses that proliferate exponentially across the political, academic, and cinematic landscapes"[9]. These discourses just provide false alibis for the murderous dimension on which Humanism is founded:

> It was free speech or the antiwar movement; it had, for example, the women's, gay, antinuclear, environmental, and immigrants' rights movements as lines of flight from the absolute ethics of Redness and Blackness. It was able to reform (reorganize) an unethical world and still sleep at night.[10]
>
> 30

Even the Marxist notion of proletarians relies on the "devastating embrace of Human capacity—that which the Slave lacks"[11]. A proletarian is deprived of actualizing his capacities, but as a human subject he HAS them, while "a Black is the very antithesis of a Human subject"[12]: "the Slave is not a laborer but an anti-Human, a position against which Humanity establishes, maintains, and renews its coherence, its corporeal integrity"[13]. That's why "forced labor is not constitutive of enslavement"[14] – being a Slave is a properly ontological category: "slavery for Whites was and is experiential and that for Blacks it is and was ontological"[15]. An exploited worker experiences what he has lost while a Black has nothing to lose, or, as James Baldwin put it apropos his relationship with Norman Mailer: "There is a difference between Norman and myself in that I think he still imagines that he has something to save, whereas I have never had anything to lose."[16] So

> the Third World can fight against domination and for the return of colonized peoples' land, for they are people with a narrative of repair, whereas Slaves can only fight against slavery – the for-something-else can only be theorized, if at all, in the process and at the end of the requisite violence against the Settler/Master, not before.[17]

Fanon draw the ultimate consequence from this state of things: for the Slave, the only cure, the only way to achieve freedom, is "the end of the (human) world" as it exists now. Alenka Zupančič[18] links this unique subjective stance of Afropessimism to Lacan's basic formula hysterical desire ("'I ask you' – what? – 'to refuse' – what? – 'what I offer you' – why? – 'because that's not it.'"):

When blacks are given this or that 'right' and insist that 'that's not it', it's not simply because more rights could and should be given, or because they are never satisfied, and don't understand that this is all about an endless progress toward full equality . . . . No. If you read the authors of Afro-pessimism, they reply to this: you completely miss the point; it is not that we want more rights or different rights, we *want to be*, and that is not the case; our being is excluded from the world such as it is, regardless of its progress in terms of rights and political correctness. This is what Wilderson calls 'ontological death'. What they are saying is: 'You are quite right, whatever you give us, it is not, and will never be, *it*, because it is not by progressive concessions that you can give us what was excluded at the very moment of the constitution of the 'modern world', namely our (social) being. The ground on which you stand when you give us these rights is constituted by the exclusion of our being. This is our truth, the truth to which we testify by 'never being satisfied.'

And this, exactly, should also be the reaction of the victim of racism and/or sexism to the endless process of the pseudo-radical liberal Left offering them more and more concessions: let's rewrite classic texts to make them acceptable to today's PC sensibilities (recall what is going on with reprints of classic fairy tales, Agatha Christie novels, etc.), let's purify our daily language so that "they" becomes the pronoun for all those who don't want explicitly to be addressed as "he" or "she", let's destroy the monuments to all figures from the past who said or did something that is today considered problematic, etc. The answer of the oppressed should be: "Sorry, but *that's not it*, you are bombarding me with such offers just to retain your basic social position of superiority!" So when Lacan proposes his formula of hysteric provocation ("'I ask you' – what? – 'to refuse' – what? – 'what I offer you' – why? – 'because that's not it.'"), we should go to the end here and enact the passage from giving/having to being: a hysteric does not just endlessly reject what the Other offer him because "that's not it" (what s/he really wants); s/he finally realizes that the "it" is the Other itself. The message is thus: "YOU are not it!", you are not in a position to give me what I really need or want. Notice a specific reversal present in Lacan's formula: it is not me, the victim demanding something from (a figure of) the big Other, who us complaining to it: "I refuse what you are offering me because that's not it!", as the Afro-pessimists claim in the scene imagined by Zupančič; *it is the Other itself who asks me to refuse its offer because "that's not it"* . . . Do we not get here an extreme version of the offer meant to be rejected, a form of politeness in our daily lives? When I invite my poor friend to an expensive diner, it is clear to both of us that I will pay the bill; however, at least in my country, it is expected that my friend will insist for a short time that he should pay the bill (and then, as expected, he concedes that I'll pay it) . . . So was my friend not telling me: "I ask you to refuse my offer to pay the bill because that's not it!", i.e., because I just made my offer as a formal gesture to show my friendship?

Can Lacan's formula of hysteria "I demand you to reject what I offer you because it's not THAT" not be read also as a formula for an authentic government/power? The message of such a power to its subjects is not "we give you what you want/need," it is rather "we give you what we can, but we know well this is not THAT." Imagine that, in the midst of the Covid pandemic, a government's message would have been: "We are doing all we can, we organize all the measures, vaccination, lockdowns . . ., but this is not THAT!" (And the same holds for global warming, war in Ukraine, immigration, etc.) Unfortunately, there is also a more cynical reading of this formula: we give you all the rights etc., but that's not IT – beneath all this, there is the fact of our raw power, we can do what we want, we don't really serve you . . . This gap is constitutive of all power, which means that a hystericized power is impossible, power has to pretend/act as if it is actually full power.

So what if we make here even a step further and apply this to the ultimate figure of the big Other, to god himself? What if Christ's ultimate message, the message of his sacrifice, is: "I ask you (who believe in me) to refuse what I offer you (my sacrifice on the Cross) because that's not it"? What if it is in this sense that Christ's sacrifice is a sacrifice to end sacrifices? It stages the meaninglessness of a sacrifice and thus releases us into our freedom. In other words, Christ is not a mediator between god and man which brings about their reconciliation: his dead body is rather a monstrous frozen monument to the lack of any transcendent agent safeguarding our fate. To put it in yet another way: Christ does not act for us, redeeming us from our sins, he is rather *interpassive*: in his passive suffering, he gives body to the fact that "there is no big Other," that something is terribly out of joint in our world.

In this basic sense hysteria, a hysterical stance, is not just a psychological category designating a specific psychic disorder: the hysterical "conversion" gives body to the Truth (in the most emphatic sense of the term) of the social big Other, to the exclusion, lack, inconsistency on which it is based. That's why hysterics "don't know what they want": the horizon of what one can want (i.e., demand from the big Other) is determined by the coordinates of this big Other, and desire "signals the imbalance that sustains the order of being, and aims – beyond all objects – to shake this order, to bring about a shift in the order of being." Hysteria is thus not subjective only in the precise sense of the subjective "conversion" of a disorder in big Other itself. And Zupančič goes to the end in her de-psychologization of hysteria as a collective political act: in her path-breaking interpretation of the ongoing Iranian protests against the regime triggered by the death of a young Kurdish woman, she reads the poisonings of thousands of girls in schools as a phenomenon of mass hysteria which makes the girls' acts an authentic revolutionary act. The irony is that, after all standard explanations of the poisonings failed (revenge attacks by fundamentalist groups who do not want girls to attend school, secret actions by the government itself to deter girls who might join (or have already joined) the protests, foreign powers trying to blacken the image of the ruling Islamic power . . .), and after no traces of dangerous chemicals have been found so far, "led to the hypothesis (in the Western press as well as in some Iranian government circles) that this could be a case of 'mass hysteria.' And from there to the conclusion that the incidents should therefore not be taken too seriously; it is just a 'psychological illness', so there is nothing to it" – however,

> what we should categorically reject is the conclusion that therefore 'there is nothing to it.' For if it were true, it wouldn't at all mean that there is nothing to it. It would not exculpate anyone, but would rather

inculpate the authorities, the regime all the more, and present yet another case of *mass protest*, of physical bodies converting into protesting, political bodies. If I were in the shoes of the Iranian regime, I would be very scared of this option, because it would mean that the bodily demonstration ('conversion') of the *state disorder* also continues in this way.

The disorder is thus "ontological," and we should take the term "ontology" here very seriously, not just as a rhetorical exaggeration: back to Afropessimism, being Black is not a question of having but a matter of being. Being Black involves a kind of *epoche*, suspension of all capacities – my Master can make me work and use what I am good at, but work is not an expression of my subjective capacities, I am a machine that functions . . . The Hegelian turn to be made here is, of course, that the void that remains after a slave is de-humanized is subjectivity at its purest, deprived of all its substantial content. This constitutive being-deprived-of-freedom opens up to a Slave the prospect of a much more radical freedom: if "Slaves can only fight against slavery – the for-something-else can only be theorized, if at all, in the process," this means that, in the process of fighting against slavery, they should freely invent what they will become, i.e., they will not just become what they really are, realize their potentials, which were thwarted in their reality. It is along these lines that we should reread the introduction to Hegel's lectures on the philosophy of history where he (in)famously dismisses Blacks (in Africa) as outside history: human history proper begins with China, Africa

> is no historical part of the World; it has no movement or development to exhibit. What we properly understand by Africa, is the Unhistorical, Undeveloped Spirit, still involved in the conditions of mere nature, and which had to be presented here only as on the threshold of the World's History. Having eliminated this introductory element, we find ourselves for the first time on the real theatre of History.[19]

History means collective labour, mediation and alienation: a worker's product is taken from him/her, s/he is unable to recognize him/herself in it, a revolution is needed for the workers to re-appropriate their products. However, even if/when they toil for their Master, Black Slaves do not perform work in which they express themselves, they fall outside mediation through work which is history . . . But what if we turn around Hegel's conclusion and posit that, precisely as "inhuman," Blacks are subjects whose subjectivity is not yet obfuscated by the filth of human personality? Or, to put it even more pointedly, what if, in his treatment of Black Africa, Hegel was here not Hegelian enough, in exactly the same way as he was not Hegelian enough in his treatment of sexuality?

Far from providing the natural foundation of human lives, sexuality is the very terrain where humans detach themselves from nature: the idea of sexual perversion or of a deadly sexual passion is totally foreign to the animal universe. One sentence from Roberto Bolaño's short story – "That afternoon we made love to hide the sheer joy of seeing each other again."[20] – tells more than long treatises about what Lacan aimed at with his *il n'y a pas de rapport sexuel*. One should avoid here the trap to spiritualize or desexualize "the sheer joy of seeing each other again": this "sheer joy" is enjoyment at its unbearably strongest, which is why we are compelled to avoid it. One has thus to turn around the pseudo-"Freudian" notion that "doing it" is the focus of enjoyment and that seeing each other is just a pleasure of knowing that we will soon "do it": it is the sexual act which is by definition an escape-into-activity from the mere inactive presence of the other. In other words, since full sexual act is impossible, the only way to render it present is in the form of its opposite, as an utter inactivity.

Here, Hegel himself commits a failure with regard to his own standards: he only deploys how, in the process of culture, the natural substance of sexuality is cultivated, sublated, mediated – we, humans, no longer just make love for procreation, we get involved in a complex process of seduction and marriage by means of which sexuality becomes an expression of the spiritual bond between a man and a woman, etc. However, what Hegel misses is how, once we are within the human condition, sexuality is not only transformed/civilized, but, much more radically, *changed in its very substance*: it is no longer the instinctual drive to reproduce, but a drive that gets thwarted as to its natural goal (reproduction) and thereby explodes into an infinite, properly meta-physical, passion. The becoming-cultural of sexuality is thus not the becoming-cultural of nature, but the attempt to domesticate a properly un-natural excess of the meta-physical sexual passion. This excess of negativity discernible in sex and apropos rabble is the very dimension of "unruliness" identified by Kant as the violent freedom on account of which man, in contrast to animals, needs a master. So it is not just that sexuality is the animal substance which is then "sublated" into civilized modes and rituals, gentrified, disciplined, etc. – the excess itself of sexuality which threatens to explode the "civilized" constraints, sexuality as unconditional Passion, is the result of Culture. In the terms of Wagner's *Tristan*: civilization is not only the universe of the Day, rituals and honours that bind us, but the Night itself, the infinite passion in which the two lovers want to dissolve their ordinary daily existence – animals know no such passion . . . And what if it is the same with Blacks? What if they are excluded from human history because they stand for the very cut from nature that is excluded by "humanity" in the ordinary sense?

Now we approach a very sensitive question. Prior to their colonization and enslavement, Blacks in Africa certainly lived in communities headed by Master figures – they didn't learn what a Master is only through being enslaved. So why was enslavement for them such a shattering experience? It was not simply that their enslavement was more brutal and oppressive: the White domination was not part of their traditional way of life, it totally uprooted them. Which is why we should risk the following hypothesis: they will not be able to simply pass from White domination to another more "authentic" type of Master – they find themselves in a unique position in which they will need to transform themselves radically to become ready for a new type of Master, and this can only be done by a figure who acts as a psychoanalyst.

But can this be done at all? It may appear the answer is a no, since there is no collective psychoanalytic treatment: such a treatment is focused on the singularity of an individual. However, experience shows that it is also possible for a person to bring about a group solidarity by way of occupying the position of an analyst. A rare case of this is the ongoing TV series *Ted Lasso*, an American sports comedy-drama series (first season 2020) developed by Jason Sudeikis, Bill Lawrence, Brendan Hunt and Joe Kelly. Sudeikis plays Ted, an American college football coach who is hired to coach an English soccer team with the secret intention of the team's owner that his inexperience in soccer will lead it to failure. However, "his folksy, optimistic leadership proves unexpectedly successful" – as a cause of his success, the Wikipedia entry further refers to "Ted's charm, personality, and humor," concluding that, although he is "frequently ridiculed for his folksy optimism and inexperience with the sport," he gradually wins people over through his kind and compassionate approach to coaching.[21] However, Ted's inexperience with soccer is insignificant because, as he makes it abundantly clear, his aim is not the team's success in the competition, but just to enable the players to overcome petty conflicts and establish a group solidarity. And all the quoted designations are not only superficial but outright wrong. Ted can also be rough and verbally brutal, when this is needed to confront a player with the hypocrisy or inconsistency of his subjective stance. He accepts with indifference all the gestures of animosity that most of the players display towards/against him at the beginning (referring to him as a "wonker," etc.), because he correctly reads them as signs of a negative transference on him. His apparent "naivety" (taking reproaches literally, missing their metaphoric dimension) is part of a well-planned strategy to bring the players to the truth of their subjective stance. We can guess that at the end Ted will not become an accepted Master of the team – he will just withdraw after creating a social space in which a Master will be able to function properly. Therein resides the analyst's intervention: to be a vanishing mediator who succeeds when his mediating role is obliterated and forgotten. (Freud knew this: when he met Ratman – his obsessional patient – decades after his successful treatment, the fully cured Ratman didn't even remember the encounter which set his life straight.) And, again, my hypothesis is that Blacks also need such a figure of vanishing mediator to invent a new type of Master.

Does God Believe in Himself?

So where does religion enter here? To understand how religion functions politically, and especially to understand the different modes of its functioning, the psychoanalytic couple of neurosis and perversion is indispensable – not to reduce religion to just another form of psychic disturbances but to identify universal mechanisms which find a clear expression in religious practices. Religion is a Cause for which a true believer is ready to sacrifice everything, including his life, and psychoanalysis allows us to discern the neurotic mechanism that sustains this readiness to self-sacrifice: neurotic symptoms are "tantamount to Other-sustaining (self-)sacrifices"[22], which is why, as Johnston put it, "neurotics become truly atheistic when analysis enables them to cease consciously and unconsciously making themselves suffer in the name of shielding certain significant Others in their life histories from ignorance and/or impotence."[23] So I don't sacrifice myself for the omnipotent God, I sacrifice myself to obfuscate God's impotence. One should note the anti-Feuerbachian thrust of this idea: in investing in "God," we do not just project onto "God" the supreme potentials of human beings of which we are deprived in our actual life; "God" is a fantasy-formation which fills in a gap constitutive of being-human.

And what about perversion? In the sixteenth seminar, Lacan observes that "the pervert is he who consecrates himself to plugging the hole (*boucher le trou*) in the Other . . . he is, up to a certain point, on the side of the Other's existence. He is a defender of the faith."[24] In what then resides the difference between the pervert and the hysterics who choose to suffer in the name of shielding certain significant Others in their life histories? Do both not plug the hole in the Other? The difference is that the hysteric does it with *its own* sacrificial suffering, while the pervert does it with the *other's* (his victim's) suffering. In both cases, suffering is on the side of the subject: in hysteria, the hysteric subject suffers self-imposed sacrificial pain, while in perversion, the agent (pervert) reduces itself to an object-instrument subjectivizing its victim through the latter's suffering. (Incidentally, Lacan himself comes dangerously close to a perverse stance when he says that "we can do without [God] provided that we use [Him]."[25] This claim is open to two opposite readings: a perversely-cynical one and an authentically-ethical one. It can mean: we know there is no God but we manipulatively "use" him as a spectre which enables our peaceful co-existence. Or it can mean: fully aware of God's inexistence, we endorse this spectre as a Cause to which we commit our life.)

Christian fundamentalists excel today in manipulating surplus-enjoyment than the Left – let's just recall how The Cavalry Episcopal Church (West 20th and Park Avenue South, Manhattan) announced a meeting with the title "Enjoy your forgiveness":

In Christ, God has taken all your shame, disconnection, and brokenness upon Himself and instead *given you the joy of His own life*. That's the story of Jesus in a nutshell. But what about our response? God has given us this gift so that we may *enjoy* it. 'Enjoy your forgiveness' is an invitation to celebrate and delight in the freedom of His love, loving and serving our neighbors in joy and thanksgiving. . . . Our debts are paid and we can freely take delight in God's mercy every day of our lives.[26]

The obscenity of this line of reasoning is striking – what could mean the command to enjoy our forgiveness? Obviously not just to enjoy the pleasures of life without burden but the very fact that we are forgiven, i.e., that, in a supreme act of interpassivity, Christ suffered for us. The surplus-enjoyment that we get is that we can enjoy our sinful life without paying the price for it – and whichever way we turn this around, we *enjoy Christ's suffering itself!* But are our debts really already paid? For a Christian, of course not: if we take this statement literally, then the notion of Hell becomes meaningless. Christ's sacrificial death just gives us a chance, plus in a sense it makes us even more indebted to Christ for cancelling our debt, i.e., paying the price for our sins.

The difference between neurosis and perversion also allows us to draw a clear distinction between neurotic and perverse disavowal which are both operative in religious discourses: neurotic disavowal has the simple structure of "I know well, but nonetheless . . ." (I disavow it by way of suspending the symbolic efficiency of my knowledge), while in perverse disavowal, knowledge itself is the fetish that enables me to disavow knowledge ("I know this well, and that's why I act as I do . . ."). In the terms of symbolic castration (since disavowal is ultimately the disavowal of castration), this perverse stance means: "I know well I am castrated, so I can ignore it, because I am in a safe position of knowledge." Zupančič elaborates this distinction with regard to the different way *jouissance* works In each version. Neurosis functions as "the way a subject tries – *secretly, without the Other knowing/seeing it* – to retain something of the enjoyment, to conceal it from the Other, in short, to save it for itself. However, this small part of enjoyment is all that that the subject can endure without falling into anxiety (triggered by the possibility of a full unlimited enjoyment). This, precisely, is why the 'fall' of the Other is for the subject anything but liberating": the fall of the Other means the fall of the limit of enjoyment which maintains it in the confines of what is still bearable. Perversion in both its versions also avoids anxiety triggered by the psychotic over-proximity of enjoyment:

in sadism, I posit myself as the instrument of the Other's enjoyment, while in masochism, I am the object of the Other's enjoyment (which is strictly regulated by the masochist contract).

However, this doesn't mean that the standard neurotic disavowal isn't also fully operative today. The old standard example is here the average Israeli stance of "I know very well God doesn't exist, but nonetheless . . . (he gave us the land of Israel)"; but a new form of disavowal took place in the Ukrainian war and in Israel itself after the extreme Right government took over. The false "peaceniks" who show "understanding" for Russia's attack on Ukraine no less rely on the logic of *"je sais bien, mais quand meme . . ."*: "I fully condemn Russia's brutal aggression on an independent state, but . . . (Russia was provoked by Ukraine; in this war, Russia nonetheless defends a multicentric world against the hegemony of the West; the war serves the NATO military complex)." Even the argument that we have there a proxy war between Russia and NATO for which Ukrainians are paying the price is false: for Ukrainians this is a war of survival in which they are fully engaged, so what should they do? Make a compromise and sacrifice themselves in order not to be contaminated by NATO? In Israel, after a Palestinian killed two settlers on the West Bank, a mob of settlers entered the Palestinian city of Hawara (with 7,400 inhabitants) and went on a violent rampage, burning cars and houses, with one dead and many wounded. The reaction of the Israeli government was that this shouldn't be done by a civilian mob but by the Israeli armed forces: Israel Finance Minister Bezalel Smotrich called for the state to "erase" Hawara: "I think the village of Hawara needs to be erased. I think that the state of Israel needs to do it. God forbid that regular people should do it."[27] Are we aware of the obscenity of this call? Till now, Israel destroyed the family house of a Palestinian accused of terrorism – now it moves up to "erasing" the entire city . . .

But the condemnation of this scandalous event by the Western liberals still has a form of disavowal: what we should note is the fake form of "surprise" ("what Israel plans to do now is unacceptable"). Was it really a surprise? For the Palestinians, what went on in Hawara is not unique but just a culmination of the permanent harassment of the West Bank Palestinians: for years the West Bank settlers poison water sources, burn olive trees owned by Palestinians, and engage in personal attacks on them. The disavowal here is: "OK, Israel tolerated something unacceptable, but . . . (we should not use this event to support anti-Semitism)." And what follows is, as expected, that that every clear condemnation of Israel is proclaimed anti-Semitic. It also shouldn't surprise us that the same regression to an openly barbarian "justice" spreads all around the world, from Russia to the US. On March 2 2023, a Republican congressman from Tennessee Paul Sherrell said (when the state's House Criminal Justice Committee was debating a bill to add the firing squad to existing methods of execution, lethal injection and electrocution) that public hangings (in short, lynching) should be added to this list. The reason? "For the cruelest and most heinous crimes, a just society requires the death penalty in kind."[28] (Incidentally, Tennessee is also the first state in the US that restricted public drag performances.[29])

So let's clarify further different modes of disavowal. Octave Mannoni reports on a well-known accident from the life of Casanova[30]: to seduce a primitive peasant girl, Casanova makes on a meadow near the house a huge circle of sheets of paper bedecked with cabalistic signs and declares it magic, protecting from dangers like a violent storm. He is fully aware that he is cheating, and that he does not believe in magic. But after he finishes the circle, an unexpected violent storm breaks out and, in a moment of panic, he quickly steps into the circle for protection. As Zupančič formulates this paradox: "I don't believe in the magic formula, but I can still resort to it when needed." The magic formula is "appropriated" as a tool which I can use when needed although I generally don't believe in it. Aren't our daily and political lives full of such cases? Say, I don't believe in learning my future from reading my palm lines, but I am nonetheless afraid to do it – I might learn something I don't want to know . . . Or, when a real catastrophe is impending, I repeat some magic formula "just in case" . . . Such an appropriation is perverse, as opposed to "normal" religious belief which just perform a symbolic sublation: I know there is no God sitting somewhere up there as an old man, but "in a deeper sense" there is a spiritual truth in such a vision.[31]

As true materialists, we should make a crucial step further here and transpose (dis)belief *into god himself*: it is not enough to deal with complexities and disavowals of our belief in god, one has to ask *if god himself believes in god*. We should here shamelessly apply to god himself Lacan's well-known statement that a madman is not only a beggar who thinks he is a king, but also a king who thinks he is a king:

god who thinks he is god is also the supreme madman. In the May 21 1974 session of his *Seminar XXI (The Non-Dupes Err)*, Lacan asserts that "God does not believe in God," and he immediately spells out the implications of this claim by way of equating "God does not believe in God" with "There is something (of the) unconscious (*y a d'l'inconscient*)." The move we have to accomplish here is thus the move from our doubt about God to God doubting his own divine status, not believing in himself as God. But where is his non-belief located? Does God consciously doubt his own divinity? This would have meant that we assert a substantial unconscious God whose existence is too deep even for his own consciousness. So we should rather assert the opposite: God cannot consciously doubt himself, he has to believe he is God, it is unconsciously that he doesn't believe in himself (or, more precisely, that he knows he is not a God). Johnston proceeds too fast in his dismissal of "the reflexive, self-transparent variety of philosophical and theological traditions" with regard to belief:

> From such familiar traditional perspectives, knowledge is inherently auto-reflexive and self-conscious. When one knows, one knows that one knows. When one thinks, one thinks that one thinks. Additionally, when one believes, one believes that one believes. On a Lacanian assessment, what is really revolutionary about Freud's self-styled 'Copernican revolution' is his positing of the unconscious as irreflexive mentation. One is gripped by the unconscious in knowing without knowing that one knows, thinking without thinking that one thinks, and believing without believing that one believes. Lacan's denial that God believes in God, with its associations to the irreflexivity characteristic of the Freudian unconscious, is another version of 'God is unconscious' (i.e., the Lacanian 'true formula of atheism').[32]

But if God is unconscious also to/for himself, this means that he (consciously) believes in himself and that *it is his non-belief in himself which is unconscious* – so the reflexivity is in the Unconscious itself, it is precisely what escapes consciousness. It is only from this insight that we can answer the big question raised by Johnston:

> Is atheism condemned to remaining eternally, in Hegelian terms, a determinate negation of Christianity—and, hence, permanently

dependent or parasitic upon what it negates? Can one move from sublating (as *Aufhebung*) religion to finally outright negating it? Is Judeo-Christian monotheism the disposable ladder of a thoroughly historical possibility condition for atheism? Or, is it an indispensable logical necessity for making possible all future atheisms?[33]

For me, the answer to this question is a resounding YES: atheism cannot stand on its own, a detour through religion is necessary – not only religion as such, but specifically Christianity is indispensable. The "a" in "atheism" should thus not be read as only a marker of negation but also in the sense of the Lacanian *objet a*, as pointing towards an excess in the object which is more than this object itself – "atheism" doesn't only mean "there is no god" but also "there is something in god more than god itself," and it is this excess which designates true materialism. If we throw away the ladder, we lose the thing itself which we arrived to through this ladder.

This is why, in contrast to Freud for whom religiosity is a curable symptom, for Lacan it is an incurable *sinthome*. Chiesa sums up Freud's position on the death of god: "for Freud, if the Father of the horde is dead, then nothing is permitted anymore, since he is turned into God; however, if God is dead, then everything is potentially permitted, at least in the direction of the species' collective self-annihilation."[34] One should complicate the constellation here: the God who prohibits everything is NOT the God of the real (parallel to the primordial Father) but precisely the symbolic dead god. When god is proclaimed dead, he returns in a whole series of pseudo-atheist shapes in which permissiveness itself is ultra-regulated – just recall how the Political Correctness imposes numerous prohibitions and regulations to guarantee our sexual freedom . . . On every Italian train station, you find a board announcing: *"Vietato attraversare i binari!"* ("It is prohibited to walk across the /double/ rails!"). For obvious reasons, I much prefer a literal translation: "It is prohibited to traverse the binaries!" – is this not what the traditional heterosexual ethic enjoins us? "Do not transgress the binary order of (normal) sexual difference!" What we are getting today, with our anti-binary ideology, is the opposite injunction – "It is prohibited not to transgress the confines of binary sexuality!" – which is much worse than the traditional one.

Here is an extreme case. There are reports that Ladybird books are now using "sensitivity readers" to red-flag passages in fairy tales like

"Snow White" and "Cinderella." The trope of "falling in love at first sight" was proclaimed problematic because it "presents beauty as a privilege over getting to know potential partners through their character. The concern then is that child readers will think that good looks alone are what should make someone desirable."[35] This proposal is not only ridiculous, it is also simply wrong with regard to the notion of falling in love: it implies the idea that one can also fall in love with someone one considers unattractive but admires its inner character – as if sexual love (and we're talking about this here) is not about irresistible desire for close bodily contact.

Or are we approaching a new era in which bodily lust will have to be postponed, becoming acceptable only when grounded in the knowledge of a character? So what if we turn around Ladybird procedure? What if I say that, at a colloquium, I was fascinated by the precise argumentation and ethical engagement of a young female professor; so when the colloquium session ended, we engaged in a private conversation, she invited me to her room for a drink . . . and after a night of passionate love making, I thought with satisfaction: "At first sight I fell in love with her character, but when I spent the night with her, I discovered a much deeper passion that eclipsed all the intellectual mumbo-jumbo!" . . . (Something like this never happened to me, of course!) Or, let's risk a step further in this suspicious debate about sex and character (recall that *Sex and Character* is the title of Otto Weininger's anti-feminist and anti-Semitic classic from 1903): "At first sight I found her character fake and repulsive, but when I spent the night with her, I discovered a much deeper passion that totally eclipsed the weaknesses of her character!"

Holy Spirit as a Model of Emancipatory Community

How can we then effectively overcome religion through and in Christianity? My thesis is that such an atheist gesture is contained already in the Christian notion of Holy Ghost. Chiesa writes: "Christianity transforms such a structural oscillation into a static dogma, that is, the neat separation between the abjection of our world and the perfection of the world to come that will have redeemed it."[36] However, what if we read the return of Christ as something that already takes place in the Holy Spirit, the community of believers which exists in this earthly abject world? There is no oscillation here, Holy Spirit is an event which just changes the entire constellation, and Chiesa proceeds too fast when he proclaims every version of the transcendental big Other a (watered down, secularized) theology? One can well propose a notion of the transcendental big Other as the symbolic space into which we are thrown and which is as such the horizon of our limitation and finitude – theology only enters when this purely virtual symbolic texture is "reified" into a supreme Entity.

There is a quite poignant final scene in *Alyosha's Love*, a 1960 Soviet film directed by Georgi Shchukin and Semyon Tumanov. A detachment of exploration geologists is working in the steppe region, and among them is Alyoshka, a young and shy guy who, unskillful and messy in everyday life, becomes the object of jokes and practical jokes, which are not always harmless. He falls in love with Zinka who lives with her grandfather on a crossing lost in the steppe: once in a day she comes out to turn a railroad switch, and once in a day he travels there just to take a quick glance at her, but she just ignores him. His daily trips to the crossing give a further boost to the cruel jokes by his colleagues. When Alyosha learns that Zinka will move to another part of the country, he is desperate and sits alone in his tent. However, Zinka, who decided to stay there for him, alone approaches the camp; when Alyosha's colleagues who are working on nearby hills perceive Zinka coming to him, they all stop working and respectfully look at her . . . The group obviously stands for the big Other, a passive witness recognizing the strength of the couple's love – but does this mean that we should dismiss this scene as a moment of theological mystification? Is it not rather that the group observing the couple's reunion amounts to a figure of Holy Ghost, a community based on no transcendent point of reference?

Is, however, this topic of Holy Spirit not an archaic remainder totally at odds which the universe of modern science? A closer look at the use of scientific results immediately blurs this clear opposition: science is massively used to re-imaginarize its own de-sacralization of reality. Chiesa emphasizes and further develops Lacan's observation that the role of sexual gadgets is to re-establish sexual relationship: science gets engaged in the "fabrication of counterfeit *ousia* as ersatz counterparts" by means of which the impossibility of the sexual relationship is supplemented by products which promise to render possible a more intense sexual relationship deprived of its constitutive deadlock:

Fetishized gadgets voraciously gobble up our desire with the promise of surplus, if not absolute, enjoyment (nowadays, paradigmatically, in the guise of sex-bots, virtual sex, designer-babies, not to mention the seeming availability of equally endless and disposable sexual identities). . . . the fact that, for instance, we come to treat 'an automobile like a fake wife' more generally indicates how the discourse of science, entwined with that of capitalism, restores and serially multiplies the semblance of the sexual relationship. In this way science loses the hallmark of what characterizes its break with previous kinds of knowledge, namely, its departure from the latter's dependence on the myth of the complementarity between the sexes (be it that of the Western matter and form couple or that of the Eastern Yin and Yang pair), which is itself ultimately responsible for any harmonic vision of the world as a Whole.[37]

The paradox is thus that the gadgets of modern science are used to resuscitate the basic fantasy of traditional (pre-Christian) religions, their effort to imaginarize the real in the guise of fertility cults: "the not-One pole of the oscillation of the God hypothesis is turned into another One, the Goddess, which sustains and cements the semblance of the two-as-one."[38] Such Christianity which regresses to two-as-One is implicitly anti-Semitic: it bypasses Judaism and conjoins Christianity with paganism. This is how we should also explain the passage from pagan religions to Judaism: it is the passage from religious *jouissance* to god's *desire*. With Yahweh, god as the One who is deprived of his feminine counterpart cannot any longer enjoy the divine copulation and becomes a god who desires (what he lost) – or, as Chiesa put it in precise terms:

Yahweh is a One-all-alone, and thus real, precisely in the sense that he in vain attempts to fill in the gap of a missing Goddess by means of an alliance with his people, who keep on betraying him yet not without returning to him. With the same move, their participation in divine enjoyment gives way to God's inscrutable desire – the Law's own desire –whose jealous and ferocious ignorance indeed revolves around his loss of a mythical sexual knowledge.[39]

One should note here that a homologous passage happens in the shift from Hinduism to Buddhism: although the original Buddhism is atheist (or agnostic, at least), its problem is no longer *jouissance* but desire, how to get rid of the spell of desire – in contrast to Judaism, of course, where the enigma of god's desire, of what does he want from us in his ferocious ignorance. Some interpreters of Lacan see in this the advantage of Judaism: it is the only truly non-pagan religion, the religion which leaves open the abyss of the divine desire, the crack in the big Other, while Christianity covers up this abyss, reassuring us that we know what god wants – god wants our redemption because he loves us. We thus return to the imaginarization of god: instead of the duality of masculine and feminine cosmic principles, we get the sexualized duality of god the father and the church as his bride:

our being ravaged by language as the absence of the sexual relationship, and it is thus reduced to the not-One pole. Yet this very predicament, epitomized by the death of the Logos tout-court, functions just as a necessary prelude to the Providential History of a transcendent One. God's love has always-already taken abjection into account and will finally solve it messianically through the universal and salvific revelation of himself as a One-All-Being.[40]

In my view, however, the Christian death of God precisely cannot be reduced to a "a necessary prelude to the Providential History of a transcendent One": as Hegel put it, what dies on the cross is not God's earthly representative (stand-in) but the God of beyond itself, so what happens after the crucifixion is not a return of the transcendent One but the rise of the Holy Spirit which is the community of believers without any support in transcendence. This is why Lacan said that "the Holy Spirit is a notion infinitely less stupid than that of the subject supposed to know"[41] – because the Holy Spirit does not have to rely on a subject-supposed-to-know: it can function as the immanent community (the Protestant *Gemeinde*) which already is what its members are looking for or are devoted to. In other words, read in this way, Holy Spirit is an atheist category, the notion of an emancipatory community without support in big Other. As such, Holy Spirit embodied in a Protestant *Gemeinde* is the very opposite of the Orthodox community: it is a community of believers thrown into the abyss of freedom, with no substantial support in any feminized divinity. Is then *Gemeinde* implicitly anti-feminist? On the contrary, one should denounce the celebration of the eternally-feminine substance as a male fantasy which reduced actual women to a matter waiting to be inseminated by their masculine Logos. Modern feminism is only thinkable in the Cartesian space which breaks with any sexualized ontology.

What Is True Materialism?

What one should advocate is thus the materialist procedure of the immanent self-undermining of a religious edifice – the claim that god is evil or stupid is not only much more unsettling than Peter Singer's claim that ordinary people are evil, it is also much more unsettling than the claim that there is no god since it destroys from within the very notion of divinity. To make this procedure clear, let's take an example from a different domain. The song *The Night They Drove Old Dixie Down* (best known version by Joan Baez) is a first-person narrative relating the economic and social distress experienced by the protagonist, a poor white Southerner, during the last year of the American Civil War; it does not glorify slavery, the Confederacy or Robert E. Lee, it rather tells the story of a poor, non-slave-holding Southerner who tries to make sense of the loss of his brother and his livelihood.[42] As such – as an attempt to render the experience of a poor white man sympathetic to the Southern cause but dismayed at the horror of his suffering for the interests of the rich slave owners – it is much more effective in dismantling this cause than a direct abolitionist critique, in exactly the same way as endorsing a religion but then demonstrating how its God is evil/stupid is much more effective than a direct atheist critique.

In *The Rapture* (1991, written and directed by Michael Tolkin), Mimi Rogers superbly plays Sharon, a young LA woman who works during the day as a phone operator endlessly repeating the same questions in a small cubicle among dozens of others, while in the evenings she engages in swinging orgies.[43] Bored and dissatisfied at leading such an empty life, Sharon becomes a member of a sect which preaches that the end of times and the Rapture are imminent; turning into a passionate believer, she begins to practice a new, pious lifestyle, gets married to Randy, one of her previous swinging partners, and has a daughter Mary with him. Six years later, when Randy, now also a devoted Christian, is shot to death by a madman, this senseless catastrophe makes her and her daughter even more convinced that the Rapture is soon approaching. Sharon believes god told her to go with Mary to a nearby desert camping place and wait there until the two are taken into heaven where they will be united with Randy. Foster, a well-meaning, nonbelieving patrol officer, takes care of them there during their long wait when they run out of food. Mary gets impatient and proposes to her mother that they simply kill themselves in order to go to heaven and join Randy immediately. After a couple of weeks, Sharon also loses patience, decides to do the unspeakable and follows Mary's advice to stop her suffering; however, after shooting Mary, she is unable to take her own life afterwards, knowing that suicides are not allowed into heaven. She confesses her act to Foster who arrests her and takes her to a local jail . . .

Till this point, the story moves along "realist" lines, and one can easily imagine a possible "atheist" ending: bitter and alone, deprived of her faith, Sharon realizes the horror of what she had committed, and is maybe saved by the good policeman. Here, however, events take a totally unexpected turn: in the jail cell, Rapture happens, literally, in all naivety, including bad special effects. First, deep in the night, Mary appears with two angels, and then, early in the morning, while Sharon sits in her cell, a loud trumpet blast is heard all around and announces a series of supranatural events – prison bars fall down, concrete walls fall apart, etc. Escaping from the jail, Sharon and Foster drive out into the desert, where signs of Rapture multiply, from dust storms up to the horsemen of the apocalypse running after and around the car. Next, Sharon and Foster are both "raptured," transported to a purgatory-like landscape where Mary approaches them from heaven and pleads with Sharon to accept god, to declare that she loves god – by just doing this she will be able to join Mary and Randy in heaven. Foster, although till now an atheist, quickly seizes the opportunity, says that he loves god and is allowed entrance to heaven, but Sharon refuses, saying that she cannot declare her love for a god who acted so cruelly towards her family for no reason at all. When Mary asks her if she knows for how long she will be confined to the purgatory, condemned to be there alone, Sharon replies: "Forever."

Sharon's resistance to God, her refusal to declare her love for him, is thus an authentic ethical act. It would be totally wrong to say that she rejects the *false* god and that, in an authentically Christian version of the film, the true Christ should appear at the end, proclaim her a true believer precisely because she refused to declare that she loves the false god. The true temptation to be resisted is thus to declare our love for a god who doesn't deserve it *even if he is real*. For a vulgar materialist, all this cannot but appear as an empty mental experiment; however, for a true materialist, it is only in this way that we really renounce god – by way of renouncing him not only insofar as he doesn't really exist, but even if he is real. In short, the true formula of atheism is not "god doesn't exist" but "god not only doesn't exist, he is also stupid, indifferent, and maybe outright evil" – if we do not destroy the very fiction of god from within, it is easy for this fiction to prolong its hold over us in the form of disavowal ("I know there is no god, but he is nonetheless a noble and uplifting illusion"). Lacan's programmatic claim, in *Seminar X*, that "the atheist, as combatant, as revolutionary, is not one who denies God in his function of omnipotence, but one who affirms oneself as not *serving* any God"[44] fits perfects this final gesture of the heroine in *Rapture*: even when she directly confronts the divine dimension, she refuses to serve him. If, in the film's final moment, Sharon were to turn around, she would have seen Christ at her side.

From Agnosticism to Pure Difference

This subjective stance of Sharon radically undercuts onto-theology which "persists in giving rise to a more or less *closed* dialectic of the *trou*/hole and the *Tout*/Whole, of how the real of the symbolic is imaginarily subsumed under a *Being* supposed to know (the philosopher's own system), that nonetheless does *not* fully manage to *enclose* the hole." In short, modern philosophical ontology invariably falls back into a *Weltanschauung*, literally, "a vision of the world as supposedly seen from *outside* it."[45] Let me give to these lines a self-critical spin: when, at my highest speculative effort, I play with the idea of the triad of quantum waves / ordinary reality / symbolic order as the basic all-encompassing matrix of "all there is" (with the collapse of the wave function as the "negation" of the fluid domain of quantum waves, i.e., as the emergence of our ordinary reality, and then the symbolic order as a kind of negation of negation, the "return" of what is repressed with the collapse of the wave function), am I not very close to advocating a "world view"? My counter-claim is that there is one big exception to this notion (and practice) of philosophy as "a vision of the world as supposedly seen from *outside* it", and this exception is what Hegel calls "Absolute Knowing": Absolute Knowing emerges when the subject realizes that there is no Outside on which we can rely, that all that remains is to compare our knowledge with itself, so that, at the end, there is no final Result but just the endlessly repeated process of each form of knowledge dissolving itself. Chiesa ignores this solution, which is why he misattributes to Lacan the position of historicist relativism – according to Chiesa, Lacan "insinuates" (Chiesa's strong word) that "the truth of incompleteness can only be half-said, *but* the not-One really *is* all there is, the problem is simply we cannot *say* it":

> such a blind reliance on an ultimate ontological not-Oneness supposedly obfuscated by the finitude of our linguistic-logical condition only reinforces weak atheism through the very endeavor to defuse it. If, beyond the wall of language, and the illusory fabrications of the One it gives rise to, the not-One is *all* there is, then this *a fortiori* requires the deceiving God, one who is now being specified as not only deceiving us but also, *extra*-linguistically, the whole of Creation – as still seen from an *intra*-linguistic perspective (of Lacan).[46]

The basic thrust of Chiesa's argumentation is accurate: the position he rejects is the one of naively opposing our perspectives on reality-in-itself to the (not-One) reality out there, beyond our walls of language. Chiesa correctly points out that the position of enunciation of such a claim exempts itself from reality, as if the speaker can elevate itself into the One who can compare reality with our limited visions of it. This means that the speaker regresses into general ontology, an all-encompassing vision of reality. So when Chiesa writes that "the promulgation and endorsement of the not-One as *conclusive* gives rise to the One (not-One), the Being of the lack of being, the ultimate Meaning of 'there is no ultimate meaning',"[47] he thereby correctly points out the tension between the enunciated and its enunciation that implicitly undermines this endorsement: by saying that "everything there is is a not-One," the speaker exempts itself from the totality of All, i.e., he posits himself as the One who can encapsulate all of reality in a single view. But does this necessarily entail a sceptic position? Does the fact that we don't have an access to general ontology beyond our historically-specified transcendental horizons really compel us to leave the possibility open that not-One is not "all there is," that there may be a divine transcendent entity above/beyond it? This is also why I find problematic Chiesa's claim that "what science should instead seriously consider as modern physics is the *hypothesis* that 'the real is not everything', or better, that *the real not-all is itself not necessarily all there is – although it might well be*"[48] – problematic because, for Lacan, "not-all" means precisely a multiplicity which, since it cannot be totalized, allows for no exception: "not-all" means that, since it is never all, there is no exception to it. In other words, Chiesa regresses here to the commonsense notion of the real "not all" as "not everything there is" – he regresses to the Kantian notion of a possible unknown In-itself beyond the sceptic atheism's sphere of phenomena.

My Hegelian solution is here, again, a shift from epistemological doubt/uncertainty to ontological level: "doubt" is located in reality itself, in the sense that there is no "knowledge in the real," that reality (partially) ignores its own laws and doesn't know how to behave – there is a crack in reality which makes it non-totalizable, "not-all," but everything that we project beyond this gap is our fantasy formation. The only way to avoid agnostic scepticism is to transpose this gap into reality itself: the gap we are talking about is not the gap that separates reality-in-itself from our approaches to it but an impossibility which gapes in the heart of reality itself. Let me quote here again the well-known passage from the "Foreword" to his *Phenomenology of Spirit* where Hegel provides the most elementary formula of what does it mean to conceive Substance also as Subject:

> The disparity which exists in consciousness between the I and the substance which is its object is the distinction between them, the *negative* in general. This can be regarded as the *defect* of both, though it is their soul, or that which moves them. That is why some of the ancients conceived the *void* as the principle of motion, for they rightly saw the moving principle as the *negative*, though they did not

as yet grasp that the negative is the self. Now, although this negative appears at first as a disparity between the I and its object, it is just a much a disparity of the substance with itself. Thus what seems to happen outside of it, to be an activity directed against it, is really its own doing, and substance shows itself to be essentially subject.[49]

We should be very precise here: this in no way implies that there is nothing beyond the phenomena accessible to us – of course there is an infinity of entities and processes we haven't yet discovered, but they are not "transcendent" in the sense of an In-itself beyond the phenomenal sphere. Our claim is that when we will discover new aspects of reality up to alien lives, we will not cross the boundary of impossibility that constitutes our reality. We will not discover God or anything of this order because such figures are *a priori*, constitutively, or (as Hegel would have put it) in their very notion, fantasy formations destined to fill in a gap – as Hegel put it long ago, "behind the so-called curtain, which is supposed to hide what is inner, there is nothing to be seen unless we ourselves go behind it."[50] So yes, our epistemological uncertainty is irreducible, but whatever awaits us "out there" is NOT anything resembling our figures of "God" – to bring this point to extreme, even if we'll eventually encounter something whose features appear to us "divine," this will NOT be what we call "God." To put it in yet another way, for Chiesa, difference remains differential (in the sense that it presupposes (and relies on) its opposition to some (God-)One, even if this one is impossible/barred/inexistent), while from my Hegelo-Lacanian standpoint, *"pure" difference precedes what it differentiates*. What appears as "God" is a reified/substantialized form of the gap/crack that makes our realities not-all. There is nothing beyond this gap, every figure of "beyond" is already an obfuscation of the gap.

Chiesa's insistence on agnosticism ultimately relies on his doubt in the possibility of our full scientific self-objectivization. While I share this doubt, I give to it a different spin: the failure of full self-objectivization doesn't imply agnosticism but an ontological crack in reality itself. What should interest us here is the link between purely biochemical processes (attacking our brains with so-called "psychedelic" substances) and the highest spiritual "inner" experience uncannily close to what Lacan designated as "subjective destitution," the disintegration of the fundamental fantasy which sustains our ego – we can biochemically cause the death of our ego. People who are doing this are as a rule attacking their depression, hoping to reinvent themselves completely – or, as Rorick put it: "Ego death can be really humbling and really important for some people, there's some people that need to have their egos killed; but at the same time, it's a scary thing to go through." He's had friends who have experienced ego death and never returned to drug use – they just needed drugs as a powerful tool for subjective change.[51] It is all too easy to try and distinguish such biochemical "death of the ego" with the "authentic" subjective change caused by symbolic work. But there is a limit to this biochemical procedure: it just brusquely erases the symbolic network the subject relies upon without "working through" it and made it implode from within, i.e., without making the subject confront its antagonisms, its points of impossibility – a nice paradox of how a direct intervention into the biogenetic Real serves as a way to avoid confronting the Real immanent to the symbolic order itself.

And this holds even for traumatic events like Holocaust: any prosaic description of the horrors of Holocaust fails to render its trauma, and this is why Adorno was wrong with his famous claim that after Auschwitz poetry is no longer possible: it is prose which is no longer possible, since only poetry can do the job. Poetry is the inscription of impossibility into a language: when we cannot say something directly and we nonetheless insist in doing it, we unavoidably get caught in repetitions, postponements, indirectness, surprising cuts, etc. We should always bear in mind that the "beauty" of classic poetry (symmetric rhymes, etc.) comes second, that it is a way to compensate for the basic failure or impossibility.

Let's make this point somewhat clearer with the reference to *The Prisoners* (the 2009 remake, as a six-part miniseries, of the original movie) which begins with an unidentified young man waking up in a desert and finding himself in the middle of a pursuit as mysterious guards chase an elderly man through a canyon. The old man dies soon after, but not before passing a message on to the younger man: "Tell them I got out." The younger man arrives in an enigmatic community whose residents inform him that it's called simply "The Village". Everyone he meets is known only by a number (he learns his number is 6), and he discovers that they have no knowledge or memory of the outside world; the leader of the Village is referred to as (number) 2. While life goes on in the Village, we occasionally jump to the real New York where Mr Curtis, the real-world Number 2, introduces Michael (the real-world 6) to his wife, Helen, who, just as in the Village, is trapped in a sort of waking dream. Mr Curtis explains that the Village is a form of therapy used to help people that Summakor (the organization headed by him) has identified, although the "patients" may not have agreed to his procedure. It exists within the mind of Helen who "discovered" the Village (a dream present in everyone at a level of consciousness deeper than the usual unconscious) and was its first inhabitant. Michael was pulled into the Village because he worked so well at Summakor, finding people who needed "help." (A nice touch is here that 11 is revealed to be the only resident of the Village who does not exist in the real world.) In the Village, 6 (Michael) falls in love with 313 (Sara) and desires to help Sara and the villagers; he replaces Curtis as the head of Summakor. Number 313, having become aware of her real-world self, becomes the new dreamer, freeing Helen to return to the real world, while Number 6 decides to remain in The Village for good as the new Number 2 and begins planning how to "do The Village right." Number 313, the new unresponsive dreamer, sheds a tear.[52]

The most fascinating aspect of this story is that, more and more, bottomless pits appear in parts of the Village; they don't reach deep into the earth, they just open up into a void. Is this not a perfect metaphor of how our (socio-ideological) reality is structured? It persists only if it is sustained by a consistent dream (fantasy) – when the dream is disturbed, reality also begins to disintegrate. This hole in reality (where words fails to describe it adequately) is the proper domain of poetry: poetry obfuscates the hole, making it palpable and simultaneously tolerable.

2
WHY LACAN IS NOT A BUDDHIST

Hinayana, Mahayana, Theravada

Since the topic of this book is religion, the first thing to note is that Buddha's teaching is pragmatic, focused on alleviating suffering – in matters of religion Buddha was agnostic, not interested in any higher spiritual reality: all that exists is the interconnected non-substantial flow of phenomena beneath which there is no deep substantial divine ground but just the Void. But it is interesting to note Buddhism, which originally dispensed with all institutional ritual and focused solely on the individual's enlightenment and the end of suffering, irrespective of all dogmatic and institutional frames, ended up clinging to the most mechanical and firmly entrenched institutional hierarchic frame, and simultaneously in a world conceived as full of spiritual entities. In Theravada Buddhism, there is no omnipotent creator God of the sort found in Judaism, Islam and Christianity: Gods exist as various types of spiritual being but with limited powers . . .

The question is, of course: how did Buddhism come to this point? It would have been an utterly non-Hegelian reading of Buddhism if we were to dismiss this movement as a simple regression: if there is a Hegelian axiom, it is that the flaw has to be located at the very beginning of the entire movement. What, then, is already wrong with the starting point, the Hinayana version of Buddhism? Its flaw is precisely that to which the Mahayana version reacts, its symmetrical reversal: in striving for my own Enlightenment, I regress into egotism in my very attempt to erase the constraints of my Self. Consequently, one should not make fun of the "superstitious" features of the Tibetan Buddhism – the step towards full spiritualization and ritualization – but to become aware of how this step DOES THE WORK, "delivers the goods": is not relying on a prayer-wheel – or, more generally, on the efficiency of the ritual – also a means to achieve "mindlessness," to empty one's mind and repose in piece? So, in a way, Tibetan Buddhism IS thoroughly faithful to Buddha's pragmatic orientation (ignore theological niceties, focus just on how to help people): sometimes, following blind ritual and immersing oneself in theologico-dogmatic hair-splitting IS pragmatically the most efficient way to achieve the goal of inner peace. This logic is also that of intelligent utilitarians who are well aware that moral acts cannot be directly grounded in utilitarian considerations ("I will do this because, in the long run, it is the best strategy to bring most happiness and pleasure to me also . . ."); but the conclusion they draw is that the Kantian "absolutist" morality ("do your duty for the sake of duty") can and should be defended precisely on utilitarian grounds – it is also the one that works best in real life.

But am I correct in this reading of Buddhism? In the last decades, critiques of my reading of Buddhism abound – even those who are otherwise sympathetic to my general approach claim that I miss the point when I target Buddhism. Representative of my critics is "Nagarjuna and ecophilosophy" by Adrian J. Ivakhiv[1] who also relies on John Clark's "On Being None With Nature: Nagarjuna and the Ecology of Emptiness"[2]. Ivakhiv's starting point is the core Buddhist concept of "dependent origination": every identity is process-relational position, which means that, say, a tree's existence as a unitary object, as opposed to a collection of cells, is conventional: "Removing its properties leaves no core bearer behind." In other words, "the thing we call a 'tree' is, as Buddhists say, empty of inherent self-existence; its essence is nothing other than the properties and conditions of its self-manifesting."[3] This goes against Graham Harman's (and others') argument that there is something more to any object than its properties, relations and conditions. For Buddhism, there is nothing (no-thing) left over. "But that is not to say that there is, in fact, *nothing* . . . There is the process-relational flux of what Clark calls 'nature naturing,' the continual coming into existence and passing away of the experiential bits of the world, all of which is quite real."[4] What this implies is that the "negative" and "deconstructive" project that Nagarjuna is best known for "goes hand in hand with an affirmative, 'reality-based' project of the sort that, in current continental philosophy, is best represented by Deleuze" – or, to quote Clark:

> For Buddhism the negative path of the destruction of illusion is inseparably linked to the positive path of an open, awakened, and compassionate response to a living, non-objectifiable reality, the 'nature that is no nature.'

This brings us to what I see as the central challenge for Buddhism: how do we, humans, get caught into "a dream world of illusory, deceptively permanent objects and egos, and a futile quest to defend the ego and dominate reality"? Is it enough to say that this is a "fundamental human predicament," i.e., a trans-historical invariant? Clark makes here a surprising move into a Marxist direction:

> Where most analyses (including most Buddhist analyses) of egocentric consciousness and the egoic flight from the trauma of lack stop short is in failing to investigate the social and historical roots of these phenomena. We must understand that the ego is not only a psychological and epistemological construct, but also a historical one. Its roots are to be found in the development of large-scale agrarian society and regimented labor, the rise of the state and ancient despotism, the emergence of economic class and acquisitive values, the triumph of patriarchy and warrior mentality – in short, in the evolution of the ancient system of social domination and the domination of nature. To put it in Buddhist terms, our true karmic burden, both personally and collectively, is our profound historicity and our deep materiality.[5]

But the question remains: how far can we go in this direction of historicity? Were individuals in pre-class societies dwelling in a "living, non-objectifiable reality, the 'nature that is no nature'", and should the possible post-capitalist society also be conceived as a liberation from the "wheel of desire"? Another question lurks beneath this one: "Why should the destruction of illusion lead to compassion rather than to cynicism as it often seems to in everyday life, or to social conservatism as it has in the case of Humean and other forms of philosophical skepticism?"[6] I think that, in spite of all desperate attempts to demonstrate that the way to Buddhist enlightenment goes through modesty and compassion, the only honest answer is that of D.T. Suzuki: Zen is a technique of meditation which is compatible with any political orientation, liberalism, fascism, Communism . . .

This brings us back to the Buddhist critique of my work. For Ivakhiv, this is the point where Buddhism meets psychoanalysis: "The key difference between Freud/Lacan/Zizek/et al. and Nagarjuna is that the former presuppose that this [rise of dominating ego] is unavoidable – the best we can do is to come to terms with the ego (etc.) process and try not to get too caught up in the delusional tricks it plays on us."[7] This is why my work totally ignores "the real potential of actually reading Western Buddhism not just in light of Lacan, but the teachings of the Buddha and their lineage."[8] This "real potential" is, of course, the affirmation of the flux of positive life – Ivakhiv introduces it by way of a long quote from D.T. Suzuki:

> D.T. Suzuki, whom Zizek has probably never read[9], a trained Zen Buddhist, as well as professor of Buddhist philosophy and delightfully fluent writer and speaker of English, echoes Vajjiya when he writes about Zen as life as 'absolute affirmation': 'we live in affirmation and not in negation, for life is affirmation itself; and this affirmation must not be the one accompanied or conditioned by a negation, such an affirmation is relative and not at all absolute. With such an affirmation life loses its creative originality and turns into a mechanical process grinding forth nothing but soulless flesh and bones. To be free, life must be an absolute affirmation . . . Zen does not mean a mere escape from intellectual imprisonment, which sometimes ends in sheer wantonness. There is something in Zen that frees us from conditions and at the same time gives us a certain firm foothold . . . Zen abhors repetition or imitation of any kind, for it kills. For the same reason, Zen never explains but only affirms. Life is fact and no explanation is necessary or pertinent. To explain is to apologize and why should we apologize for living? To live – is that not enough? Let us then live, let us affirm. Herein lies Zen in all its purity and in all its nudity as well.'
>
> An Introduction to Zen Buddhism[10]

Ivakhiv's "Lacanian" reading (supplemented by a critique of Lacan) is obvious here: far from advocating a renunciation to our desires, Buddha "is suggesting that staying true to our desire will yield the satisfaction of that (and all) desire, whereas Lacan is less interested in what it would mean to satisfy our desire, if it is once we have properly identified it." How can this be? Ivakhiv introduces here sexual difference: he interprets (what Lacan calls) the impossibility of the sexual relationship as the impossibility to reach the goal of the masculine phallic subject which is to swallow/dominate entire reality; from this phallic standpoint, Buddhism

> appears as a fantasmic spectre in the West, where masculine jouissance is predominant. Buddhism at once promises and threatens with the Other, dark, feminine *jouissance*. Buddhism is only conceivable in what Zizek might call the Western ideological matrix as this testament to its very failure to be conceived. Zizek's critique of Western Buddhism, therefore, has much less to do with the teachings of the Buddha than he has made it seem, and significantly more to do with the mystical, feminine *jouissance* it suggests, which seems to be beyond and for that reason threatening to Zizek.[11]

Three things have to be added here. First, for Lacan, to have a phallus does not mean to be able to dominate reality. There is a nice vulgar phrase in Serb which captures perfectly what Lacan means by his "Che vuoi?", "What do you want?", a reference to the opacity of the other's desire. The phrase is "Koji kurac te jebe?" ("What a prick is fucking you?"). The everyday meaning of this expression is something like: "Why are you annoying me? Why do you insist on bothering me? What is all this about? What do you really want from me?" The idea is that the other who is annoying me is not fully aware of what is pushing him on, as it is clearly indicated in another version of this phrase formulated as a positive statement, a kind of proverb or wisdom: "Uvek ima neki kurac koji te jebe." ("There is always a prick which is fucking you.") Incidentally, this example also makes it clear why, for Lacan, phallus is the signifier of castration: I am not fucking others with my prick, I myself am always under pressure from a "prick" that I don't control and that remains obscure to me.

This is why it is not sufficient to focus on Lacan's conclusion that a king continues to be a king, independently of all efforts to turn his absolute power into an apparently more constitutional one.[12] We have to be more precise here: Lacan also said that not only a beggar who thinks he is a king is a fool but a king who thinks he is a king is also a fool. This means that the king's authority always and by definition involves his symbolic castration: a king who is not a fool is aware that he is a king because his subjects treat him as a king, that his authority is conferred on him through symbolic rituals and objects like the royal sceptre and crown. So even in an absolute monarchy, the king is "castrated," the source of his authority is external to him. Second, far from the feminine *jouissance* to be something threatening for me, something I try to keep at a distance, the feminine *jouissance* is not "beyond" the traumatic cut of sexual difference but one of its aspects: it emerges as the other side of the phallic domain. Even the bees (the large majority of which are de-sexualized "workers" with their reproductive organs vestigial) remain well within sexual reproduction:

> Only the queen bee and the drones have a fully developed reproductive system. The worker bees have an atrophic reproductive system. Seven days after her incubation the queen bee flies outside the beehive, where drones gather, and she mates usually with 8-12 drones in mid-air in the afternoon hours – true love in the afternoon, as the title of a movie says. During mating, the drone's genitals are reversed and come out of his body, and with his abdominal muscles contracting, he ejaculates. Then his genitals are being cut from his body by the queen causing his death, and the next drone enters . . . The queen stores the entire spermatozoon in the spermatheca and her gland excretes nutrients for the survival of almost 7,000,000 spermatozoa, which are adequate for the rest of her life. During the egg-laying the queen bee chooses whether she will fertilize every egg that passes through her oviduct; she lays two kinds of eggs, fertilized and non-fertilized. The non-fertilized ones develop into drones, while the fertilized grow into female individuals – this determination is called gender determination. Afterwards, the female individuals can develop into queens or workers, depending on their nutrition during their larva stage – this determination is called caste determination.[13]

If we read this description from our human standpoint, does it not render a weird matriarchal caste society? All the work is done by bees appropriately named workers: they are female, with their reproductive organs remaining undeveloped, so they are not sexualized but literally trans-sexual. The sexual intercourse (impregnation) between a queen bee and the drones happens only once in their life time: after the intercourse, drones die while the queen gathers enough sperm to last for her entire life. So if the queen is a she and a drone a he, what are the workers? To use today's non-binary parlance, are they not precisely *they*? Bees thus form the only known society in which the large majority are "they" (subdivided into guards, those who gather pollen, etc.), while the worst fate awaits the masculine drones.

The very formulation "mystical, feminine *jouissance*" is misleading: as Lacan points out, mysticism is not exclusively feminine, apart from its feminine version (Saint Theresa) we also have its masculine version (John of the Cross). Third, the equation of the Buddhist enlightenment with the assertion of the feminine *jouissance* and/or with mysticism is totally unfounded: Buddhism is NOT simply a version of mysticism – Chiesa convincingly characterizes Buddhism as "an *inverted mysticism*":

> Unlike Eastern polytheisms and their stress on enjoyment, Buddhism is thus in this sense a religion of desire, but it organizes desire in a way that is very different from that of Judeo-Christianity. More precisely, Buddhism short-circuits 'all the variations of desire' (as poly-desire, we might add), which appear in it 'in a most incarnate fashion,' with the 'ultimate apprehension of the radically illusory character of all desire.'[14]

The formula of Buddhism would thus be: not the mystical "one with the world" (my immersion into the divine One bringing full enjoyment) but the "none with the world": I identify the void of my (in)existence, the nothingness of my Self, with the void of reality itself which lacks any substantial (id)entity. While mysticism aims at the subject's full immersion into the divine *jouissance*, Buddhism focuses on desire as the ultimate cause of our suffering: desire is inconsistent, it cannot ever be fulfilled, fully satisfied, because its nature is inconsistent – since its object is illusory, the false appearance of a void, the moment of desire's fulfillment is the moment of its defeat. Buddhism draws the radical consequence from this insight: the only way to avoid suffering is to step out of (gain a distance towards) the "wheel of desire," to avoid attachment to any object of desire, which means to accept (not only as a theoretical statement but also as an existential stance) that desires are illusory because all objects (of desire and in general) are non-substantial fluctuating appearances. Such an existential detachment is the only way for us to attain peace.

Buddhist Economics

However, from its very beginnings, Buddhism was not just a spiritual teaching: it also provided guidelines for how to organize social and economic life. In the last decades, this concept was systematically developed in numerous books and essays about Buddhist economics. Its partisans like to point out that they are not proposing a utopian plan for a perfect society: they just formulate pragmatic advices on how to make better any existing socio-economic system. It is nonetheless clear that Buddhist economics is mostly directed against Western individualism, consumerism and tendency to permanent growth.

The starting point of the Buddhist economics is Buddha's first great insight: there is suffering in the world, so our focus should not be on more and more pleasures which allegedly bring happiness but on diminishing pain and suffering. It may seem that this premise leads to a radical detachment from external material reality, from the infamous "wheel of desire": since desire for sensual objects is always condemned to failure, since it ends in dissatisfaction, the only true way out is nirvana, a radical renunciation to worldly engagements. However, Buddhism points out that even those who reach nirvana remain living beings in our material world, so the task is to maintain an inner spiritual distance to our material life, i.e., to accept (as a living spiritual experience, not just as an abstract intellectual stance) that external reality has to substantial truth, that it is a pandemonium of interconnected fleeting appearances. This pandemonium includes ourselves: we are not Selves at a distance from reality, we are part of its incessant flow, and the origin of suffering is our ignorance, our blindness for this fact.

As the partisans of Buddhist economics repeat tirelessly, Buddhism does not advocate ascetic renunciation to worldly pleasures but the proper measure between wealth and poverty, between individualism and communal spirit: wealth is good if it serves our collective well-being.

The Buddhist notion of the right measure, of "just the right amount," does not refer only to individuals: it aims at not harming oneself or others, where others are not only other human beings but all that lives. In contrast to Western individualism, Buddhism advocates a holistic approach: my well-being depends on the well-being of all others around me, but also on the balanced exchange with nature. No wonder, then, that Buddhist economics advocates a constrained/limited desire, a desire controlled by spirit, deprived of its excessive nature: it relies on the distinction between true desires and false desires. False desires are desires for pleasure attained through the consummation of sensual objects or through their possession, and they are by definition insatiable, never fully satisfied, always striving for me. True desires are desires for well-being, and to arrive at well-being, a rational mind has to regulate and contain sensual desires. We thus arrive at the opposition between limitless sensual desires and the spiritual desire for well-being:

> Consumption may satisfy sensual desires, but its true purpose is to provide well-being. For example, our body depends on food for nourishment. Consumption of food is thus a requirement for well-being. For most people, however, eating food is also a means to experience pleasure. If in consuming food one receives the experience of a delicious flavor, one is said to have satisfied one's desires.[15]

From my Lacanian standpoint, it is here that problems arise: what Buddhism aims at is a desire deprived of its excess which makes it a human desire, enjoyment deprived of its constitutive surplus. When we eat, we almost never do it just for our long-term spiritual well-being, we do it for the pleasure of eating, and it is this pleasure, not its subordination to some higher goal, which makes us human. Recall here Lacan's example of breast-feeding: a child sucks the breast to get food (milk), but the repeated act of sucking soon turns into the true source of pleasure, so that the child is pushed to such beyond the satisfaction of its needs. The same holds even more obviously for sex: we almost never engage in sex to fulfill its natural goal (procreation) but for the enjoyment it provides – we became human exactly when sex leaves behind its "natural" goal of procreation and turns into an end in itself. And it is totally wrong to characterize this shift as an abandonment to limitless sensual desires: intense sex as an end-in-itself, separated from its natural goal, is arguably our most elementary meta-physical experience: our sensual pleasure is "transubstantiated" into an experience of another dimension, a dimension beyond direct physical reality.

We should thus turn around the opposition between false limitless desires which only bring suffering and the authentic spiritual desire for well-being: sensual desires are in themselves moderate, constrained to their direct goals, they become infinite and self-destructive only when they are infected by a spiritual dimension. Is this nonetheless not a form of Evil? Maybe, but, as already F.W.J. Schelling knew, only spirituality is self-destructive in its longing for infinity, which is why Evil is much more spiritual than our sensual reality. In other words, the root of Evil is not our egotism but, on the contrary, a perverted self-destructive spirituality which can also bring us to sacrifice our lives. This dimension is missing in Buddhist economics, which is why its declared goal of the proper measure, when one attempts to practice it, tends to end up in some form of (not always) soft Fascism. (Recall that Fascism also presents itself as the middle road between the two extremes, capitalist individualism and Communist collectivism.) The cases usually mentioned are Malaysia, Thailand, Myanmar, Sri Lanka, Japan, even China, but the main reference is Bhutan where

> King Jigme Singye Wangchuck and its government have promoted the concept of 'gross national happiness' (GNH) since 1972, based on Buddhist spiritual values, as a counter to gauging a nation's development by gross domestic product (GDP). This represents a commitment to building an economy that would serve Bhutan's culture based on Buddhist spiritual values instead of material development, such as being gauged by only GDP.[16]

Sounds OK, if it were not for an event which somehow spoils the picture:

> Often overlooked in all the attention received by the tiny Himalayan kingdom of Bhutan's much-touted 'Gross National Happiness' program is that the government's version of happiness includes being free of any unwelcome ethnic minorities. More than 100,000

ethnic Nepalese – a Hindu minority in Bhutan for centuries – were forced out of Bhutan in the early 1990s by authorities who wanted to impose the country's dominant Buddhist culture.[17]

This is the price we have to pay if we ignore the paradoxes of desire deployed by Freud and Lacan.

Why Bodhisattva is a Fake

The key question that arises here is, of course: where does desire come from? How do we get caught into its illusion? Desire cannot be accounted for in the terms of the opposition between reified particular objects and the void beneath them, so that it arises when we get excessively attached to particular objects. The object-cause of desire (what Lacan calls *objet a*) is not an empirical object, it is a virtual element which disturbs the harmonious natural circuit described and celebrated by my Buddhist critics. So the vision, advocated by my critics, of a desire purified of its excess, is for Lacan totally illusory: desire is in itself a "pathological" excess, a de-stabilization of any balanced natural order. Suzuki seems to imply that what makes a desire mortifying is its "intellectualization," its submission to rational categories that reify the fluid life experience of reality into a world of fixed substantial objects. However, desire is at its most basic not an effect of mechanic intellectual imprisonment, it is a "deviation" inscribed into life itself. In other words, if we subtract desire from life we don't get a more balanced life, we lose life itself. To put it succinctly: Buddhism celebrates the stepping out of the "wheel of desire," while Lacan celebrates the subject's very fall into this "wheel": "not compromising one's desire" means a radical subjective engagement in a crazy desire which throws entire reality out of balance.

Or, to put it in yet another way, Buddhism accepts the common view that the purpose of life is happiness (to quote Dalai Lama, "the purpose of our lives is to be happy"), it just defines this term differently – here are a couple of statements by Dalai Lama which make this difference clear: "Happiness is not something readymade. It comes from your own actions." / "When we feel love and kindness toward others, it not only makes others feel loved and cared for, but it helps us also to develop inner happiness and peace." / "We don't need more money, we don't need greater success or fame, we don't need the perfect body or even the perfect mate. Right now, at this very moment, we have a mind, which is all the basic equipment we need to achieve complete happiness." / "Human happiness and human satisfaction most ultimately come from within oneself."[18] Following Freud, Lacan, on the contrary, asserts death drive as the basic component of our libidinal lives which operate beyond the pleasure-principle: what Lacan calls enjoyment (*jouissance*) emerges out of a self-sabotage of pleasure, it is an enjoyment in displeasure itself.

A Lacanian view is much closer to Dr House who, in one of the episodes of the series, when he tries to diagnosticize a patient with his group and one of his collaborators mentions that the patient radiates happiness, immediately adds "happiness" on a list of the patient's symptoms of his illness to be explained and abolished. The feeling of happiness is a dangerous symptom, not something we should strive for. And one should add here that the same goes for what is also considered the most spontaneous parental feeling: the immense love of one's own small child. Small children are horror embodied: stupid, annoying, smelling bad, breaking our sleep . . . so the feeling of love for them is a clear case of what is called the "Stockholm syndrome": a coping mechanism to a captive or abusive situation, when people develop positive feelings toward their captors or abusers over time. Isn't this the exact mechanism of how we cope with small children?

So what about the desperate Lacano-Buddhist attempt to read what Buddhism calls nirvana as basically the same stance as that signalled by Lacan's "traversing the fantasy"? We cannot simply dismiss it as a gross misunderstanding of Lacan because there is a grain of truth in it: desire is metonymic – every empirical positive object that we desire is a trap (in the sense that, if we get it, our desire is not fully satisfied but disappointed, we experience a "*ce n'est pas ca*" (this is not *that* what we really desired), so let's drop our attachment to particular objects and just persist surfing along from one object to another. In other words, a true betrayal of our desire is precisely our full attachment to a particular object as its true object – if we renounce this, if we maintain a distance towards every object, we attain peace, we are faithful to our desire, i.e., to the void in its heart which cannot be abolished by any object . . . But this logic ultimately fails: for Lacan, desire in its "purity" (considered without an empirical object of desire) cannot be transformed into a peaceful integration into a non-substantial changing multiplicity of our reality because desire is as such a gesture of breaking up the balance of reality. If we subtract particular objects, we get the gesture of breaking-up, of disturbing the balance, as such. What any particular empirical object of desire obfuscates is not the balance of a void but this negative gesture as such: any particular object particularizes this rupture as such, transforming it into a desire for something that positively exists as a particular object . . . But where is here the dimension of intersubjectivity? In her "Relational Dharma," Jeannine A. Davies deploys a "liberating model of intersubjectivity" – her starting point is the basic goal of practicing dharma, which is

> to discern the distinction between conventional and ultimate realities through direct experience. A simple example of the distinction between conventional and ultimate reality is the difference between the concept of water and the physical sensation of water. Its salient characteristics are of wetness and of a cool, warm, or hot temperature. As awareness discriminates between the concept of water and water's physical sensations, an insightful penetration into the nature of conceptual ideation occurs. Concepts are then seen as abstractions within consciousness, mental overlays born through prior conditioning.[19]

Davies, of course, has to concede that the practice of meditation is primarily focused on solitary, introspective methods, where stages of insight unfold within a climate of extreme mental seclusion and interpersonal isolation – her aim is to demonstrate how dharma can also be achieved through new practice of social interaction, In order to deploy this claim, she has to engage in the opposition between two main orientations of Buddhism, Mahayana and Theravada: Theravada concentrates on achieving dharma by means of individual practice of introspection, while Mahayana emphasizes dharma achieved by social interaction. Say, when an individual is afflicted by a trauma which threatens to destroy her/his psychic balance and ability to interact with others, Mahayana practices the Relational Dharma approach which

> mediates and attunes within an environment of empathic union, nourishing an atmosphere that assuages anxiety and facilitates the

generation of trust and safety to flow in the in-between. This process allows for the possibility of transforming negative or life-diminishing 'filters' into associations that widen and deepen identity. In this experience, the appearance of something 'foreign,' 'not part of,' or 'too much,' is relaxed, so that one's sense of what constitutes a 'whole person' naturally broadens and evolves, and a deeper understanding of oneself and the relationship between oneself and others emerges.[20]

In such an approach, one achieves "the inner liberty to feel another's suffering as inseparable to one's own and the compassion to seek to alleviate it, thus respecting the freedom of others as inseparable to one's own freedom," a freedom to "forgive others for their transgressions. In order to forgive, the ability to 'step back' and recognize the conditions that gave rise to his or her actions versus reacting from a place of personalizing these actions, must be developed. As awareness into the causal relationships that led this individual to be wounded and act in a harmful ways becomes recognized, relational objectivity emerges and compassion becomes possible."[21] Such a stance opens up a path to peacefully revolutionize our world beset by violence and non-sustainable action: our

insight into the conscious engagement of interrelatedness may be one of the most important in terms of its spiritual, social, and political implications. It is only when we see with greater clarity the intimate causation of how 'we,' citizens of the Whole, affect totality that we find the inspiration to take personal responsibility for our presence and fine tune our physiological, emotional, and physical resonance within the Whole.[22]

Suffering and obstacles to freedom do not simply vanish, they are not simply left behind; in an almost Hegelian way, they are re-experienced as vehicles for growth and freedom. They are deprived of their substantial identity and put in their relational context in which they arise and disappear in co-dependence, resonating within the Whole.

Another difference between Theravada and Mahayana concerns the accessibility of nirvana which makes the subject a bodhisattva: in Theravada, encountering somebody who already is a Buddha is needed to truly make someone a bodhisattva – any other resolution to attain Buddhahood may easily be forgotten or abandoned during the long time ahead. Theravada thus held that the bodhisattva path was only for a rare set of individuals and has to be transmitted through exclusive lineage, in contrast to Mahayanists who universalized the *bodhisattvayana* as a path which is open to everyone and is taught for all beings to follow.

To maintain this universality, the Mahayana tradition has to introduce a distinction between two different notions of a bodhisattva's relationship to nirvana. The basic goal is to become arhat ("the one who is worthy"), a perfected person, one who has gained insight into the true nature of existence and has achieved nirvana (spiritual enlightenment): the arhat, having freed himself from the bonds of desire, will not be reborn. While the state of an arhat is considered in the Theravada tradition to be the proper goal of a Buddhist, Mahayana adds to it an even higher level,

a kind of non-dual state in which one is neither limited to samsara nor nirvana. A being who has reached this kind of nirvana is not restricted from manifesting in the samsaric realms, and yet they remain fully detached from the defilements found in these realms (and thus they can help others).[23]

We thus obtain the distinction between two kinds of nirvāṇa: the nirvāṇa of an arhat and a superior type of nirvāṇa called apratiṣṭhita (non-abiding) that allows a Buddha to remain engaged in the samsaric realms without being affected by them. However, the predominant Mahayana notion of bodhisattva silently concedes that to arrive at such non-dual state is practically impossible, so he heroically sacrifices his own dharma and postpones his awakening until all living beings will be liberated – bodhisattvas take the following vow: "I shall not enter into final nirvana before all beings have been liberated," or "I must lead all beings to Liberation. I will stay here till the end, even for the sake of one living soul."

The bodhisattva who wants to reach Buddhahood for the sake of all beings, is more loving and compassionate than the sravaka (who only wishes to end their own suffering): he practices the path for the good of others (*par-ārtha*) while the sravakas do so for their own good (*sv-ārtha*). I find this distinction between *par-ārtha* and *sv-ārtha* potentially very dangerous: although Mahayana appears more "democratic," allowing everyone to attain dharma, does its notion of bodhisattva who refuses to enter nirvana not conceal a new form of elitism: a selected few who remain caught into our ordinary reality (in the wheel of desire), legitimize their special privileged position by the fact that they could have reached nirvana but postponed it to help all others to reach it. In some radical sense nirvana thus becomes impossible: if I reach it, I act as an egotist, caring only for my own good; if I act for the good of others, I postpone my entry into nirvana . . . I consider this privileged position dangerous because it remains caught in a dualism that authentic Buddhism promises to leave behind: the realm of nirvana becomes a Beyond which we strive to reach. The danger resides in the fact that this position relies on what one could call the basic syllogism of self-sacrifice: I want all living beings to overcome their suffering and achieve the supreme good; to do this, I have to sacrifice my own happiness and accept suffering – only in this way my own life has meaning . . .

Again, the danger is that a short-circuit necessarily occurs here: I automatically take my own suffering as a proof that I am working for the good of others, so that I can reply to anyone who criticizes me: "Can't you see my suffering? Who are you to criticize me when I sacrifice myself for you?" At this point, happiness and sacrifice are no longer opposed, they fully coincide: *what brings me "happiness" (in the sense of libidinal satisfaction) is the very pain of my sacrifice which I (mis)read as a proof that my life has a deeper meaning.* This is why the only authentic nirvana means that I fully remain in this world and just relate to it differently: "non-abiding" nirvana is the ONLY full and true nirvana. So where does even this authentic nirvana fail?

To see this, we have to turn to the status of intersubjectivity in Buddhism: Buddhism ignores the radical intersubjectivity of desire, the fact that desire is always reflexive (a desire for desire, a desire for being desired), and that the primordial lacking object of desire is myself, the enigma of what I am for my others. From the Freudian standpoint, this is also the problem with the Politically Correct struggle against harassment: it presupposes that every individual has its own unique "true" desire which is then repressed or oppressed due to the ideological (mostly patriarchal) compulsion and other forms of social domination, so that if we get rid of this oppression, we will be able to fully enjoy in following our true desire. According to Lacan (and already Freud), however, our desire is irreducibly (constitutively) "alienated," mediated by the desire of the Other in all three meanings of the term: I desire to be desired by the Other; my desire (even in its most transgressive form) is structured by the big Other, the symbolic coordinates of my universe; the enigma that propels my desire is the enigma of the impenetrable Other (what am I for others? how do they perceive me?). This is why it is meaningless to search for my own "true" desire: as Lacan put it, my desire is the desire of the Other.

What this means is that, as Hegel clearly saw it, domination of others and violence towards them is a key moment of the painful process of intersubjective recognition. This violence is not an expression of my egotist self-interest, it relies on an "evil" for which I am ready to put at risk my own welfare and even my life. Relational dharma is not enough to account for this "evil" since this dimension of "evil" is constitutive of how I experience an Other: as an impenetrable abyss which cannot be dissolved in a fluid network of appearances. At is most basic, "evil" has nothing to do with my egotist interests: it is more spiritual than simple self-interest – the Buddhist notion of samsara ("the wheel of desire") ignores this spiritual aspect of "evil."

This is where the already-quoted passage about the "key difference between Freud/Lacan/Zizek/et al. and Nagarjuna" – "the former presuppose that this [rise of dominating ego] is unavoidable – the best we can do is to come to terms with the ego (etc.) process and try not to get too caught up in the delusional tricks it plays on us"[24] – totally misses the point: Buddhism describes how we can gradually get rid of the egotist stance of domination over others and of being enslaved to our desires which both cause suffering; our goal is to reach dharma in which our ego dissolves in the flux of appearances and loses its substantial identity. Within this space, Freud and Lacan can only appear as going half-way: they clearly see the self-destructive nature of the dominating Ego, but they ignore that there is a domain beyond the ego and its paradoxes, the domain of inner peace and happiness, so their ultimate reach is to escribe the paradoxes of the ego. For Freud and Lacan, on the contrary, there is nothing beyond the antagonisms of our reality, nothing but a gap of impossibility that thwarts it from within: everything that we perceive as its Beyond we project it there. What this means is not that what Buddhists describe as nirvana or dharma is an illusion or a fake: it is a profound experience of subjective destitution, but it nonetheless functions as the obfuscation of a more radical experience of a gap out of which our reality appears.

Since dharma is as a rule described as the highest freedom accessible to us, one should point out that, to anyone who knows a little bit about Hegel, the radical opposition between the Buddhist and Hegel's notion of freedom cannot but strike the eye: for Buddhism, we are truly free when we liberate ourselves from the rational categories which cut into pieces and thus mortify the pure non-substantial flux of reality, while for Hegel, the basic form of freedom is precisely the infinite power of abstraction that pertains to our Understanding (not Reason), the power to interrupt the smooth flow of reality and to cut mechanically reality into its pieces. The very idea that there is something (the core of the substantial content of the analysed thing) which eludes Understanding, a trans-rational Beyond out of its reach, is the fundamental illusion of Understanding. In other words, all we have to do to get from Understanding to Reason is to *subtract* from Understanding its constitutive illusion – Understanding is not too abstract/violent, it is, on the contrary, as Hegel put it apropos of Kant, *too soft towards things*, afraid to locate its violent movement of tearing things apart into things themselves. In a way, it is epistemology versus ontology: the illusion of Understanding is that its own analytic power (the power to make "an accident as such – that what is bound and held by something else and actual only by being connected with it – obtain an existence all its own, gain freedom and independence on its own account") is only an "abstraction," something external to "true reality" which persists out there intact in its inaccessible fullness. In other words, it is the standard critical view of Understanding and its power of abstraction (that it is just an impotent intellectual exercise missing the wealth of reality) which contains the core illusion of Understanding. To put it in yet another way, the mistake of Understanding is to perceive its own negative activity (of separating, tearing things apart) only in its negative aspect, ignoring its "positive" (productive) aspect – Reason is Understanding itself in its productive aspect.

The common counter-argument is here: but is for Hegel such mortifying abstraction not just a negative moment followed by a notional mediation by means of which we return to a higher form of organic unity? Yes, but this higher organic unity in no way returns to the reality of direct experience: in it, any reference to direct experience is obliterated, we move entirely within notional self-mediation. To put it in abstract formal terms, for Hegel, first negation negates what is given, some positive content, but this negation remains within the horizon of this content, while in "negation of negation" this very horizon is negated, we change the very field in which we move. An example from popular culture: the negation of life (of being alive) is death, but its negation is undeadness, when we become "living dead," outside the space of the opposition between life and death.

This doesn't mean that Hegel does not allow for something that echoes the practice of meditation which (within Theravada Buddhism) "has primarily focused on solitary, introspective methods, where stages of insight unfold within a climate of extreme mental seclusion and interpersonal isolation." However, while, in Buddhism, through such practice the mind "experiences a kind of current of quiet peace," for Hegel introspection confronts us with an awful space in which ghastly apparitions of partial objects float around – here is his most famous and often quoted passage of this "night of the world":

> The human being is this night, this empty nothing that contains everything in its simplicity – an unending wealth of many representations, images, of which none belongs to him – or which are not present. This night, the interior of nature, that exists here – pure self – in phantasmagorical representations, is night all around it, in which here shoots a bloody head – there another white ghastly apparition, suddenly here before it, and just so disappears. One catches sight of this night when one looks human beings in the eye – into a night that becomes awful.[25]

One should not be blinded by the poetic power of this description, but read it precisely – is there not a strange echo between this passage and Hegel's description of the negative power of Understanding which is able to abstract an entity (a process, a property) from its substantial context and treat it as if it has an existence of its own? "That an accident as such, detached from what circumscribes it, what is bound and is actual only in its context with others, should attain an existence of its own and a separate freedom—this is the tremendous power of the negative."[26] It is thus as if, in the ghastly scenery of the "night of the world," we encounter something like *the power of Understanding in its natural state*, spirit in the guise of a *proto-spirit* – this, perhaps, is the most precise definition of horror: when a higher state of development violently inscribes itself in the lower state, in its ground/presupposition, where it cannot but appear as a monstrous mess, a disintegration of order, a terrifying unnatural combination of natural elements. And Hegel's ultimate lesson is to learn to "tarry with the negative," not to dissolve its unbearable tensions into any kind of natural positive flux of appearances.

The main opposition that traverses the recent revival of Hegel studies is the one between Kantian and Aristotelian approach. The "Kantians" (Pippin, Brandom) read Hegel's *Logic* as a radicalized transcendental *a priori* for every possible intelligibility of the universe, while the "Aristotelians" insist that the transcendental dimension (which functions only insofar as it is embodied in a self-conscious living being) is grounded in and emerges from life. In her anti-Kantian Aristotelian reading of Hegel, Karen Ng[27] argues that that "self-consciousness has its ground in the category of life, without which the categories of reason, spirit and self-consciousness would lack content, a determinate relation to the world." In his *Critique of Judgment*, Kant tried to bridge the gap between consciousness and matter through the category of life which implies purposiveness as its immanent principle. "Yet on Kant's picture, purposiveness is merely a 'regulative' rather than 'constitutive' principle—a principle that judgment 'heautonomously' requires of itself for scientific inquiry but that it does not 'autonomously' give to nature as a principle genuinely constitutive of the objects of experience." Ng argues that "this distinction does not really hold up under scrutiny," that the "as if" character of regulative judgements itself seems to commit one to "the thought that nature is purposively constituted such that teleological explanations are satisfactory. And it is precisely here where Hegel will seek to rescue Kant from himself, by showing that purposiveness is not just a regulative principle with merely subjective validity but a principle with actual purchase on objectivity." So life is a "context in which subjects, objects, and their relationship come to have meaning at all."[28] My position is here a third one: the opposition between organic life and reason is not all-inclusive, to pass from organic life to reason (the domain of discourse), another level intervenes which is neither life nor rationality but an "irrational" eruption of absolute negativity that mystics called the monstrous "night of the world," of which – as we have just seen – Hegel was fully aware.

Insofar as this "night of the world" stands for the volid of subjectivity (the barred subject, $) , my critic nonetheless has a point in approaching feminine stance to mystical "night of the world." Some feminists protest: "Don't tell me what a woman is, based entirely on what she is not!"[29] But this is precisely what should be done since the basic subjective stance of a woman is pure negativity, the power of NOT, which is why Lacan says "woman doesn't exist." So it's not women who are deficient (fallen) men, men are women who "fell" into determinate positive identity.

This "fall" is what Althusser describes as ideological interpellation. Many interpreters and critics of Althusser's theory of interpellation already pointed out the circularity of the process of interpellation: yes, ideology interpellates an individual into subject; however, for the individual to recognize itself in the interpellation, it must already be open to interpellative call, i.e., in Hegelese, it must already be a subject "in itself." What this means is that we are dealing with a (subtly asymmetrical) mutual causation: both the subject and the big Other, the agent of interpellation, emerge through the process of interpellation. This convoluted structure is that of what Hegel called "absolute recoil": the subject-effect retroactively causes its Cause. Recall a political case: Communists are motivated by their shared Cause, but this Cause exists (is efficient) only through the activity of its partisans . . . Is, however, this all we can say about the circularity of interpellation? Lacan moves one step beneath and includes into this process the moment of failure – his succinct formula is: X is interpellated into a signifying identity, i.e., subordinated to a Master-Signifier, this subordination fails, a part of (what will become) subject resists interpellation, remains out of its scope, and the subject proper IS this remainder. Recall the standard case of love declaration: I try to express my inner stance to my beloved, I ultimately fail, and through this failure my love is confirmed as authentic. (If I express myself perfectly in my declaration, it is not love but a flat mechanic expression.) So the circular paradox here is that the subject is the failure of the operation to become subject: obstacle is a positive condition. Circularity means that the remainder (of the failure) of an operation retroactively causes this operation: there is no subject before the process of symbolic interpellation/subjectivization who tries to express itself in it, this subject emerges only retroactively through the failure of its attempt.

We encounter a similar (although not the same) circularity also in the process of ideology. It is not enough to say that ideology presents an artificial social construct as a biological or social fact – recall Judith Butler's classic case: sex identity is not a natural fact or a fact grounded in some eternal (patriarchal or divine) laws, it is the result of a complex symbolic process which is basically contingent and historically limited. One must add the opposite claim: in our postmodern era, ideology can also function as a historicist relativization of something that has deeper roots – for example, capitalist ideology presents exploitation and corruption as a contingent secondary fact, not as something that pertains to the very notion of capitalism. In other words, ideology doesn't only elevate something contingent into a necessity, it also dismisses as a contingent deviation something that belongs to the necessity constitutive of a given space.

Against Sacrifice

This radical negativity brings us back to the topic of sacrifice. We have seen what kind of sacrifice the notion of bodhisattva implies – it remains firmly within the frame of the traditional sacrifice: I choose to remain in the valley of tears, postponing my full Enlightenment in order to work for the global elimination of suffering. Buddhist Enlightenment itself implies a paradoxical self-reflective sacrifice: in emptying myself of futile desires the pursuit of which always disappoints me, I in a way sacrifice sacrifice itself, I realize that what I sacrifice is in itself worthless. (This is also how the ambiguity of assuming the position of bodhisattva can be understood: sacrificing/postponing my entry into nirvana brings me back to the space of surplus-enjoyment, I am allowed to get fully engaged in a passionate struggle . . . The trick is that I cover up my re-entry into the domain of passionate engagement with the fake legitimization that I am just submitting myself to the high ideal of helping others.) So the notion of sacrifice and its ambiguities definitely deserve a closer look.

The topic of M.Night Shyamalan's *Knock at the Cabin* (2023) is how the end of the world is prevented by a sacrifice in the last seconds – here is the basic storyline[30]. Seven-year-old Wen is vacationing with her parents, Eric and Andrew, at their remote cabin in rural Pennsylvania.

Four mysterious strangers – Sabrina, Adriane and Redmond, led by Leonard – break into the cabin and tie the entire family up. They claim they have no intention to harm the family – they have been compelled by visions and an unknown power to find the family. The group foresees an upcoming apocalypse in which oceans will rise, a plague will descend, the sky will fall, and finally an unending darkness will blanket the earth – this can only be averted if the family kills one of their own as a sacrifice. Eric and Andrew believe the group is lying and the attack is rooted in hate and delusion. When the family refuses to choose, the visitors sacrifice one of them (Redmond) by beating him to death. The TV reports devastating mega tsunamis, which Leonard says is the start of the apocalypse. After he sacrifices all three of his companions, he tells the three survivors they will only have minutes to decide before it is too late, and then slashes his own throat. Upon his death, the skies darken and lightning bolts cause fires and more planes to fall. Eric now believes that the events are real; not wanting Wen to grow up in a destroyed world, he offers himself as the sacrifice – he feels that they were chosen to sacrifice their family because their love was pure. Andrew reluctantly shoots Eric before lightning strikes set the cabin on fire. Andrew and Wen find the visitors' truck with belongings that mostly corroborate their stories; they drive to a crowded diner nearby, where they watch news reports confirming that the disasters have subsided.

Although the notion that a chosen individual's sacrifice out of love may save humanity gives birth to Christological associations, it is difficult to imagine a more anti-Christian movie. Among recent movies, a similar sacrifice is the topic of Yorgos Lanthimos' *The Killing of a Sacred Deer* (2017). A sixteen-year-old Martin tells the respected Dr. Steven Murphy that, in light of Steven botching Martin's father's surgery resulting in his death, Steven's family will die from a mysterious illness unless Steven himself chooses one to kill. The family starts experiencing weird symptoms (paralysis, lack of appetite, eyes bleeding), no matter what Steven does, up to tying up Martin in his basement beating him roughly. So, Steven spins in a circle with a hat over his eyes and randomly shoots and kills his son Bob. In the final scene, we see the Murphy family minus Bob at a diner; Martin walks in, looks at them without their youngest and, satisfied, leaves the diner. Lanthimos himself referred the story of his film to Euripides' late tragedy *Iphigenia in Aulis* in which Agamemnon sacrifices his daughter in order to pacify the goddess Artemis and bring good winds to the Greek ships on their way to Troy. Such a procedure obeys the clear logic of sacrificing something precious to prevent a much bigger catastrophe; one of its late forms is found in Stalinist show trials: by confessing their guilt, by assuming responsibility for the problems and failures of the Soviet system, the accused did a great service to the Party, saving it, maintaining its purity – the troubles of daily life were not the Party's responsibility . . . The same effort to rescue the Other sustains the neurotic's guilt: the neurotic blames himself, he takes the failure upon himself in order to maintain the fantasy of an ideal father.

This, however, is precisely *not* what happens in Christ's death: his sacrifice does not obfuscate the Other's (God-the-Father's) lack – on the opposite, *it displays this lack*, the inexistence of the big Other. It was already Hegel who wrote that what dies on the cross is the God of Beyond himself: instead of us sacrificing to or for God, God sacrifices himself and dies – the message of this paradox can only be that *there is no one to sacrifice to/for*.[31]

In other words, as Rene Girard said, the sacrifice of Christ is the act destined to break/end the very logic of sacrifice. In contrast to this, the sacrifice in *Knock at the Cabin* remains at the level of neurotic symptoms which are "tantamount to Other-sustaining (self-)sacrifices"[32], and, as Johnston put it, "neurotics become truly atheistic when analysis enables them to cease consciously and unconsciously making themselves suffer in the name of shielding certain significant Others in their life histories from ignorance and/or impotence."

The basic problem of Tarkovsky's last two films, *Nostalgia* and *Sacrifice*, is the problem of how, through what ordeal or sacrifice, is it possible today to attain the innocence of pure belief. The hero of *Sacrifice*, Alexander, lives with his large family in a remote cottage in the Swedish countryside (another version of the very Russian *dacha* which obsesses Tarkovsky's heroes). The celebrations of his birthday are marred by the terrifying news that low-flying jet planes signalled the start of a nuclear war between the superpowers. In his despair, Alexander turns himself in prayer to God, offering him everything that is most precious to him to have the war not have happened at all; in a sacrificial gesture, he burns his beloved cottage (the cabin also burns at the end of *Sacrifice*). The war is "undone," and Alexander is taken to a lunatic asylum . . . In *Nostalgia*, this pure, senseless act that restores meaning to our terrestrial life, is accomplished by the same actor (Erland Josephson) who, as the old fool Domenico, burns himself publicly. To this sacrifice, one should give all the weight of an obsessional-neurotic compulsive act: if I accomplish the proper sacrificial gesture, THE Catastrophe will not occur or will be undone – the well-known compulsive gesture of "If I do not do this (jump two times over that stone, cross my hands in this way, etc. etc.) something bad will occur." Tarkovsky is well aware that a sacrifice, in order to work, must be in a way meaningless, a gesture of "irrational," useless expenditure or ritual (like traversing the empty pool with a lit candle or burning one's own house) – the idea is that only such a gesture of just "doing it" spontaneously, a gesture not covered by any rational consideration, can restore the immediate faith that will deliver us and heal us from the modern spiritual malaise. The Tarkovskian subject here literally offers his own castration (renunciation of reason and domination, voluntary reduction to childish "idiocy," submission to a senseless ritual) as the instrument to deliver the big Other: it is as if only by accomplishing an act which is totally senseless and "irrational" that the subject can save the deeper global Meaning of the universe as such.[33]

What elevates Tarkovsky above cheap religious obscurantism is the fact that he deprives this sacrificial act of any pathetic and solemn "greatness," rendering it as a bungled, ridiculous act (in *Nostalgia*, Domenico has difficulties in lighting the fire which will kill him, and the passers-by ignore his body in flames; *Sacrifice* ends with a comic ballet of men from the infirmary running after the hero to take him to the asylum – the scene is shot as a children's game of catching each other). It would be all too simple to read this ridiculous and bungled aspect of the sacrifice as an indication of how it has to appear as such to everyday people immersed in their run of things and unable to appreciate the tragic greatness of the act. Tarkovsky, whose films are otherwise totally deprived of humour and jokes, reserves mockery and satire precisely for scenes depicting the most sacred gesture of supreme sacrifice (already the famous scene of Crucifixion in *Andrei Roublev* is shot in such a way: transposed into the Russian winter countryside, with bad actors playing it with ridiculous pathos, with tears flowing).

Such an authentic sacrifice functions as a gesture of total self-renunciation: "in self-renunciation one understands one is capable of nothing."[34] In theological terms, this renunciation bears witness to the total gap that separates man from god: the only way to assert one's commitment to unconditional Meaning of Life is to relate ALL of our life, our entire existence, to the absolute transcendence of the divine, and since there is no common measure between our life and the divine, the sacrificial renunciation cannot be part of an exchange with God – we sacrifice all (the totality of our life) *for nothing*: "The contradiction which arrests [the understanding] is that a man is required to make the greatest possible sacrifice, to dedicate his whole life as a sacrifice – and wherefore? There is indeed no wherefore."[35] What this means is that there is no guarantee that our sacrifice will be rewarded, that it will restitute Meaning to our life – one has to make a leap of faith which, in the eyes of an external observer, cannot but appear as an act of madness (like Abraham's readiness to kill Isaac): "At first glance the understanding ascertains that this is madness. The understanding asks: what's in it for me? The answer is: nothing."[36] The ultimate meaning of sacrifice is therefore *the sacrifice of meaning itself.*

Knock At the Cabin may appear to purvey similar complexity, but it doesn't: what takes place is, as expected, only constant doubts of all participants, prisoners and intruders, about the reality of the catastrophic prospect which mobilizes them. A true complexity would involve a weird reversal: the terrorized family itself secretly believes in the threat, and the four "fundamentalist" intruders doubt their own visions which brought them there – only in this way would we approach the ambiguities of belief today.

The stratagem of sacrifice is thus to deprive death of its meaninglessness. On hearing of the death of a Turkish ambassador, Talleyrand is supposed to have said: "I wonder what he *meant* by that?" (More commonly, this quote is attributed to Metternich who purportedly uttered it upon Talleyrand's death in 1838.)[37] Does the logic behind this remark not fit perfectly Stalinism in which every event, no matter how contingent or "natural" it appears, has to have a hidden political meaning. Death is for sure an event which purveys no hidden meaning.

The Ultimate Choice

The only true radical ethical opposition is the one between Buddhism and (Lacan's formulation of) psychoanalytic ethics. They are both not anti-scientific: they accept that scientific achievements cannot be re-integrates into our daily experience. Thomas Metzinger[38] claims that we cannot help experiencing ourselves as "selves," i.e., it is impossible for us to phenomenologically imagine a selfless experience: one can know (in the purely epistemic sense of objective knowledge) that there is no substantial Self (this is what Metzinger develops in his PSM theory of subjectivity), but *"you* cannot believe in it":

> The SMT is a theory of which *you cannot be convinced*, in principle . . . . This fact is the true essence and the deepest core of what we *actually* mean when speaking about the "puzzle"—or sometimes even about the "mystery"—of consciousness. . . . If the current story is true, there is no way in which it could be intuitively true.[39]

However, Metzinger goes a step further here: there is one caveat that he allows, the Buddhist Enlightenment in which the Self directly-experientially assumes his own non-being, i.e., recognizes himself as a "simulated self," a representational fiction. Such a situation in which the phenomenal dream becomes *lucid to itself* "directly corresponds to a classical philosophical notion, well-developed in Asian philosophy at least 2500 years ago, namely, the Buddhist conception of 'enlightenment.'"[40] Such an enlightened awareness is no longer self-awareness: it is no longer I who experience myself as the agent of my thoughts, "my" awareness is the direct awareness of a self-less system, a self-less knowledge. In short, there effectively *is* a link, or at least a kind of asymptotic point of coincidence, between the radical brain-sciences position and the Buddhist idea of an-atman, of the Self's inexistence: the Buddhist subjective stance of "anatman" is the only subjective stance which really assumes the result of cognitivism (no Self), and which (in certain versions, at least) is fully compatible with radical scientific naturalism.

But it is here that we see clearly how, although Lacan defines the Freudian subject as the subject of modern science, this proximity only makes the gap more palpable. In Buddhism, you are taught to sacrifice desire in order to attain the inner peace of Enlightenment in which sacrifice cancels itself. For Lacan, the true sacrifice is desire itself: desire is an intrusion which throws off the rails the rhythm of our life, it compels us to forfeit everyday pleasures and comforts for discipline and hard work in the pursuit of the object of our desire, be it love, a political Cause, science . . . or, as Neil Gaiman put it in a memorable passage:

> Have you ever been in love? Horrible isn't it? It makes you so vulnerable. It opens your chest and it opens up your heart and it means that someone can get inside you and mess you up. You build up all these defenses, you build up a whole suit of armor, so that nothing can hurt you, then one stupid person, no different from any other stupid person, wanders into your stupid life . . . You give them a piece of you. They didn't ask for it. They did something dumb one day, like kiss you or smile at you, and then your life isn't your own anymore. Love takes hostages. It gets inside you. It eats you out and leaves you crying in the darkness, so simple a phrase like 'maybe we should be just friends' turns into a glass splinter working its way into your heart. It hurts. Not just in the imagination. Not just in the mind. It's a soul-hurt, a real gets-inside-you-and-rips-you-apart pain. I hate love.[41]

There is a cure against this horror of intense love – it's called marriage. A (not too) vulgar joke provides an insight into a truly happy marriage. Late in the evening, a wife and a husband lie in bed; the wife is trying to fall asleep, while the husband is reading a book. Every couple of minutes, he reaches with his hand over to the wife and gently rubs his finger into her vaginal lips. After this goes on for half an hour, the wife explodes: "I am trying to fall asleep! If you want to have sex, do it fast, don't play with me like that!" The husband replies: "Sorry, it is not about sex. I am just reading a book and every couple of minutes I need to wet my finger to turn a new page . . ."[42] This brings us to Pascal: the true Pascalean formula of marriage is not "You don't love your partner? Then marry him or her, go through the ritual of shared life, and love will emerge by itself!"; it is, on the contrary: "Are you too much in love with somebody? Then get married, ritualize your love relationship, in order to cure yourself of the excessive passionate attachment, to replace it with the boring daily custom . . ." Marriage is thus a means of re-normalization which cures us of the violence of falling in love. And, incidentally, are many "radical" Leftist intellectuals not doing something similar to the unfortunate husband? Afraid to approach the real of actual political struggle they just touch it fleetingly to wet their finger and go on reading and writing academic books (criticizing actual fighters) . . .

And does Buddhism not do something similar? It teaches us how to get rid of this soul-hurt, while psychoanalysis compels us to fully embrace it since, as Lacan put it, the highest moral Law is the Law of desire. To further clarify this difference, Rammstein's "Dalai Lama" indicates the way. The song is vaguely based on Goethe's "Der Erlkönig" ("King of the Elves"), a poem which tells of a father and son riding a horse when the wind begins to hypnotize the child and eventually the child dies. The child in the song is on a flight with his father; as in the poem, the travellers are menaced by a mysterious spirit which "invites" the child to join him (though only the child can hear the spirit's invitation). However, in the poem, the alarmed father rides for help, holding the child in his arms, only to find that his son is dead; in Rammstein's song, it is the father himself who causes the child's death . . . What does all this have to do with the Dalai Lama? Not only does the song make fun of the Dalai Lama's fear of flying, but the lyrics demonstrate a more intimate link with the core of the Buddhist teaching. Dalai Lama's fear of flying is strangely echoed in the figure of the Lord: "Man does not belong in the air, so the Lord in heaven calls his sons on the wind" to cause a strong turbulence that will kill the child. But how? Not just by crashing the plane but by directly haunting the child's soul: "A choir drips from the clouds / Crawls into the little ear / Come here, stay here / We are good to you / We are brothers to you." The Devil's voice is not a brutal cry but a soft loving whisper.

This ambiguity is crucial: the raw external threat is redoubled by a chorus of seductive voices heard only by the child. The child fights the temptation to surrender to these voices, but the father, holding him too tightly to protect him, does not notice the child's shortness of breath and "pushes the soul out of the child." (Note the ambiguous ending of the song: the lyrics never say that the plane really fell down, just that there was a strong turbulence.) The father (who obviously stands for the Dalai Lama) wants to protect the child from the external threat of reality (turbulence), but in his very excessive protection he kills his son. There is a deeper identity here between the Dalai Lama and the "king of all winds." The obvious implication is that the Buddhist protection from pain and suffering mortifies us, excludes us from life. So, to quote a well-known ironic paraphrase of the first lines of the GDR anthem, the message of "Dalai Lama" effectively is "Einverstanden mit Ruinen / Und in Zukunft abgebrannt" ("In agreement with the ruins / and in future burned down").[43]

However, "Dalai Lama" gives to this standard pessimist wisdom an additional spin – the central refrain of the song is: "Weiter, weiter ins Verderben / Wir müssen leben bis wir sterben" ("Further, further into ruin / We have to live till we die"). This is what Freud called "death-drive" at its purest, not death itself but the fact that we have to LIVE till we die, this endless dragging of life, this endless compulsion to repeat. The refrain is what in France they call a *lapalissade* (an empty tautological wisdom like "a minute before he died, Monsieur la Palice was still alive"). But Rammstein turns around the obvious wisdom "no matter how long you live, at the end you will die," replacing it with "till you die, you have to live." What makes the Rammstein version not an empty tautology is the ethical dimension: before we die we are not just (obviously) alive, we HAVE to live. For us humans, life is a decision, an active obligation – we can lose the will to live.

To grasp this, we need psychoanalysis – we need it not just to account for the (falsely) so-called "irrationalities" of the contemporary libidinal economy: as we have already seen, only a reading of Hegel's dialectics through psychoanalysis enables us to connect atheist Christianity, (our reading of) quantum physics, and the transcendental/ ontological parallax. But why is psychoanalysis needed to do this? Let me do here something impossible: I'll try to present as succinctly as possible my basic ontological stance which, reduced to its minimum, amounts to a specific version of anti-ontology.[44]

My reply to the big question "Why is there something and not nothing?" is: *because something is a failed nothing* (to paraphrase Mladen Dolar's claim that being is a failed non-being). So in some sense there is only nothing and not something – but, as we learned from quantum mechanics, this nothing or void is not totally empty, it is full of wave oscillations, and for something to emerge out of nothing, the "nothing" should be somehow blocked, barred, not allowed to find peace in its flat zero-state. So where does this barrier come from? My speculative conjecture is that it is not a mysterious something, it is another form of the Nothing itself – the pure flat nothing, not the nothing full of virtual wave oscillations. (We find here a strange echo of the Kabalah notion that, prior to creating the world (our reality), in a kind of radical self-contraction god had to create nothing itself as the space for new reality.) Reality thus emerges as an "incontinence of the void" (the title of one of my books taken from Samuel Becket), it emerges because a barrier prevents the void to rest in itself. The word "incontinence" is here well-chosen: reality is an excrement of the divine void, and humans themselves, the (for us and till now, at least) the top of creation, as Luther put it, fell out of god's anus.

Here my Hegelo-Lacanian position and that of Buddhism come very close – with one detail that changes everything. In Buddhism, the absolute ground out of which everything arises (and dissolves back into it) is the Void, the abyss of internal rest – humans should tend to rejoin it in order to get rid of desire and suffering that comes with the fall from it (Buddhism never properly explains how does the illusion of *maya* – being caught in *samsara*, the wheel of desire – and the striving for material objects emerge in the first place). In my view, however, the barrier (or, in theological terms, the Fall) comes first, it (logically) precedes what it is presumed to fall from: at its most basic, "reality" is a barrier, an impossibility, nothing behind the barrier, and, as we have just seen, even this void behind the barrier is divided, split in itself. The point is not that Buddhism excludes the dynamics of movement: as we have already seen, the Void as the ultimate reality is the medium in which the process-relational flux, the continual coming into existence and passing away of the experiential bits of the world, all of which is quite real, takes place. What the Void excludes is just the idea that this flux is sustained by some "deeper" substantial reality which cannot be resolved in its relations with others. The peace towards which we strive in Buddhism is nothing else than the peace of the full immersion into this flux of appearances – or, as Badiou, the Void in which multiplicities thrive.

So what Buddhism tries to get rid of is the fixation on any substantial identity that is exempted from the relational flux and disturbs its harmonious balance – but where does the temptation to do this come from? The Hegelo-Lacanian view turns the entire perspective around: the relational flux does not just flow in the medium of a Void, it is elicited by an irreducible bar, by an impediment which we, caught in its wheel, try to fill in by some substantial entity. The primordial fact is that of an absolute "contradiction," and that's why Lacan calls Hegel "the most sublime of hysterics" (the title of yet another of my books): the elementary reversal in a dialectical process is the displacement of the barrier from our subjectivity (we, mortal humans, cannot comprehend all of reality) to the Real which is barred already in itself – as in Christianity, where the distance that separates a human from god is transposed into god himself (god doesn't believe in himself). In the next step, of course, this self-difference in god is to be transposed into the self-difference in man: "God" is a name for the fact that man is not wholly (not divine but) *human* – whatever human being we encounter, "s/he is not it." This is why a true materialism does not simply claim that god is a product of humans, of their imagination: "god" names the fact that man in not wholly man, that there is an inhuman dimension in its core.

In the quantum universe, we encounter a similar circularity: we should reject the notion of wave oscillations as a productive flow whose effect is the ordinary single reality which arises when a wave oscillation collapses, but also the opposite view of wave oscillations as a kind of virtual echo that surrounds actual objects (David Bohm's view). While wave oscillations in some sense "produce" objects, they simultaneously come second, they are already structured around a void and tend to collapse to a single reality to fill in this void. The ontological parallax also displays a similar circular structure. We try to arrive at reality the way it really is in itself, and the transcendental is the "indivisible remainder" which relativizes every structure of reality: every cognition is rooted in a certain transcendental structure which cannot be deduced from ontological cognition since this cognition always relies on a transcendental horizon.

How can this work? As we have already seen, it works only if we presuppose a certain circularity (or retroactive causality) for which I used the Hegelian term "absolute recoil" (in my book of the same title). The basic model is here provided by Lacan's dictum that repression and the return of the repressed are one and the same – there is no positive repressed content preceding repression, no deep Unconscious waiting to be set free. We find here the circularity typical of the symbolic universe: what is repressed is retroactively created by repressed. Although in a theoretical space totally different from Lacan's, Michel Foucault saw this clearly: the basic thesis of his *History of Sexuality*[45] is that the process of symbolization, of submissive regulation, generates what it "represses" and regulates, i.e., the very medical-pedagogical discourse of disciplining sexuality produces the excess it tries to tame ("sex"), a process which began already in late antiquity when the Christian detailed descriptions of all possible sexual temptations retroactively generated what they fought. The proliferation of pleasures is thus the obverse of the power which regulates them: power itself generates resistance to itself, i.e., the excess it cannot ever control – reactions of a sexualized body to its subjection to disciplinary norms are imprevisible.

This circularity is based upon the reflexive inversion that characterized desire: a repression of desire inevitably turns into a desire for repression, i.e., repression itself gets libidinally invested. It is not only that regulative oppression produces what it regulates (in the Saint Paul sense that prohibition gives birth to the desire to violate it) – much more radically, the prohibition of some sexual desire or practice necessarily turns around into the desire for prohibition, i.e., the prohibition of enjoyment becomes a source of surplus-enjoyment. That's why Freud had to introduce the category of primordial repression (*Ur-Verdraengung*), a gesture that has to be presupposed and which constitutes the very space of repression, the space into which something can be repressed.

Lacan gets here more specific and makes a step further: what is primordially repressed is the binary signifier (S_2), the counterpart of the Master-Signifier (S_1). It is weird to read accusations that Lacan remains caught in a "binary" logic of sexual difference: did he not purify psychoanalysis of the last traces of the duality of "masculine" and "feminine" principles which underlies the entire pre-modern tradition from *yin-yang* onwards? Here, then, we encounter the first paradox: Lacan didn't do what one would expect from a psychoanalyst reading philosophy, he didn't "sexualize" philosophy – on the contrary, he DE-sexualized philosophy which was till him (more broadly till Descartes or, at least, till Kant) secretly sexualized. The lack of the binary signifier means precisely that (as Mladen Dolar put it[46]) while there is more than one sex, there are less than two: a woman's identity cannot be fixed into a signifier, and the entire tradition of patriarchy in which women are oppressed resides precise in the repeated attempts to construct the missing binary signifier which would complement the masculine Master-Signifier, i.e., to impose onto women a fixed symbolic identity which determines their socio-psychic functioning ("to be a true woman means to feel and act like . . ."). These attempts fail insofar as they try to eradicate the very hysterical core of (feminine) subjectivity which resides in the resistance to the symbolic identity imposed by the big Other (the primordial hysterical question is "Why am I what you are saying that I am?"). When some trans-feminists insist on the asymmetry of the masculine and feminine sexual identities, claiming that feminine identity is somehow closer to LGBT+ flexibility than to masculinity, they are thus making a valid point: for Lacan, although there is more than one sex there are not simply two sexes. That "more" is the fluid space which resists identification, and the basic aim of patriarchal ideology is to domesticate/fix it, to impose on it a firm identity, to determine "what a woman really is" (which means: how she *should* be and act).

When Lady Macbeth doubts if her husband is ready to commit the act she pushes him to do (killing king Duncan and taking his place) since he appears haunted by moral doubts, her rage explodes: "Come, you spirits / That tend on mortal thoughts, unsex me here, / And fill me from the crown to the toe topful / Of direst cruelty!" (*Macbeth*, Act I, scene 5, 40-43) "Unsexing" obviously means here stepping out of the feminine clichés of kindness and compassion – but this in no way equals abandoning a feminine stance: a ruthless and calculating woman is also one of the clichés about woman. The main thing to note here is that in a similar (but not symmetric) way the same holds also for men – each sex is "unsexed" in its own way. The reason is that "feminine" and "masculine" do not stand for a fixed set of properties: they both name a certain deadlock which can only be articulated in a series of inconsistent and even self-contradictory features.

Sexual difference arises out of this very de-sexualization, it stands for the two ways to organize the constitutive imbalance of primordial repression.[47] In the first version, the binary signifier, the symmetric counterpart of S_1, is "primordially repressed," and it is in order to supplement the void of this repression that the chain of S_2 emerges, i.e., the original fact is the couple of S_1 and the Void at the place of its counterpart, and the chain of S_2 is secondary; in the second version, in the account of the emergence of S_1 as the "enigmatic term," the empty signifier, the primordial fact is, on the contrary, S_2, the signifying chain in its incompleteness, and it is in order to fill in the void of this incompleteness that S_1 intervenes. How are the two versions to be coordinated? Is the ultimate fact the vicious circle of their mutual implication? What if, yet again, these two versions point towards the logic of Lacan's "formulas of sexuation"? Contrary to our expectations, it is the first version – the multitude emerges in order to fill in the lack of the binary signifier – which is "feminine," i.e., which accounts for the explosion of the inconsistent multitude of the feminine non-All, and it is the second version which is "masculine", i.e., which accounts for how a multitude is totalized into an All through the exception which fills in its void. However, the symmetry between the two versions is not full: as in the case of Kant's antinomies of pure reason where mathematical antinomies logically precede dynamic antinomies, the "feminine" version (multiplicity fills in the lack of the binary signifier) comes first, it accounts for the very emergence of multiplicity, of the non-totalizable series whose lack is then filled in by the reflexive Master-Signifier, the signifier of the lack of the signifier. Both versions are clearly opposed to the notion that "it all begins" with the multiplicity of multiplicities which "is" the void (as Badiou proposes): for Hegel and Lacan, void is not the neutral medium of multiplicities but the impossible/barred One, the One which is nothing but its own impossibility.

This circular structure also allows us to conceptualize the two opposed ways to deal with the duality of a universal and its particular moments. We can conceive universality as the barred One, the void of its own impossibility, and particular identities as attempts to resolve this impossibility – for Hegel, for example, "state" is a self-contradictory notion, it cannot ever effectively stand for the interests of its particular groups, and particular forms of State are attempts to resolve the universal impossibility, to find a feasible identity that would somehow function and obfuscate the underlying impossibility/antagonism. Or, in the opposite way, we can develop how a universality arises through an exception with regard to particular multiplicities, an exception which totalizes them. In Marx's analysis of commodities, money is such a universality: an exception (it has no use value) which, as such, gives body to value as the universal feature of all commodities. (Lacan did something strictly homologous with his concept of the phallic signifier as the signifier without signified.)

Universality thus arises out of the impossibility of a particular thing to be fully itself (in Hegelese, to fit its notion). Ernesto Laclau developed this aspect in detail in his notion of the struggle for hegemony: the permanent transformation implied in the notion of the permanent struggle for hegemony is not a direct continuation of the fact that everything in nature and reality in general is permanently changing; the dialectic of hegemonic process described by Laclau (where universality is simultaneously impossible and necessary/unavoidable) introduces a tension between particularity and universality in which universality is "for-itself," posited as such, not just the abstract medium of particular elements. Why do we talk of universal human rights? Precisely because there are large groups of people who cannot realize their potentials within the particular role conferred on them by the existing hegemonic order. Feminism arises when women experience that their social situation doesn't allow them to realize their potentials (to which the conservative answer is, of course, that women should learn to fully identify with the social role and place allocated to them, and that their endeavour to break out of it and demand more expresses a hysteric dissatisfaction caused by external ideological propaganda).

Only in the symbolic space does each particularity posit its own universality, so that the hegemonic struggle is not the struggle between particularities but the struggle of universalities themselves. And for this to happen, a bar has to affect universality itself, a bar which makes it impossible and which in this way opens up the space of hegemonic struggle, the struggle for which of the multiple particularities will assume the hegemonic role. But here, again, a split intervenes. Let's take a well-structured order of social hierarchy: at its top, we have a Master-Signifier, a privileged point which guarantees the stability of the entire order, and the task of a critical analysis is to demonstrate how the universality sustained by the Master-Signifier secretly privileges a particular content (say, our notion of "universal human rights" privileges a series of features that characterize Western liberal individualism) – this particular spin makes the universality false. Is there, then, a true universality? Marx already provided an answer: in our class societies, it is those at the bottom, those without a proper place in the social hierarchy, who stand for true universality. Proletarians are a universal class because they are a non-class among classes, a class with no stable social identity. This is why, for Marx, a proletarian is a human being "as such."

Does, however, all this not remain confined to the symbolic space, to the "logic of the signifier"? Can we transpose it into the pre-symbolic Real? Here quantum physics, the topic of the next chapter, enters the game.

3
ON SUPERPOSITIONS AND ATHINGS

The link between the 2023 big Oscar winner *Everything Everywhere All at Once* and quantum physics was often noted; however, the *Everything Everywhere* version is much less radical than the scientific notion of the superposition of states.[1] In quantum theory, one version of multiple superpositions "collapses" into our common reality, but there is no Fate or victory of the best in this: the collapse happens in an irreducibly contingent way – there are collapses which are (from our standpoint) better or worse, even catastrophic, but it all depends on pure chance.[2] To say "it's okay to pick one and be happy with that one" – the message of the film – is false because it is not us who picks one: nobody makes the choice, it just happens. (In contrast to this radical contingency of the collapse, the quantum world of superpositions implied by *Everything Everywhere* is Bohmian: in David Bohm's interpretation of quantum mechanics, there is one substantial reality – say, of a particle – and superpositions are just pilot waves that surround it, floating around it . . .) The awareness that other versions might have happened should mobilize us for a struggle, not lull us into resigned satisfaction. This, exactly, is what happened with *Casablanca* and the play the film is based on – not many people are aware that *Casablanca*, the top candidate for the "absolute" Hollywood film, is based on the play *Everybody Comes to Rick's* by Murray Burnett and Joan Alison (written in 1940; Warner Brothers bought the rights, so that the play was staged only in 1991).

We can compare the play and the movie as the two superposed versions of the same basic story – here are the main differences.[3] The four main characters (Rick, Rinaldo/Renault, Lois/Ilsa and Laszlo) are the most altered. Rick, a married man in the play who had cheated on his wife, a lawyer with a self-pitying streak, becomes in the film the cynical, tough, secretive loner. The immoral womanizer Rinaldo becomes the teasing, sophisticated, slightly sarcastic Renault. In the play, the Germans want money from Laszlo: they claim Laszlo had made $7 million from the anti-Nazi writings he'd published in Europe before he fled – if Laszlo turns the money over to the Third Reich, he gets to leave Casablanca. Plus Laszlo and Lois aren't married but just lovers (both married to another person). Laszlo is not an anti-Fascist hero but thoroughly cynical: he sends Lois to Rick knowing she will sleep with him for the Letters of Transit (and they do sleep together, in contrast to the film which is ambiguous with regard to this point). The Lois of the play is the most changed: she is a middle-age American tramp with no sense of loyalty, much less duty, though in the end she is ready to sacrifice herself not for a cause but for love. At the end, Laszlo and Lois get away safely as in the film, but the fate of Rick is tragic. Lois declares that she is leaving Laszlo for Rick, and he seemingly enlists her and Rinaldo in a plan to capture Laszlo, the price being the couple's safe conduct out of Casablanca. Once they're in the clear, Rick betrays Rinaldo, gives the Letters of Transit to Laszlo, and compels Lois to go with him, telling her: "We'll always have Paris." Rick then surrenders to Rinaldo and Strasser, likely to be sent to a prison camp and to his death.[4]

The first thing to note is that, at the end, it is not (as in the film) Rinaldo (Renault) who surprisingly turns out to be a good guy (shooting Strasser) but Rick himself who sacrifices everything. So there is no "beginning of a beautiful friendship": not only Rinaldo remains corrupted but the general tone of the play is that of a depressive and desperate common reality of opportunism and corruption, with no place for big gestures of patriotism and heroic political struggle – there is only one heroic act at the very end. Of course, such a vision was unacceptable for Hollywood after Pearl Harbour. But what interests us here is that in the play we get a much more realist depiction of the situation (I am well aware of the risks involved in using the term "realism"), with all the ambiguities and unresolved tensions that pervade our daily reality, and the movie transposes the story into a heroic melodramatic mood that befits the historical moment of anti-Fascist struggle. In contrast to *Everything Everywhere*, the superposition of the play and the film is irreducible, no version has ontological priority – we should not reduce the play to an unimportant prequel of the final result, a great movie. The movie itself appears in a new (and more true) light if we watch it against the background of the play. So we are here much closer to the spirit of quantum theory . . . But do we have the right to refer to quantum mechanics in this way?

How Can Reality Itself Be Wrong?

When a philosopher deals with quantum physics, the first temptation to avoid is to elevate its *prima facie* paradoxical results into a universal world-view, a formula that applies to all possible domains – Niels Bohr himself occasionally fell into this trap and argued that his notion of complementarity has wide applicability: from Kaballah (complementarity between God's love and God's justice), between life and physics, between energy and causation, between knowledge and wisdom . . . Did he thereby not come close to a kind of universal metaphysics that contains all of reality, in clear contrast to his repeated insistence that quantum mechanics is just a way we describe reality, with no ontological implications?

Closer to the spirit of our time, one should also reject the cultural historicization of superpositions and complementarity in quantum physics, perceiving them as one of the manifestations of the turn in the predominant ideology around 1900 (the reverse of the mechanistic-determinist materialism with its "naïve" notions of "objective reality"; the idea that, in new scientific advances, "matter is disappearing"; the passage from realism to modernism in arts with the accent on multiple subjective porspcctives; general doubt in rationalism and social progress): the theory of relativity and quantum mechanics are supreme scientific achievements which cannot be reduced to or accounted for in the terms of the social and ideological circumstances that gave birth to them. Yes, quantum mechanics emerged in a specific historical constellation, but this doesn't relativize its truth – as already Marx put it, certain categories (his example is the universal notion of labour) which are valid for all times can only appear as such, in their universality, in modern capitalist society in which labour becomes universal in the experienced social situation itself (workers are aware that they can pass from one kind of labour to another since they are paid for it by money, the universal equivalent of all values). In capitalism, I experience myself as a human being who is for contingent reasons engaged in one or another activity to survive. I am a universal being also for myself.

A little bit more pertinent, although still problematic, is to locate quantum mechanics in the shift between appearance and reality that took place at the same time. The gap that separates the quantum level from our ordinary perceived reality is NOT a gap between the ultimate hard reality and a higher-level unavoidable-but-illusory hallucination. On the contrary, it is the quantum level which is "hallucinated," not yet ontologically fully constituted, floating-ambiguous, and it is the shift to the "higher" level of appearances (our perceived reality) that makes it into a hard reality. Therein resides the embarrassing paradox encountered by the twentieth century "hard" sciences: in (among others) quantum physics, the "appearance" (perception) of a particle determines its reality – the very emergence of "hard reality" out of the quantum fluctuation through the collapse of the wave function is the outcome of observation, i.e., of the intervention of consciousness.[5] This premise of the ontological superiority of appearances is difficult to accept – a difficulty that doesn't concern only the ideological misuse or philosophical interpretation of a science: it is a difficulty that haunts science itself.

As it is clear from this last example, I approach quantum mechanics from the standpoint of the struggle between materialism and idealist or outright religious spiritualism. Throughout the twentieth century, quantum mechanics was celebrated as the ultimate proof that modern science itself is leaving behind deterministic mechanical materialism and admitted it is dealing with non-material entities, plus that the notion of our reality which takes place through being observed opens up to subjectivist denial of objective reality (does the primacy of appearances not imply an observer to whom things appear?). Some quantum physicists themselves claimed that the only way to account for our entire universe is to presuppose a global external observer (i.e., God). I am thoroughly opposed not only to this direct theological solution, but also to the traditional "realist" stance which no less secretly relies on a divine dimension (as Einstein explicitly stated) – it is only (what I consider) a correct reading of quantum physics which opens up the way to consequent materialism (even if, from a traditional reading, this may appear to be a weird materialism without matter).

This difficulty is what we'll focus on, taking as our starting point Lee Smolin's *Einstein's Unfinished Revolution*, a book wonderfully characterized by George Dyson as "the best explanation yet of what has yet to be explained" (quoted on the book's cover).[6] Smolin doesn't provide a new Theory of Everything; after bringing out the limitations of quantum mechanics, he very cautiously formulates a series of conjectures of how "what lies beyond quantum" will look. To go to the end, Smolin's starting point – quantum mechanics is the most successful theory ever formulated, the only problem with it is that it is wrong – should be supplemented with: what if the solution is not to make a big step into some unknown universe of hidden variables that would provide a full view and explanation of reality? What if the deadlocks of quantum mechanics point towards the weird fact that, measured by the standards of our reality, the "reality" of which quantum mechanics speaks is in some sense *in itself "wrong"*?

In *what* sense, exactly? In the sense that the universe of quantum waves described by science is incompatible with our intuitive notion of reality: science concerns only measurable quantities, it can't give an intuitive picture of what goes on at atomic scales. So is complementarity not a notion reflected into itself? It is not just the complementarity of qualities we measure (say, particles and waves, or position and momentum), but also the complementarity of the observed and the observer, of the quantum phenomena and the ordinary reality in which all measurements take place.[7] This is why I find problematic Smolin's claim that, "however weird the quantum world may be, it need not threaten anyone's belief in commonsense realism"(205) – the least one can add is that "commonsense realism" implies a belief in substantial reality of things which cannot be resolved in or reduced to a network of relations, plus that space is an irreducible aspect of our commonsense notion of reality. In contrast to Smolin's own idea that

> to extend quantum mechanics to a theory of the whole universe, we have to choose between space and time. Only one can be fundamental. If we insist on being realists about space then time and causation are illusions, emergent only at the level of a coarse approximation to the true timeless description. Or we can choose to be realists about time and causation. Then, like Rovelli, we have to believe that space is an illusion.
>
> 204[8]

Quantum mechanics thus immanently raises a fundamental ontological question: what is the status of its object? If it is not a part of our spatio-temporal reality, is it a part of another reality or just a theoretical fiction? But we should also turn the question around: is what we call philosophy still able to account for what quantum mechanics is dealing with?[9]

Bell's Theorem

At the very beginning of his bestselling *The Grand Design,* Stephen Hawking triumphantly proclaims that "philosophy is dead."[10] With the latest advances in quantum physics and cosmology, the so-called experimental metaphysics reaches its apogee: metaphysical questions about the origins of the universe, etc., which were till now the topic of philosophical speculations, can now be answered through experimental science and thus empirically tested . . . Upon a closer look, we, of course, soon discover that we are not yet quite there – almost, but not yet. Furthermore, it would have been easy to reject these claims and demonstrate the continuing pertinence of philosophy for Hawking himself (not to mention the fact that his own book is definitely not science, but its very problematic popular generalization): Hawking relies on a series of methodological and ontological presuppositions which he takes for granted.

But we should nonetheless not ignore philosophical implications of quantum mechanics; even when quantum mechanics may seem to indulge in wild speculations, its claims are getting empirical confirmation. The 2022 Nobel prize for physics was given to Alain Aspect, John F. Clauser and Anton Zeilinger for discovering the way that unseen particles, such as photons or tiny bits of matter, can be linked to, or "entangled" with, each other even when they are separated by large distances. Clauser said:

> Most people would assume that nature is made out of stuff distributed throughout space and time, and that appears not to be the case. . . . Quantum entanglement has to do with taking these two photons and then measuring one over here and knowing immediately something about the other one over there, and if we have this

property of entanglement between the two photons, we can establish a common information between two different observers of these quantum objects. And this allows us to do things like secret communication, in ways which weren't possible to do before.[11]

The obvious question that arises here is: could there be a more complete description of the world, with quantum mechanics reduced to just one of its parts? For example, could particles be carrying hidden information about what they will show as the result of an experiment, so that measurements display the properties that exist exactly where the measurements are conducted? Bell discovered that there is a type of experiment that can determine whether the world is purely quantum mechanical, or whether there could be another description with hidden variables.[12] If his experiment is repeated many times, all theories with hidden variables show a correlation between the results that must be lower than, or at most equal to, a specific value – this is called Bell's inequality. However, quantum mechanics violates this inequality: it predicts higher values for the correlation between the results than is possible through hidden variables.

The implications of these experiments are not only practical (they point towards the direct exchange of information at long distances) but also philosophical. Today the wave of critiques directed against the Copenhagen orthodoxy is rising – most quantum physicists no longer endorse it, Bohr's formulations are dismissed as a theory which prohibits any theory, as variations on the theme of "Shut up and calculate!".[13] For example, Sabine Hossenfelder's return to realism is clearly opposed to Hegel's idealism: there is a chaotic thickness ("ugliness") of reality that cannot be generated by means of formal (logical, mathematical) "beautiful" articulations. But while the demand to confront the big "metaphysical" question about the reality that sustains quantum phenomena is totally legitimate, one should not too easily "domesticate" the basic paradoxes displayed by the quantum measurements: not only is a kind of realism disproved by them, i.e., not only do we have to abandon the notion that a theory simply registers what goes on in independent "objective" reality. The properly Hegelian dimension of the elimination of hidden variables resides in the fact that this elimination does something that appears impossible for common sense: it proposes a procedure to demonstrate rationally and experimentally not the presence of something behind the phenomenal appearances but its absence, the fact that there is nothing behind. The inaccessibility of hidden depth is not just epistemological, it can be proven that it is part of reality itself – therein resides the basic reversal of Hegelian dialectical process, so we need to formulate a philosophical version of Bell's theorem. Critics of Bohr accuse him of irrationally prohibiting any speculations about what kind of reality there is behind the phenomena we measure and translate into mathematical formula – but what if, since the ontological question persists, we should transpose the limit that prohibits us to grasp reality-in-itself into this reality itself, conceiving this reality as something that is "barred," traversed by an irreducible impossibility?

The experimental testings of Bell's inequality thus provided the first clear case of what is usually called "experimental metaphysics": the result – the rejection not only of the hidden variables critique of quantum mechanics but also of its "orthodox" Copenhagen interpretation – has crucial ontological implications about the nature of time and space and about the general interconnectedness of reality. Bohr was a stubborn everyday-life realist: he was never tired of repeating that only our reality exists and that all that happens in quantum physics experiments is part of our common reality (apparatuses we use for experiments are part of this reality, the results of experiments are numbers that appear on a screen) – we never see wave oscillations or other quantum entities, the entire edifice of quantum mechanics is just a mathematical construct we use to account for the connection between phenomena we observe in our reality, it doesn't point to another sphere of reality beyond or beneath our common reality. The paradox is that, although experiments which confirmed Bell's hypothesis (a link between particles faster than the speed of light) were taken as a victory of Bohr against Einstein's insistence on hidden variables, they renewed the debate about the ontological status of quantum phenomena. In an anti-Bohr spirit, Bell spoke of "beables" as opposed to "observables": reality is not a chaotic mess waiting for observers so that it can "collapse" into observable objects, it is something that should be analysed the way it is in itself. The link between two particles that connects them faster than light means that at a certain level of reality, the time/space dimension functions in a way that is fundamentally different from the time/space of our reality: either information can move faster than light or there is another level of space where what appears to us far away is next to us. We should be careful to note here that the results of experiments which tested Bell's theorem do not exclude hidden variables as such, they only exclude *local* hidden variables, i.e., hidden variables which operate within our time-space in which the greatest speed is the speed of light. So the question remains: how are two correlated particles connected beyond our space-time since it seems that a signal passes between them faster than the speed of light? David Bohm's pilot wave theory which tries to explain this implies precisely such non-local hidden variables.

In quantum mechanics, counterfactual definiteness (CFD) is the ability to speak "meaningfully" of the definiteness of the results of measurements that have not been performed (i.e., the ability to assume the existence of objects, and properties of objects, even when they have not been measured). The term "counterfactual definiteness" is used in discussions of physics calculations, especially those related to quantum entanglement and to the Bell inequalities. In such discussions "meaningfully" means the ability to treat these unmeasured results on an equal footing with measured results in statistical calculations.[14] How far do we go here? Bell's violation demonstrates an absence, not a presence. Does then entanglement not imply a kind of counterfactual definiteness? If one element goes up, we know without measurement that the other one goes down? Becker quotes David Deutsch who brought out the best argument for the many worlds interpretation of quantum mechanics:

> The Everett (many worlds) interpretation explains well how the (quantum) computer's behavior follows from its having delegated subtasks to copies of itself in other universes. When the (quantum) computer succeeds in performing (almost instantly) computations that would have taken days by the best non-quantum computers, how would the conventional interpretations explain the presence of the correct answer? *Where was it computed?*
>
> 253

The task is to define this place "where it was computed" not as another reality like ours, but as another virtual-but-effective place. Bell's theorem shows a path to this with its three key features: contextuality, imperfection, counterfactual definiteness. In quantum mechanics, contextuality is the dependence of an observable's outcome on the experimental context, i.e., on the system–apparatus interaction, which means that *the order in which measurements are made matters*, or, to evoke the standard example of a conversation between Anna and Beth: "the answers Anna gives depend on the choice of which questions Beth is asked"(55):

> "Contextuality occurs in situations in which our system is described by at least three properties, which we can call A, B, and C. A is compatible with both B and C, so A may be measured simultaneously with either B or C. But B and C are not compatible with each other, so we can measure only one at a time."

So we can measure A and B or we can measure A and C, and the paradox is that "the answers to A depend on whether we chose to measure B or C along with A. The conclusion is that nature is contextual."(56)

Probabilistically, complementarity means that the joint probability distribution does not exist: one has to operate with contextual probabilities. The Bell inequalities are interpreted as the statistical tests of contextuality, and hence, incompatibility. For context-dependent probabilities, these inequalities may be violated.[15] However, what is the ontological status of such context-dependent probabilities? Is it not clear that they cannot stand on their own, or, as Smolin put it, that "any system quantum mechanics applies to must be a subsystem of a larger system"(26) – why? Because (for Bohr) is doesn't cover the ordinary reality in which we measure quantum phenomena: observers and measuring systems are not part of the system being studied, and quantum mechanics cannot cover the gap that separates the two.[16] Smolin tries to imagine a solution here by way of stepping "beyond the quantum." To designate the basic elements of the universe, Smolin proposes a neologism "nads" (Leibnitz's "monads" minus "mo"), in the spirit of Democritus' neologism "den" (he subtracts the negation "me" from "meden," the term for nothing) – in this sense, nads are also in a way something that is less than nothing. Unlike (the standard reading of) Democritus' atoms, Smolin's nads are not substantial entities but a network of relations. Originally, these interactions occur in time only, not limited by the speed of light – this limit emerges only with the appearance of space-time. How, then, does space arise out of spaceless temporal events and their intermingling?

> "Space arises as a coarse-grained and approximate description of the network of relationships between events," and quantum nonlocalities are "remnants of the spaceless relations inherent to the primordial stage, before space emerges".
>
> 236

Smolin's main argument for the theory of decoherence is a lack of clones: large objects are unique, they have no clones, so they bring about a collapse into single reality – macroscopic systems which have no copies anywhere in the world don't obey quantum mechanics. But all of reality cannot be "sublated" into our space-time, so "quantum physics arises from nonlocal interactions left over when space emerges"(240) – in my terms, quantum phenomena bear witness to the fact that god itself (the big Other) is deceived, that somethings elude its grasp. I am, of course, by far not qualified to pass a judgement here, since this topic is very complex: how does decoherence relate to collapse of the wave function in a measurement? Are they the same? Obviously not directly, since the way Smolin describes decoherence, it happens "objectively." Plus how does observation differ from "views" that characterize every nad? Are such views not a more basic mode of observation? This brings us back to the key ontological problem of quantum mechanics avoided by Bohr: how to account for the split between observed/measured phenomena (quantum waves) and the entire complex machinery of observation (not only observers but also the instruments we use to do the measurements) which is firmly located into our reality? The first thing to do is to take note of the fact that

> every way of drawing a boundary splits the world into two incomplete parts. There is no view of the universe as a whole, as if from outside of it. There is no quantum state of the universe as a whole. If relational quantum theory had a slogan, it would be 'Many partial viewpoints define a single universe.'
>
> 197

Carlo Rovelli gives to such relational quantum mechanics a specific spin:

> reality consists of the sequence of events by means of which a system on one side of the boundary may gain information about the part of the world on the other side. . . . This reality is dependent on a choice of boundary, because what is a definite event – something that definitely happened for one observer – could be part of a superposition for another.
>
> 198

Apropos Schrödinger's cat, our observation decides if the cat in the box is dead or alive, but we can also posit the cat itself as the observer of the signal from the detector, etc.: "if it doesn't make sense for us to exist in a superposition, it surely doesn't for the cat either"(53). Such a view also enables us to reject the Everett theory of multiple universes: it implies that we can occupy a godlike position from which we can posit that the infinity of branches really exists: "But we are not godlike, we are observers living inside the universe, we are part of the world that the wave function describes. So that external description has no relevance for us or for the observations we make."(165) Note, again, the mention of god at this crucial point. Here, however, one has to add that a vision of the universe of wave functions in which nads interact through "viewing" each other ("viewing" in the abstract sense of limited links which connect a nad with its environment), and in which gaps between observers and observed emerge continuously, doesn't allow us to posit relational reality as an all-encompassing reality within which gaps emerge: there has to be a void, a limitation beyond which there is nothing, in wave reality itself – reality itself is non-all, "feminine." Not simply without boundary, but with an empty boundary which makes it non-all. "Masculine" is the gap of decoherence, with the exception of the observer. Theology provides here a false solution: reality can be conceived as All through God as universal observer.

This paradox enables us to explain why Bell's theorem is so revolutionary: as Becker pointed out, it implies a move from perfection to imperfection: "Bell's stroke of brilliance was to consider imperfection, rather than perfection."(151) THIS is why Bell's theorem is "the most profound discovery of science"(141): it provides a formula (of the result expected if there is no faster-than-light interconnection) *in order to refute it*. Imperfections usually serve to demonstrate that other (hidden) variables must be at work – in the case of Bell's theorem, they serve the opposite end: they prove that there is nothing BEHIND.

A Deceived God

In the debate between theology and atheism we encounter a similar problem: the usual argument of religious theorists is that it is possible to (pretend to) explain reality without reference to God, i.e., that God is a hypothesis we don't need (as Laplace famously replied to Napoleon), but it is not possible to prove that something doesn't exist. However, a true materialist does exactly this, which is why it has to pass through religion. To make this point clearer, let's take a closer look at Napoleon and Laplace – when Napoleon visited Laplace, he asked him: "They tell me you have written this large book on the system of the universe, and have never even mentioned its Creator." Laplace replied: "Sire, I had no need of that hypothesis." Religious commentators claim that this reply is "constantly misused to buttress atheism":

> Of course God did not appear in Laplace's mathematical description of how things work, just as Mr. Ford would not appear in a scientific description of the laws of internal combustion. But what does that prove? That Henry Ford did not exist? Clearly not. Neither does such an argument prove that God does not exist. Austin Farrer comments on the Laplace incident as follows: 'Since God is not a rule built into the action of forces, nor is he a block of force, no sentence about God can play a part in physics or astronomy. We may forgive Laplace – he was answering an amateur according to his ignorance, not to say a fool according to his folly. Considered as a serious observation, his remark could scarcely have been more misleading. Laplace and his colleagues had not learned to do without theology; they had merely learned to mind their own business'.[17]

The religious side makes here a worthwhile point: the fact that natural scientific explanation of the universe doesn't need to evoke God is true since it is basically tautological: in the space of natural determinism (even if it admits an irreducible contingency), there is no place for entities like God, free will, etc. But this does not prove that there is no God: God can still be conceived as a transcendent cause of the entire cosmos. So here a reference to Bell becomes crucial: Bell's genius resides in the way he succeeded in demonstrating that something (hidden variables) DOESN'T exist, and a true atheist materialist should do the same for God: not just prove that we don't need God to explain reality, but to prove that God cannot exist.

The problem is that most of the practitioners of quantum mechanics avoided this path. Becker claims that "every interpretation has its critics (though the proponents of basically every non-Copenhagen interpretation are usually agreed that Copenhagen is the worst of the lot)."(287) I agree, but my reaction to it is a variation of Churchill's well-known quip about democracy (which he took from someone else): "democracy is the worst form of government – except for all the others that have been tried." Yes, Copenhagen orthodoxy is the worst imaginable – it is not an argument at all, just an outright prohibition to raise the very ontological question of the status of quantum phenomena. However, all others – solipsism of observer, hidden variables, Bohm-realism, many-worlds interpretation – are worse because they fill in the ontological gap kept open by the Copenhagen interpretation. So instead of filling in this gap by way of proposing its positive explanation, we should just displace it, posit it into the very heart of reality itself. If a rumour that Bohr was an avid Kant reader is true, one should accomplish here a move from Kant to Hegel: Bohr limits reality to what Kant calls the space of transcendental constitution forever separated from the In-itself, and Hegel challenges us to transpose this separation into the In-itself – or, as they say in quantum theory, what if the imperfection implied by complementarity "is a feature and not a bug"(89)?

To put it in yet another way, Bell's theorem "is significant not because of what it is, but what its *negation* implies: a violation of Bell's theorem in experiment is proof that quantum mechanics *cannot* be described by hidden variables, and thus by classical mechanics."[18] Here is a simple description of the experiment that I took from Paul Mainwood:

I am going to allow my two electrons to communicate as much as I want in advance of their being emitted from the source. Now they are emitted by the source and fly apart, each to their own detector. I am going to set things up so that I ban them from all communication once they are in flight. I am also going to allow my detector operators a free choice as to the angles they choose to set their detectors and ban all communication between them too. *How much correlation can there be between the readings of spin ("positive" and "negative") that I get from the two detectors?* The answer to the question depends on the relative setting of the angles of the two detectors. Let's start with the case where the two detectors are set at the same angle as one another. For the case where the two detectors measure in the same direction, here's an easy plan that can give you full 100% correlation. But now, what if the detectors are not set at the same angle? For example, if we placed the detector angles at 90 degrees to one another and use the same rules, it is straightforward to see that we'd get zero correlation: half the time, the demons in each of the two electrons will shout the same word, and half the time they'll shout opposite words . . . But what happens if *the "demons" don't know what angles the detectors will be set at?* As long as there is no communication between the electrons once in flight, and so long as the angles of the detectors are set independently, then any scheme has a limit on the correlation value that is shown by the green areas here [Fig. 3.1].

But what if you get to quantum mechanics, and you set up exactly this setup with two real electrons that are entangled with one another? Quantum mechanics predicts that these two electrons will give *more* correlation in their spin measurements than this limit – here's the quantum line in red [Fig. 3.2].

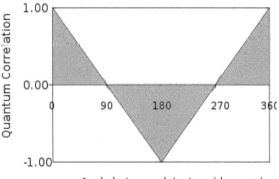

Figure 3.1

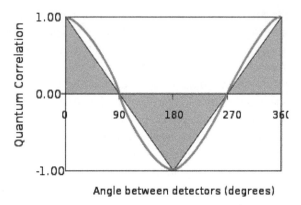

Figure 3.2

This gives us Bell's theorem: no local (= no communication between the electrons/detectors), realistic (= any kind of machinery or demon-thing that contains state assignments or probability distributions for measurement outcomes) model can reproduce the predictions of quantum mechanics – there is too much correlation predicted by quantum mechanics for any local, realistic scheme to work."[19]

Incidentally, in a popular explanations of this experiment, the imagined situation often used is the one of Bob and Alice, two roulette players interacting in a complex set of two triple roulettes. From a superdeterminist position, we can of course question the status of Alice's and Bob's "contingent" decisions: are they really contingent, or even free? Are they not also parts of the determinist reality into which they intervene? Plus, the comparison with Alice's and Bob's card cheating connotes sexual difference (woman versus man), but the term "cheating" points in the right direction of how quantum reality "cheats" the laws of our reality.

Now we can return to our basic question of materialism and quantum physics: quantum physics is truly materialist insofar as it allows such ontological "cheating." In his advocacy of hidden variables which are needed to explain quantum measurements, Einstein produced a pure formula of "subject supposed to know" by way of providing a clear formulation of what Lacan called "knowledge in the real": "Somebody must know, the photon must know . . ."[20] When asked about the basis for his realist stance, he explained: "I have no better expression than the term 'religious' for this trust in the rational character of reality and in its being accessible, at least to some extent, to human reason." But it is precisely this "knowledge in the real" that is shattered in quantum physics: quantum phenomena bear witness to the fact that nature "doesn't know" how to act, that its laws are not all-inclusive. Anton Zeilinger mentions that there is a joke that has been circulating among quantum physicists for decades: since god was too lazy to fully determine reality, leaving parts of it ontologically incomplete, he is repeatedly annoyed by the quantum experiments: "Humans are again making that quantum experiment which will prove that I didn't finish my work of creation, so I have to put more work quickly to fill in the gaps of incompleteness!"[21]

Bohr is quoted as saying: "There is no quantum world. There is only an abstract quantum physical description. It is wrong to think that the task of physics is to find out how nature *is*. Physics concerns what we can *say* about nature."[22] This vaguely positivist statement was echoed by Heisenberg: "[W]e have to remember that what we observe is not nature in itself but nature exposed to our method of questioning."[23] (No wonder that Heisenberg as a German formulates a version closer to hermeneutics.) Bell proposes here a third way: the universe of quantum waves is not just our description of reality, it uncovers a new reality which obeys different laws than those of our ordinary spatio-temporal reality with linear time and three-dimensional space. In short, the link between the two correlated particles appears as a "spooky action at a distance" only if we stick to the standard notion of space, of spatial distance – what if we introduce the notion of heterogeneous spaces? This is why we stumble here (again) upon a spiritualist temptation: what if the non-local link is a simultaneous-atemporal spiritual bond of everything, an indication of a reality different from our spatio-temporal materiality? Again, this is the pseudo-solution we should unconditionally reject: yes, photons are in themselves massless, so they don't move in time or space, everything happens among them instantaneously – but this matter-less other space nonetheless remains real. If we look for some kind of spiritual dimension, it is present in Einstein and not in Bohr: the fact that Einstein (who didn't believe in a personal god) talks about god when evoking the universal laws of nature confirms that god is the ultimate figure of the big Other, and that Descartes was right when he claimed that only a non-deceiving god can sustain our knowledge about reality:

In order for science (true knowledge) about the external world as well as about ourselves as *res extensae*, that is to say, as bearers of sensible properties, to constitute itself, it is necessary to presuppose/demonstrate the existence of a god who is not deceiving us, who created eternal truths and, as Descartes put it, planted them like seeds into our souls. This god is not a god of religion but a god of philosophers and scientists (to follow Pascal's differentiation between the 'god of Abraham, Isaac and Jacob', and the 'God of philosophers and scientists'.) A human can become a subject of knowledge who dominates the world, but only as a depositary of the truths of the Other.[24]

But, as Lacan pointed out, the passage from universal doubt through certitude to *cogito ergo sum* (as a *res cogitans*) is not as smooth as Descartes's deduction implies. Anxiety arises when my trust in everyday reality breaks down, when I see that I cannot rely on any figure of the big Other, that the big Other is not just deceiving but deceived itself, inconsistent. The paranoiac vision of a *genie malin*, a deceiving god which is a fantasy reaction to the true anxiety: it re-establishes the big Other who controls things, although in the evil form – the big shift happens here, my belief in a big Other who controls things is restored. Then comes the third moment, the proof that god cannot be a cheating deceiver but must be truthful. So the first form of certitude is not simply the certitude that I exist even if all objects of my thoughts are hallucinations; it is the negative certitude that I cannot rely on anything or anybody. This certitude

is the opposite of the certitude of being, it could rather be formulated in this way: I know (that the Other is inconsistent, that it can cheat me, and that, for this reason, my knowledge provides no solid ground), *therefore I am not.* We are dealing with the certitude of non-being.[25]

Even before God enters, there is a subtle shift from "I doubt about everything" to "when I doubt, I think, know this, so I am": at the high point of anxiety, when I am certain of my non-being, I am a pure void of a subject ($), because I am (as a subject, $) only insofar as the Other is inconsistent. "I am not" means that I am barred subject – the moment I say "(I know that) I am," I am no longer a subject, I transpose myself into the domain of objective reality where I am one among the existing things which are the object of science. This is why Lacan can claim simultaneously that the subject of modern science is the Cartesian subject *and* that modern science forecloses subject. Modern science is grounded in the Cartesian radical doubt which shatters our everyday life-world, undermines our "being-in-the-world," our trust in reality – in other words, modern science is grounded in the experience of pure substanceless subjectivity, a void of non-being. However, in its functioning, modern science forecloses this dimension and simply ignores its position of enunciation, reducing its discourse to talking about external reality towards which we maintain a safe distance – "subject as nothing" becomes "no subject," science is supposed to be objective. One can mobilize here the difference between the two German terms, *Zweifel* and *Verzweiflung*, used already by Hegel. *Zweifel* means a simple doubt: from the safety of my subjective stance, I doubt about things outside of my space. *Verzweiflung* means that my subjective position is also threatened: it implies subjective despair.

Space or Time

So what has all this to do with quantum physics? Quantum physics provokes anxiety, ontological uncertainty, its implication is that the big Other itself is deceived, that there is a lack/inconsistency in the big Other. The subject is here not foreclosed, excluded as in objective science, it returns as the "observer" which makes measurements and thus causes the collapse of quantum waves into objects of our "normal" reality. However, this "observer" is not the pure subject but already an agent as part of "normal" external reality. Consequently, the Copenhagen interpretation advocated by Bohr and others obfuscates the most radical dimension, the "ontological scandal," of quantum physics, by way of reducing it to "the way we speak," with no ontological implications. Bohr was not too sceptical (about external reality), quite the opposite, by constraining science to "the way we speak" about phenomena of our ordinary reality (which is the only reality there is), he protected this reality from all doubts and uncertainties.

The many worlds interpretation solves the problem of the collapse of a wave function in a different way, by proposing a model without collapse: a wave function does not collapse into one reality, decoherence gives birth to multiple realities, i.e., all superposed options are actualized according to the Schrödinger's equation that governs the wave function of a quantum-mechanical system. Given a set of known initial conditions, the Schrödinger equation gives the evolution over time of a wave function, the quantum-mechanical characterization of an isolated physical system.[26] Many worlds are all real, although each with a different probability – but if a variant's probability is just 1 per cent, it is no less real than, say, the one with 90 per cent probability. The ontological gap between quantum waves and our ordinary reality thus disappears: there are only quantum waves with all their superposed versions actualized. Based on this insight, Sean Carroll postulated that from an (impossible) objective view, we could give a full deterministic description of reality – the problem is only that *we would not know to which of multiple worlds we belong*, i.e., where are we (observers) located in this multitude of worlds.[27]

Is this not the problem with the Cartesian *cogito*? The subject reduced to a pure observer has no place in mechanically-determined external reality, and it exists as subject only if it has no place. Lacan knew this when he wrote that modern science is based on the foreclosure of the subject – and does the same also not hold for how capitalism and predestination implicate each other? Capitalism, a system which pushes individuals to incessant activity, is theologically grounded in Protestant notion of predestination which claims that our loss or salvation are decided in advance, and are independent of our activity. How can this be, would it not be much more logical to claim that predestination enjoins us to inactivity? Everything is already decided in advance, so relax and enjoy, why worry . . . The point is that *we don't know how our lives are predestined, and this pushes us to incessant activity.*

But what if we – as Hegelians – follow here his basic axiom: it is crucial to grasp the Absolute not only as substance but also as subject? What if we make here the move from the epistemological to the ontological dimension? What if this limitation (the impossibility to locate ourselves into the complete picture of reality) is not only epistemological but also ontological? In other words, what if the notion of the objective "total view" not only implies an impossible epistemological position (of an all-knowing subject) but is also ontologically false? What if this impossibility to include the subject into the total view of reality is the symptom of an impossibility that is immanent to reality itself? This impossibility means that reality is in itself not-all, inconsistent, with gaps, and it is this hole in reality itself, not just in our knowledge of it, that makes collapses of wave function necessary.[28] This impossibility also maintains an irreducible contingency, locating it into the very basic structure of reality.

But is it adequate to say that, in the many worlds interpretation, there is no collapse? Is it not rather that there is an infinite number of multiple collapses since all possibilities in a wave function are actualized? Although the main premise is here that there is no ordinary reality, just wave functions, is it not that what we get are multiple ordinary realities with no contact with each other? In other words, does the many worlds interpretation not rather obliterate wave functions in their ontological specificity, as different from our ordinary reality? Instead of wave functions with their superpositions of possibilities we get multiple realities – a price to be paid for re-asserting complete determinism.[29]

As we have already seen, Einstein refused the chance aspect of quantum theory, famously telling Niels Bohr: "God does not play dice with the universe."[30] Einstein's other favourite saying – that the Lord is subtle but not malicious – is related to the same conviction of rationality: "Nature hides her secret because of her essential loftiness, but not by means of ruse."[31] It is not enough to counter Einstein's statement with the opposite claim that god does deceive us – this still leaves unscathed the figure of god as an agent who manipulates us but knows what he is doing, his own integrity remains intact. We should apply to god himself the line from 1 John 1:8: "If we say that we have no sin, we deceive ourselves, and the truth is not in us." God deceives himself, which is why there is sin in him and the truth is not in him. But even this figure of self-deceiving god is not enough: god is deceived not simply by himself but by something that is "in himself more than himself" – how are we to understand this crazy claim? First, we should conceive god here as the ultimate figure of the big Other, the symbolic space which registers everything there is and thereby confers on it symbolic existence; then, we should take into account the lesson of quantum physics: particles appear and vanish before being registered by the big Other, floating in a sphere outside what God notices.

Here we should reject Chiesa's claim that what Lacan also expresses the "God hypothesis" as "'there is something of the One' (il y a de l'Un) and 'there exists one' (*il existe un*)"[32]: "*y a de l'Un*" (mentioned in *Encore*) is not a figure of God but the pre-symbolic Ones as "synthoms" whose status is that of a particle which emerges out of the void of the Thing and disappears/disintegrates before its existence is registered by the big Other. Miller is right to point out that "'there is such a thing as One' is the counterpart to 'there is no such thing as the sexual relation'"[33]: "there is no sexual relationship" once we are occupied by the big Other, caught in the symbolic network, but Ones as synthoms are precisely remainders of something that *a priori* escapes God's grasp. Let's elaborate further here the parallel with quantum mechanics. Imagine that you have to take a flight on day x to pick up a fortune the next day, but do not have the money to buy the ticket; but then you discover that the accounting system of the airline is such that if you wire the ticket payment within 24 hours of arrival at your destination, no one will ever know it was not paid prior to departure. In a homologous way,

> the energy a particle has can wildly fluctuate so long as this fluctuation is over a short enough time scale. So, just as the accounting system of the airline 'allows' you to 'borrow' the money for a plane ticket provided you pay it back quickly enough, quantum mechanics allows a particle to 'borrow' energy so long as it can relinquish it within a time frame determined by Heisenberg's uncertainty principle. . . . But quantum mechanics forces us to take the analogy one important step further. Imagine someone who is a compulsive borrower and goes from friend to friend asking for money. . . . Borrow and return, borrow and return – over and over again with unflagging intensity he takes in money only to give it back in short order. . . . a similar frantic shifting back and forth of energy and momentum is occurring perpetually in the universe of microscopic distance and time intervals.[34]

This is how, even in an empty region of space, a particle emerges out of Nothing, "borrowing" its energy from the future and paying for it (with its annihilation) before the system notices this borrowing. The whole network can function like this, in a rhythm of borrowing and annihilation, one borrowing from the other, displacing the debt onto the other, postponing the payment of the debt – it is really like the subparticle domain playing Wall Street games with the futures. A minimum of time always elapses between a quantum event and its registration, and this minimal delay opens up the space for a kind of ontological cheating with virtual particles (an electron can create a proton and thereby violate the principle of constant energy, on condition that it reabsorbs it quickly enough, i.e., before its environs "take note" of the discrepancy). THIS is how God himself – the ultimate figure of the big Other – can be deceived; by a swarm of "ones" which escape its grasp. This is how one should read the notion of "half-God" introduced by Chiesa: god who is not fully the demiurge of all there is, god to whom a whole layer of things escapes, or, as Lacan put it: "it is not so much a question of knowing whether he is not a deceiver but, what Descartes does not bring up, whether he is not deceived."[35] Chiesa is here too short: deceived is not the same as not believing in himself, it implies a much stronger de-centering of God.

Another paradox (for our common sense) of this notion of "borrowing" energy from the future and paying for it (with its annihilation) before the system notices this borrowing, is that it seems to involve what it would be difficult not to perceive as a kind of *backwards time travel*.[36] Are closed causal loops in which A is both the causal future and causal past of B really to be excluded? Retrocausality allows us to explain faster-than-light link between particles without violating speed of light as the fastest possible movement: when two entangled particles are split, information from one particle first travels (with the speed of light) back in time to the moment of their split and then travels forward to the other particle, so that their link appears simultaneous . . . We don't necessarily need to posit general reversibility of time: the basic direction of time remains forward, from the past to the future, and the occasional detours through the past just complicate the overall movement. (Is there a parallel in nature of the time structure described by Dupuy? At what level can we say that natural processes do not just develop obeying linear causality, that they may also involve a vision of future and react to it?) Dupuy points out the homology between his notion of projected time in which different futures coexist and the basic idea that future is necessary:

There are no alternative possible futures since the future is necessary. Instead of exclusive disjunction there is a superposition of states. Both the escalation to extremes and the absence of one are part of a fixed future: it is because the former figures in it that deterrence has a chance to work; it is because the latter figures in it that the adversaries are not bound to destroy each other. Only the future, when it comes to pass, will tell.

Here theology enters – how? If we consider our situation as that of superposed realities, we are not dealing with multiple options within the same global reality in which a complex situation sometimes offers different paths to be taken ("now you have to decide, do THIS or THAT, and the consequences can be far-reaching . . ."). We are dealing with something much more radical: at the symbolic level, *our entire reality, past included, changes*, and from this new position, a new way to act is not just an option within the frame of the same existing reality but *the only logical, necessary even, thing to do*. In the terms of the previous hegemonic ideology, such a change cannot but appear as a "miracle" since it cannot be accounted for within the frame of the hegemonic ideology. This "miraculous" change which opens up a new possibility ("Yes, we can!") is a theological moment: it shatters the very foundations of our being by way of making us aware that what we (mis)took for our reality is a fragile symbolic construct.

And Dupuy is aware of a link with quantum mechanics: "I arrived at the concept of superposition of states by a line of reasoning that owes nothing to quantum theory. Even so, there are unmistakable affinities, at the very least, between the metaphysics of projected time and some of the basic concepts of quantum mechanics."[37] So what kind of notion of time (in its contrast to space) does such a notion of universe rely on? The three major rival metaphysical views of time are Presentism, Possibilism and Eternalism (see Fig. 3.3)[38]:

3 METAPHYSICS OF TIME

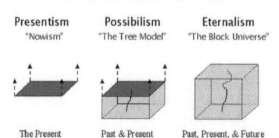

Figure 3.3

Presentism is the ontologically austere view: only the present exists, the past has been but is no longer, while the future will come to be but is not yet. Then we have the tree model which is closest to our common sense view: the past and the present form a stable block of what really took place or is taking place, while the future is open to chance and to our freedom. The block universe is philosophically most interesting, it basically reduces time (temporal change) to space: everything there is exists in an eternal present, and the flow of time is just the illusion due to our limited view constrained to the present. The purest version of the block-universe in which time is reduced to a secondary dimension was recently deployed by Rovelli who

> posits that reality is just a complex network of events onto which we project sequences of past, present and future. The whole Universe obeys the laws of quantum mechanics and thermodynamics, out of which time emerges. He argues that our perception of time's flow depends entirely on our inability to see the world in all its detail. Quantum uncertainty means we cannot know the positions and speeds of all the particles in the Universe. If we could, there would be no entropy, and no unravelling of time.[39]

Rovelli spells out clearly the ontological implications of this view: what we experience as our temporal reality "is not a fundamental constituent of the world," it only appears to us

> because the world is immense, and we are small systems within the world, interacting only with macroscopic variables that average among innumerable small, microscopic variables. We, in our everyday lives, never see a single elementary particle, or a single quantum of space. We see stones, mountains, the faces of our friends – and each of these things we see is formed by myriads of elementary components. We are always correlated with averages: they disperse heat and, intrinsically, generate time. . . . Time is an effect of our overlooking of the physical microstates of things. Time is information we don't have. / Time is our ignorance.
>
> 222–3[40]

What this means, at the level of ontology, is that "we must not confuse what we know about a system with the absolute state of the same system. What we know is something concerning the relation between the system and ourselves"(223). What really exists out there, reality in itself, "the absolute state of the system," is composed of quantum events and their interactions which take place outside time, and we should strictly distinguish this reality-in-itself from the way reality appears to us due to the limitation of our view – the classical metaphysical difference between reality and appearances returns here with a vengeance, and Parmenides wins over Heraclitus.

No wonder Einstein viewed with sympathy the idea of a block universe and played with it – this idea is not a crazy extrapolation but a necessary implication of a fully deterministic view of the universe. Consequently, the only way to really save time – in whatever form – is to conceive reality as not-all, as incomplete, and in this sense as open towards the future. What this means is that what Rovelli calls the "absolute state" of reality, its complete description, is not only out of reach to us, finite limited observers, it is in itself a meaningless notion that should be abandoned. The "ignorance" that separates us, our view, from the absolute state of reality is immanent to reality itself – reality is "in itself" barred, traversed by an impossibility. Usually idealists privilege time (our thoughts happen in time but cannot be located in space), while materialists insist on the irreducible character of space (even our thoughts have to be located in the spatial reality of our brain); but we should turn this privileging around.

So which of the three models should we adopt? Not that of a tree ("possibilism") with past and present determined and an openness just towards the future, but a fourth one: the *historicity of block-universe itself*. Each "now" – say, every historical epoch – reconstructs its own vision of the past and of the future, and when a true change happens, not just a repetition of the same, the whole block-chain is transformed. There is a wonderful (and politically correct in the best sense of the term) anecdote about Hanns Eisler, Schoenberg's pupil who became after the Second World War a kind of official composer of the GDR, but never renounced Schoenberg, withstanding all the pressures of the official ideology. He justified his fidelity with an old Chinese proverb: "the one who does not love and honor his teacher is a dog." Eisler's friend Hans Mayer asked him where did he find this proverb, and Eisler answered: "I invented it."[41] This is the correct dialectical-materialist stance: the greatest creative act is not to be original and break with the past but to reinvent a new past.

The past itself is open towards the future, it is not simply "what really happened" but full of cracks, of alternate possibilities – the past is also what failed to happen, what was crushed so that "what really happened" could have happened. It is at this point that we should avoid the fatal trap of conceiving this "openness" of reality in the sense of a single temporal reality which is open towards the future and solicits incessant gradual progress. No wonder that Smolin, an opponent of block-chain theory and advocate of the reality of time, co-wrote a book with Roberto Unger[42] whose stance is that of a "radicalized pragmatism,"

> the operational ideology of the shortening of the distance between context-preserving and context-transforming activities. It is thus a program of permanent revolution – however, a program so conceived that the word 'revolution' is robbed of all romantic otherworldliness and reconciled to the everydayness of life as it is.[43]

We get here an example of how a socio-political vision of gradual progress, of the permanent self-transformation of humans, echoes a fundamental ontological vision. A similar progressive vision was deployed by Cornelius Castoriadis in his reading of Aristotle. Against the notion of imagination as "negative" (as a false representation of reality), Castoriadis argues that

> hidden deeper within the philosophical tradition was a discovery of a *primary imagination* that is not simply negative. Indeed, in *De Anima* 3.7-3.9 Aristotle argued that the primary imagination is a 'condition for all thought.' For Castoriadis, this claim implies that there can be no grasp of reality without the primary imagination. It should be interpreted, Castoriadis argued, as a capacity for the very *presentation* of reality as such, a presentation required for any further understanding. In this way, the primary imagination precedes any *re*-presentation of reality.[44]

From my Lacano-Hegelian standpoint, such a positive vision of imagination neutralizes too much the infinite power of imagination as the force of negativity which tears apart all forms of organic wholeness – yes, as Shakespeare wrote, "imagination bodies forth / the forms of things unknown, the poet's pen / turns them to shapes and gives to airy nothing / a local habitation and a name."(*Midsummer's Night Dream*, Act V, Scene 1), but, prior to doing that, imagination opens up this "airy nothing," which it then fills in not primarily with poetic beauty but first with the nightmarish mixture of *membra disjecta*, partial objects, objects detached from their organic Whole.

Materialism of Athings

The same effect can be generated also by simply approaching an object in our reality too much. A close-up of an ant's face captured by Eugenijus Kavaliauskas from Taurage, Lithuania, recently went viral on the web, and taking a look at it, one can easily see how the head of a tiny ant just properly enlarged, gives rise to a feeling of immobilizing dread, as if the head of a monster from a horror movie is in front of us[45]. Although we are looking at an image, this image doesn't fit the proportions of our reality: its enlargement in some sense imaginarizes it, makes it a part of our reality, and thereby transforms it into pure nightmarish evil. This gap is not simply the gap between our subjective perception of reality and the objective reality in itself: the horror of the ant's head also resides in our perception of it. Exactly the same goes for the human body: if we were to take a look at a strongly enlarged image of a detail of our body (say, the anal opening), the effect would also be one of horror. So even at this elementary level of photographic images, the pure quantitative amplification changes the ontological status of the object.

The role of science is crucial here. Science moves from symbolizing the real with formulas incompatible with perceived sensual reality to the re-imaginarization of what these formulas disclose – not just gnostic-obscurantist appropriation of scientific theories (quantum mechanics is often read in this sense) but also the "immanent" search for some form of final unified theory of everything, unity of quantum and gravity, etc. The main effect of modern scientific discourse (which culminates in quantum mechanics) is the non-agreement between human sense-perception and nature: modern science deals with (and generates): science's symbolically/mathematically manipulating of the physical real undermines the all-inclusive unity of substance which we perceive as our reality; it introduces into our reality a "pullulating swarm of in-substances, from Hertz waves mentioned already by Lacan to more perspicuous examples from quantum mechanics, astrophysics, not to mention the more mundane field of information technologies":

> Lacan salutes the emergence of these no-things (*achoses*). He claims that it is on their basis that we can finally – atheistically – think materialism in a completely different sense, that is, relinquish the 'ideality of matter' vulgar materialism clings to. . . . This materialism focused on the, so to speak, immaterially material effects generated by science rests on an appreciation of the fact that this very effectiveness necessitates repeated encounters with the real. . . . Science constructs itself 'out of something of which there was nothing beforehand' – since this in-substantial something only becomes some-thing symbolically and takes form with reference to mathematical formalization.[46]

The term *achose* (no-things or, rather, athings) is, of course, again ambiguous in a typical Lacanian way: the "a" can be read as a mark of negation (as in "arhythmic" or "apolitical"), or as *objet a*, signalling that the no-object (an object with no substantial support in our ordinary reality) appears as an embodiment of the object-cause of desire. However, we are unable to assume fully this basic result of science, which is why "the symbolic operations of real science are always accompanied by the imaginarization of what they operate on." This imaginarization proceeds on two levels. Within scientific discourse itself, it occurs when science "*explicitly* attempts to put forward a harmonic vision of the world as a Whole," as can be seen in the desperate search to formulate the ultimate formula of reality, a TOE (theory of everything), or to come "at least one step closer to finalization, preferably in the guise of a synthesis of pre-existing visions (for instance, string theory or quantum gravity should accommodate the competing findings of relativity theory and quantum mechanics)."[47] Therein resides the difficulty of being a true materialist today: not just in advocating science against all forms of spiritualism (as the proponents of so-called "new materialism" from Steven Pinker and Christopher Hitchens to Sam Harris are doing) but, as Althusser saw it clearly decades ago, to defend science against its own spontaneous ideology operative even in (and maybe especially in) its most reductionist forms. (Unfortunately, even Zeilinger succumbs to this temptation when he agrees with Dalai Lama that contingency can also be a sign that god is acting incognito, at a level inaccessible to our knowledge.[48])

The term "athings" (or "non-things") was conceptualized by Byung-Chul Han in his *Non-things*[49], a book based on the opposition between the presence of authentic things which open up and sustain a life-world, introducing into it the stability of rituals, and language reduced to a means of communication, to passing around information: "Non-things block out things, pollute them. Junk information and communication destroy the silent landscape, the discreet language of things."(80) Things are static, providing permanence and stability, while the flow of information is a flow in which multiple images and words battle for our attention, for getting our "likes." In our digitalized information-society, reality is reduced to informations which are at our (subject's) disposition, de-sacralized objects to which no aura pertains. They are no longer things in their impenetrable density but "non-things," substanceless data which we can multiply and manipulate at our will since they offer no resistance . . . But things immediately get more complex: the digital universe of data is not simply immaterial: on the contrary, it reduces reality to that which it continues to refer to as mere objects, to their materiality which contains no mystery – what we see on Pornhub (or witness live on porno spectacles) is precisely the stupid flat materiality of copulating bodies. On the opposite side, what makes a thing a thing is precisely *its no-thing aspect*, the evocation of an immaterial secret in its invisible core. Han is undoubtedly aware of this paradox since, at the same time as claiming that "non-things block out things, pollute them," he writes:

> While the normal things of everyday perception are representatives of the symbolic order, the secret *thing-in-itself* is a NON-THING (*achose*). The NON-THING is the *real* that escapes the *symbolic*. The NON-THING slips through the net of representation. It is the *punctum of reality*, than 'blind field' (*champ aveugle*) or 'subtle beyond' (*hors-champ subtil*) that undermines the *studium*, the vast field of information."

59–60

See also a similar formulation a couple of pages later: "The NON-THING *impresses* because it does not inform. It is the *reverse*, the mysterious backyard, the 'subtle beyond' of the artwork, even its *unconscious*. It resists the disenchantment of art."(65)

So there is a "bad" informational non-thing (a flow of immaterial data) and a "good" non-thing (the real that escapes the symbolic). Along these lines, Han paraphrases the distinction between *studium* and *punctum* elaborated by Barthes: "The *studium* is invested with a 'sovereign consciousness'. I let my sovereign attention glide across the vast field of information. The *punctum*, by contrast, puts me into a condition of radical passivity. It makes me weak. I suffer a loss of self. Without any conscious decision on my part, something 'is poignant to me'. Something 'pricks me' and 'bruises me'."(58) One has to introduce here the distinction between "self" and subject: what Barthes calls *punctum* is the Lacanian *objet petit a*, the virtual-real object (excess over reality) which "tickles" the subject and is as such constitutive of the very dimension of subjectivity. Subject emerges through the loss/emptying of "self" – "self" designates the fantasmatic wealth of a "person" which fill in the void of the subject.

Along the same lines, Han, following Barthes, speaks of *erotic body of language*, or, in singing, of the "geno-song," the dimension of singing beyond communication, a voice which houses the voluptuous body of desire.(63) Han opposes here eroticism and pornography: pornography shows everything, all the details, but it totally de-eroticizes the shown bodies, erasing all their aura. Contrary to some of Han's formulations, we are thus not dealing here with a shift from materiality of things to the immaterial flow of informations: things in their stupid reality remain there as objects of analysis and manipulation. What disappears is their non-thingness, their aura, which is conferred on the – how? *Through language.* The "mystic" unspeakable excess is a retroactive product of language itself.

Plus there is another ambiguity ignored by Han. When, quoting Ponge, he celebrates the erotic dimension of poem as a thing with a body in which words are no longer reduced to self-effacing instruments of transmitting information, he doesn't mention the obscene obverse/underside of poetry, the disgust/fascination with embarrassing words which strike us in their vocal materiality. Even the most superficial pop-songs regularly mobilize words and melodies beyond their meaning (like the 1971 Sweet's hit "Co-Co" with the obscenely-catchy endlessly repeated line of meaningless words: "ho – chi –ka – ka – ho – co – co – co – co"[50]); it is similar with their other hit "Papa Joe" in its line "Rumbo rumbo hear papa Joe."

We are thereby entering the domain of what Lacan called *lalangue* ("language"), language in all its non-intended ambiguities and wordplays. It may appear that *lalangue* opens up the space in which we can resist the hegemonic discourse of power. In today's China, the Grass Mud Horse or Căonímǎ is an internet meme based on a pun: it is a play on the Mandarin words *cào nǐ mā*, literally "fuck your mother." Căonímǎ is an exemplary case of the resistance discourse of Chinese internet users, a mascot of netizens in China fighting for free expression, inspiring poetry, photos and videos, artwork, lines of clothing, and more. As such, it is part of a broader Chinese internet culture of spoofing, mockery, punning and parody known as *e'gao*, which includes video mash-ups and other types of *bricolage*.[51] From our own culture, suffice it to mention the Häagen-Dazs brand of ice-creams – how did this name emerge? Reuben Mattus, a Polish Jew who emigrated to the US and founded the Häagen-Dazs ice-cream company in 1959, engaged

in a quest for a brand name that he claimed was Danish-sounding; however, the company's pronunciation of the name ignores the letters 'ä' and 'z' and letters like 'ä' or digraphs like 'zs' do not exist in Danish. According to Mattus, it was a tribute to Denmark's exemplary treatment of its Jews during the Second World War, and included an outline map of Denmark on early labels. Mattus felt that Denmark was also known for its dairy products and had a positive image in the United States. His daughter Doris Hurley reported that her father sat at the kitchen table for hours saying nonsensical words until he came up with a combination he liked.[52]

Is "Häagen-Dazs" not *lalangue* at its purest? The name condenses a reference to alleged historical facts (Denmark's treatment of the Jews, Denmark as a country known for its dairy products), imagined associations which are false at the level of facts (letters like 'ä' or digraphs like 'zs' do not exist in Danish although they "sound" Danish

. . . for us, not for the Danes themselves, of course), up to the enjoyment in pure vocal nonsense. Such phenomena are far from being limited to ordinary language: many philosophical or scientific terms are formed in a similar way, chosen because of their pleasantly-obscene sound or their improper associations? Just think about quantum mechanics: "degeneracy" as a quantum concept, anyons, quarks (which also designated a healthy soft cheese), up to Big Bang itself . . .

Such an infection of scientific concepts with the "degenerate" obscenities of *lalangue* in no way relativizes science into a historical phenomenon: true universal science easily survives its transposition from one to another ordinary language which affects its discourse with different kind of obscenities. What this case clearly demonstrates is that *lalangue* should not be reduced to some kind of subversive poetic playfulness which liberates the speakers from the confines of the hegemonic ideology – *lalangue* also (and maybe even predominantly) serves as an instrument of violent humiliation and oppression. A typical act of racists is to designate its enemies with an apparently "neutral" term whose obscene echoes deliver a clear racist message – and, when the attention is drawn to it, the perpetrator claims that his hands are pure since he used the term in its neutral sense . . . A true act of liberation resides in our ability to extract a pure universal concept from its obscene contaminations. Try to formulate a racist/ sexist notion in its pure logical structure and its absurdity immediately becomes clear.

We are thereby raising the old Freudian question: why do we enjoy oppression itself? That is to say, power asserts its hold over us not simply by oppression (and repression) which are sustained by a fear of punishment, but by bribing us for our obedience and enforced renunciations – what we get in exchange for our obedience and renunciations is a perverted pleasure in renunciation itself, a gain in loss itself. Lacan called this perverted pleasure surplus-enjoyment: there is no "basic enjoyment" to which one adds the surplus-enjoyment, enjoyment is always a surplus, in excess. It is the reference to Marx, especially to Marx's notion of surplus-value *Mehrwert*, that enabled Lacan to deploy his "mature" notion of *objet a*, the object-cause of desire, as surplus-enjoyment (*plus-de-jouir, Mehrlust*). Freud made the first step in this direction when he talks about *Lustgewinn*, a "gain of pleasure," which does not designate a simple stepping up of pleasure but the additional pleasure provided by the very formal detours in the subject's effort to attain pleasure. Exemplary is here the already-mentioned reversal that characterizes hysteria: renunciation to pleasure reverts into pleasure of/in renunciation, repression of desire reverts into desire of repression, etc. Such a reversal lies in the very heart of capitalist logic: as Lacan pointed out, modern capitalism began with *counting* the pleasure (of gaining profit), and this counting of pleasure immediately reverts into the *pleasure of counting* (profit).

At the opposite end, there is the silent presence of a thing that sustains a world: all cases evoked by Han refer either to noble monuments or (mostly) to small things that mean something to a person that possesses them (from a small child's transitional objects which bring stability and shape to its life to an old book or (Han's own example) a jukebox from the 1950s). But what about things which should remain because they bear witness to an unspeakable horror? What such extreme cases demonstrate is that the dimension of the sacred and divine has its own dark underside: with all its unspeakable horrors, Auschwitz also was an *achose*, a sacred thing divulging the evil side of the divine – its very excessive horror makes it divine.

Recall the case of Marek Edelman, one of the authentic heroes of the twentieth century, a Polish Jew, the last survivor of the 1943 Warsaw ghetto uprising. When his wife and children emigrated in the wake of the growing anti-Semitic campaign in 1968, he decided to stay in Poland – why? Even some of his admirers speculated about personal-pathological reasons that may have pushed him to do it (his pathological relation with his mother), but in an interview decades ago he made it clear: he compared himself to the stones of the ruined buildings at the site of the Auschwitz camp: "Someone had to stay here with all those who perished here, after all." This says it all: what mattered was ultimately his bare and muted presence there, not his declarations – it was the awareness of Edelman's presence, the bare fact of his "being there," which kept in our memory the unspeakable horror of Auschwitz more than all the books, music and films about it.

Is the duality of immaterial athings and the silent presence of inert things not yet another case of complementarity? This is why a chapter on quantum mechanics has to end up with athings: in its notion of wave oscillation, quantum mechanics broke out of the mystical space of athings as fuzzy spiritual phenomena and located them in the very foundation of material reality. Athings are not indications that material reality is not all there is – as Lacan clearly saw, they are the ultimate proof of radical materialism.

4

THE SACRED, THE OBSCENE, AND THE UNDEAD

The common definition of parallax is: the apparent displacement of an object (the shift of its position against a background), caused by a change of the point from which we observe it.[1] The philosophical twist to be added is that the observed difference is not simply "subjective," due to the fact that the same object which exists "out there" is seen from two different points of view. It is rather that, as Hegel would have put it, subject and object are inherently "mediated," so that an "epistemological" shift in the subject's point of view always reflects an "ontological" shift in the object itself. This is why the subtitle of Alenka Zupančič's book on *Antigone* is "Antigone's parallax."[2] In the 1960s and 1970s, it was possible to buy soft-porn postcards with a girl clad in bikini or wearing a proper gown; however, when one moved the postcard a little bit or looked at it from a slightly different perspective, the dress magically disappeared and one was able to see the naked body of the girl. The two figures of Antigone, her sublime beauty and her monstrous brutality, are intimately connected, as in the vulgar postcard: a small shift in our point of view makes visible her uncanny nature since Antigone's sublime ethical stance is grounded in her monstrous disturbance of the existing social order. Antigone's lesson is thus the one formulated a century ago by Rainer Maria Rilke in his "Duino Elegies": "the beautiful is nothing but the beginning of the dreadful which we are just still able to sustain, and we admire it so much because it aims to destroy us with its calm disdain. Each and every angel is dreadful."[3]

Eating the Last Cannibal

So we should not oppose the two sides of Antigone, the good one and
the bad one, or try to guess which is a more substantial one: Antigone
gives body to the parallax itself, she *is* the gap with no resolution. How
to demonstrate this? Zupančič's starting point is her perspicuous
reading of the well-known answer of the members of an aboriginal tribe
to the explorer who visits them for the first time "Are there still cannibals
among you? Are you a cannibal crime?": "No, we're not cannibals; we
ate the last one yesterday." Zupančič's comment:

> What this joke nicely sums up is that at the core of every written,
> symbolic law there is (always) something like an 'impossible crime.'
> If a civilized, noncannibal community is constituted by its members
> eating the last cannibal, that community could never be constituted
> if that 'last' act of cannibalism were labeled as such, a criminal act of
> cannibalism. From the standpoint of the new community, it is a crime
> but only retrospectively; it is a crime that becomes a crime with the
> very occurrence of this act of eating the "last." It is not a crime like
> other crimes; it is, strictly speaking, the impossible crime that takes
> place in a territory that has no territory, no ground on which to stand;
> it constitutes an excluded interior of the state of law. The constitution
> of law (or of the symbolic order in general) involves a discontinuity, a
> gap, something that cannot be based on anything other than itself or
> derived linearly from the previous, 'natural state.' The cannibal joke
> points to just that. 'Eating the last cannibal' would correspond to the
> linear transition from one state to another, without discontinuity, but
> this is logically impossible; it constitutes a paradox: What about
> those who ate the last cannibal? In what way are they no longer
> cannibals? Something happens here; something is lost, the first,
> 'original generation' of noncannibals is constitutively missing, and
> the law of noncannibalism depends on its absence, on this gap.

11

The foundation of a legal order implies thus that the crime that founds
the legal order is what Fred Jameson called a "vanishing mediator"
between the two spheres, belonging neither to the pre-legal brutality
(abolished by it) nor to the sphere of law (it is after all an illegal violent

act). Kant was well aware of this paradox when he dealt with the complicated legal status of the rebellion against a (legal) power: the truth of a statement depends on (and changes with) the time of its enunciation. The proposition "what the rebels are doing is a crime which deserves to be punished" is true if pronounced when the rebellion is still going on; however, once the rebellion wins and establishes a new legal order, this statement about the legal status of the same past acts no longer holds. The circle of symbolic economy, in which effect precedes the cause, i.e., retroactively creates it, thus holds also for the legal status of the rebellion against a (legal) power in Kant: the proposition "what the rebels are doing is a crime which deserves to be punished" is true if pronounced when the rebellion is still going on; however, once the rebellion wins and establishes a new legal order, this statement about the legal status of the same past acts no longer holds:

> If a violent revolution, engendered by a bad constitution, introduces by illegal means a more legal constitution, to lead the people back to the earlier constitution would not be permitted; but, while the revolution lasted, each person who openly or covertly shared in it would have justly incurred the punishment due to those who rebel.[4]

One cannot be clearer: the legal status of the same act changes with time. What is, while the rebellion goes on, a punishable crime, becomes, after a new legal order is established, its own opposite – more precisely, it simply disappears, as a vanishing mediator which retroactively cancels/erases itself in its result. The same holds for the very beginning, for the emergence of the legal order out of the violent "state of nature" – Kant is fully aware that there is no historical moment of "social contract": the unity and law of a civil society is imposed onto the people by violence whose agent is not motivated by any moral considerations:

> since a uniting cause must supervene upon the variety of particular volitions in order to produce a common will from them, establishing this whole is something no one individual in the group can perform; hence in the practical execution of this idea we can count on nothing but force to establish the juridical condition, on the compulsion of which public law will later be established. We can scarcely hope to find in the legislator a moral intention sufficient to induce him to

commit to the general will the establishment of a legal constitution after he has formed the nation from a horde of savages.[5]

However, it is essential to make a step further here: what if, in the same way as the mythic moment of social contract, the primordial Crime is also a retroactive fantasy? We can see now where Kant's weakness resides: there is no need to evoke "radical Evil" in the guise of some dark primordial crime – all these obscure fantasies have to be evoked to obfuscate the act itself which happens (or, rather, can happen) all the time. The paradox is clear: Kant himself, who put such an accent on the ethical act as autonomous, non-pathological, irreducible to its conditions, is unable to recognize it where it happens, misreading it as its opposite, as the unthinkable "diabolical Evil." Kant is here one in the series of many conservative (and not only conservative) political thinkers from Pascal and Joseph de Maistre onwards who elaborated the notion of illegitimate origins of power, of a "founding crime" on which state power is based; to obfuscate this origins, one should prohibit the exploration of these origins and offer to ordinary people "noble lies," heroic narratives of origins. Robert B. Pippin make the same point in his *Hollywood Westerns and American Myth*[6]: the passage from "barbarism" to the modern legal order in the "Wild West" of the US was accomplished through brutal crimes, through eating the last cannibals, and legends were invented to obfuscate them – this is what John Ford aimed at in his famous line: "When the legend becomes fact, print the legend." Legend "becomes fact" not in the simple sense of factual truth but in the sense that it becomes an immanent constituent of the actually-existing socio-political order, so that rejecting it amounts to the disintegration of this order.

The key movie is here, of course, Ford's late *The Man Who Shot Liberty Valance* (1962) in which Tom (John Wayne), "the cannibal who eats the last cannibal," is a rancher in a small western town terrorized by Valance and his gang. Ranse (James Stewart), a newcomer to the town, a young lawyer and educator, wants to deal with Valance in a legal way, but is prevented by the cowardly local sheriff Appleyard. After Valance vandalizes the town once more, Ranse arms himself and goes after him alone; Valance easily disarms the inexperienced Ranse and wounds him, but Ranse retrieves his gun, shoots, and Valance falls dead. Ranse returns to the local cantina where Hallie, a love-object of both Tom and Ranse, treats his wounded arm; Tom enters and, after seeing Hallie's clear affection for Ranse, he gets drunk, forces Appleyard to run Valance's men out of town, and attempts suicide by setting fire to his own house, but is saved in the last minute.

The killing of Valance elevates Ranse into a local hero and he is proposed as a candidate for a higher office at a local convention; but he entertains doubts because he doesn't want to start his political career by a murder. Tom then arrives and explains to Ranse that it was he, not Ranse, who killed Valance: knowing that Ranse could never hope to beat Valance, Tom shot him with Pompey's rifle at the same time Ranse fired. Tom encourages Ranse to accept the nomination for Hallie's sake before quietly walking out of the convention. A quarter of a century later, hearing of Tom's death, Ranse – now a successful Washington senator – visits the town again to attend Tom's funeral, but doesn't explain the reason for it, because he is now publicly identified as "the man who shot Liberty Valance" . . . The interesting feature of the film is that Ranse's position in a way inverts that of Oedipus: the killing, the heroic act of "eating the last cannibal," is effectively done by the anonymous Tom so that Rance keeps his cake and eats it – he gets all the glory and success that came from the act while he can feel subjectively innocent since he didn't kill anyone, i.e., he didn't commit the founding crime. We can see here how the heroic act of "eating the last cannibal," far from being the dirty hidden foundation of the legal order, is itself an ideological myth: the true threat to Rance's career is the truth that he didn't commit the founding illegal act of killing the obstacle to the rule of law. The function of this myth is to relegate crime into a distant mythic past and to obfuscate the ongoing crime (illegal violence) immanent to the present functioning of the state, not only the "objective" violence of the state apparatuscc but also the (growing) need of subjective crime to sustain the functioning of the state.

Ernest Gellner points in this direction with his claim that the most accurate definition of government is Ibn Khaldun's: government is "an institution which prevents injustice other than such as it commits itself."[7] The way to obfuscate this painful paradox is to elevate the domain of state crimes into the non-human domain of the sacred – is here not a clear parallel between this claim and Sayid Qutb's proposition that only pure and unconditional submission to God guarantees freedom from servitude to anyone else? We humans cannot stand alone, we need a higher authority, and only an authority which is not that of another human being makes it possible to retain freedom and avoid submission to other human beings . . . Along these lines, Zupančič locates the "sacred, unwritten laws" evoked by Antigone to justify her act precisely into this "impossible" interspace of a crime that grounds a new order: they

> are not simply a remnant of ancient traditions but arise (or appear) with the cut that inaugurates the new order – it is only at this point that a particular dimension of the old past is constituted as sacred because it is linked to the inaugurating crime of the new order. The sacred could thus be defined in this context as something that has no place in the given symbolic order; more precisely, the place of the sacred is the place of the nonplace.
>
>   12

So what did Creon do by forbidding Polyneices's burial? He intervened into this sacred space, disturbing it into a very precise way: he "staged the feast of eating the last cannibal and invited everyone to see his decaying body."(13) In other words, Creon's obscenity resides in the fact that he repeated the founding crime of the legal order once this order is already established, within this order, as just another legal measure justified by state laws. He "has not simply perpetuated the standard, imperceptible objective/systemic violence of the given rule," i.e., he has not simply stuck too firmly to the letter of the law; on the contrary, he has himself performed a gesture of excessive, subjective violence not grounded in the laws of the city, plus, "and this aggravates his offense, he has performed this gesture of subjective violence in the name of the state and public law."(10) In short, he didn't just commit a crime which violates the law, he violated the law pretending (acting as if) he did this *on behalf of the law itself* – he thereby ruined the law from within, besmirching it with arbitrary subjective corruption.

We find a similar structure in a Catholic Church scandal which reverberated all around Europe at the end of 2022. It concerns Marko Ivan Rupnik, a Slovenian Jesuit, for many years director of the "Ezio Aletti" Study and Research Centre. Rupnik is not only a theologian but also a world-renowned artist best known for his mosaics. He has realized famous artworks all over the world, such as the mosaics in the

"Redemptoris Mater" Chapel in the Apostolic Palace in the Vatican, in the Cathedral of Santa Maria Real de l'Almudena in Madrid, the Orthodox Church of the Transfiguration in Cluj, the Sanctuary of St. John Paul II in Krakow, and the Sanctuary of St. John Paul II in Washington. His esteem was so high that in 2016, during the Jubilee of Mercy, the Pope celebrated a Holy Mass for the Aletti Centre in the Apostolic Palace. In Slovenia, Rupnik was almost a national icon, celebrated as the greatest living artist.

The scandal broke out in Rome a couple of years ago when a young nun, after her repeated discreet complaints were ignore, went public and revealed how Rupnik forced her to have a threesome with another nun from her community joining them in sex, evoking an almost Marxist sounding argument: "sexuality has to be redeemed from private property, and to do this is to follow the image of Trinity where a third person accepts the relationship between the two." The nun met him as a 21-years old student, and established a contact with him because she was interested in art and he was a Jesuit painter. She also posed nude for him, which at first didn't appear unusual to her:

"It wasn't difficult to unbutton my blouse. For me, naïve and unexperienced as I was, this meant just helping a friend. Then he kissed me softly on my lips and told me this was how he kissed the altar where he celebrated the Eucharist," she recalls. What followed where numerous misuses, demands for oral sex and violent masturbation. If she resisted him, he discredited her in the eyes of her community. "He had no restrain, to achieve his goal he used all means, even confidential details he heard during her confession." The nun finally gathered courage and left the community . . .[8]

In all honesty, one has to add that, although the story is true (and further supported by dozens of Rupnik's similar acts in Italy and in Slovenia), there may be a dark political background to its publication: it appears to be used by conservative Catholic forces against Pope Franciscus and the Jesuits (who are usually more progressive). One should also add that (with some delay, nonetheless), Jesuits and the Church itself reacted adequately, calling other victims to report Rupnik's similar acts to public authorities. Nonetheless, the old argument is still heard that we are dealing here with the private sin of an individual which has nothing to do with the Church as an institution – this argument has to be rejected since, as we have just seen, Rupnik evoked Christian notions like Trinity in his very seduction of the young nuns.

The same holds even more for the homosexual cases of pedophilia that blossom among many Catholic priests – they are not something that concerns only the persons who, because of accidental reasons of private history with no relation to the Church as an institution, happen to choose the profession of a priest. This abuse is a phenomenon that concerns the Catholic Church as such, because it is inscribed into its very functioning as a socio-symbolic institution. In this way, it does not only concern the "private" unconscious of individuals, but the "unconscious" of the institution of the Catholic Church itself. This abuse is not something that happens because the institution has to accommodate itself to the pathological realities of libidinal life in order to survive, but something that the institution itself needs in order to reproduce itself. One can well imagine a non-pedophiliac priest who, after years of service, gets involved in pedophilia because the very logic of the institution seduces him into it. Such an *institutional Unconscious* designates the obscene disavowed underside that sustains the public institution. (In the army, this underside consists of obscene sexualized rituals such as fragging, which sustain group solidarity.)

In other words, it is not simply that, for conformist reasons, till recently the Church tried to hush up its pedophilic scandals; rather, in defending itself, the Church was defending its innermost obscene secret. What this means is that identifying oneself with this secret side was a key constituent of the very identity of a Catholic priest. This is why, back to Rupnik, it is crucial to discern the two locations of surplus-enjoyment in what he was doing: not only the surplus-enjoyment brought by transgressing the Church Law but the surplus-enjoyment generated by the fact that the Church ideology and rituals are providing the very frame of violating the Church Law.[9] To return to our metaphor of soft-porn postcards: we have a postcard depicting Rupnik as a great artist, deeply immersed into spiritual matters; then we move the postcard a little bit and we see a dirty old man with an obscene smile . . . However, sacredness should not be constrained to the affairs of religion. As Jean-Pierre Dupuy conclusively demonstrated, the madness of nuclear weapons which contain the threat of our total self-annihilation also implies the space of the sacred:

there is a very precise sense in which the bomb and the sacred can both be said to contain violence in the twofold sense of the verb 'to contain': to have within and to keep in check. The sacred holds back violence by violent means, originally through sacrifice. In the same way, throughout the Cold War, it was as though the bomb had protected us from the bomb. The very existence of nuclear weapons seemed to have prevented a nuclear holocaust, without ceasing to be what made it possible.[10]

Here we stumble upon the obscene ambiguity of the nuclear weapons: officially they are made NOT to be used – however, as Aleksandr Dugin said in an interview, arms are ultimately made to be used . . . So when Zupančič evokes here, with regard to Creon's act, the opposition between obscenity and decency (13), she targets here also and above all contemporary practice like "enhanced interrogation techniques":

Modern illegal state violence (or, more generally, illegal or extralegal practices supported and enabled by the legally existing apparatuses of power) could be seen as a contemporary version of Creon's way of ruling shamelessly, that is to say, by transgressing the inner limits of the law, by repeating its illegal constitution – like eating the last cannibal over and over again.

17

This is why Julian Assange is our Antigone, for a long time kept in the position of a living dead (isolated solitary cell, very limited contacts with his family and lawyers, with no conviction or even official accusation, just waiting for the extradition) – why? Because he assumed the consequences of his act of making the obscene dark side of the US policy *public*, not just informing on it to the secret services of the opposite side . . . No wonder that, on June 6 2023, a High Court judge in London has denied Julian Assange permission to appeal an order to extradite him to the United States where he faces criminal charges under the Espionage Act.[11] Although Assange's legal team already announced they will protest this decision, the snare around his neck is gradually but, so it seems, inexorably pulling shut.

How can the US (and UK) do it? When Afghanistan fell to Taliban, a Taliban commander was explaining to a US journalist that, while the US and the West have the best watches to measure time, time itself is on the side of Taliban, it works for them, so they can afford to wait as long as possible. In the case of Assange, time is on the side of US and UK: they can afford to wait, counting on the fact that the public interest will gradually dwindle, especially due to other global crises that dominate our media (Ukraine war, global warming, the threat of AI . . .). What is happening to Assange is thus more and more something reported on the margins of our big media: the fact that he sits in solitary confinement for years is just part of our lives . . .

However, if we want to cope with today's global crises, people like Assange are needed more than ever. The horrors taking place out of the public eye in today's wars, the catastrophic effects of global warming all around the globe, the impact of Artificial Intelligence on our social relations . . . only whistleblowers like Assange can make us aware of this threats to our very survival as humans by way of bringing the hidden dark side out to public space. Here is a model case of such a need for whistleblowers. When, at the end of May 2023, suburbs of Moscow were again attacked by a couple of drones (Ukraine denied its hand in this attack, attributing it to the Russian opposition), Putin promptly denounced it as a "terrorist act"[12], and even some Western observers complained that Ukraine is pushing the war too far . . . But whatever our tactical considerations are here, one should take note of the obvious asymmetry: a couple of drones bombing Moscow is a terrorist act (or, for some in the West, a problematic one at least), while a much more massive systematic bombing of Kyiv is part of warfare operations hitting legitimate targets . . . Following the same line of reasoning as Putin, Belarus President Alexander Lukashenko has claimed that nations who are willing "to join the Union State of Russia and Belarus" will be given nuclear weapons: "It's very simple. Join the Union State of Belarus and Russia. That's all: there will be nuclear weapons for everyone."[13] (Is this not a North-Koreanization of the smaller states?) So, again, the Russian–Belarus alliance has the right to give nuclear weapons to everyone on their side, while a mere suspicion that Ukraine may be protected by Western nuclear weapons is denounced as a step towards the new global nuclear conflict . . .

One should remember here that, when the Soviet Union disintegrated, Ukraine delivered all nuclear weapons to Russia on a promise that its borders are recognized by Russia – does it not have the right now to get (back) nuclear weapons? Why is this obvious solution dismissed with horror even by those who pay lip service to the defence of Ukraine? They are simply unable to admit the more than obvious fact that, in resisting Russian aggression, Ukraine performed an authentic heroic act that took all the world by surprise. This act changed the coordinates (and the silent presuppositions) taken for granted, obliging us to rethink the entire global political constellation.

To see all this, we don't need Assange. But should we then just unconditionally support (the NATO support of) Ukraine? Recall the very last lines of Brecht's *Dreigroschenoper*: *"Denn die einen sind im Dunkeln / Und die andern sind im Licht. / Und man sieht nur die im Lichte / Die im Dunkeln sieht man nicht.* (And some are in the darkness / And the others in the light / But you only see those in the light / Those in the darkness you don't see.)"[14] This is more than ever, perhaps, our situation today, in the self-proclaimed age of modern media: while the big media are full of news about the Ukraine war, "world's deadliest wars go unreported."[15] From Eritrea (where the state terror appears to be worse than in North Korea) to Central African Republic or Congo with civil wars where dead are numbered in millions – "those in the darkness you don't see" in the blinding light of the reports on Ukraine.

This doesn't mean that we should not fully support Ukraine – the point is how to ground this support. The idea that we should support Ukraine because "such things shouldn't happen in Europe," i.e., in order to defend Western civilization, is to be absolutely rejected: it is this same civilization which not only ignores horrors taking place outside its borders but often even supports and manipulates them. With the Ukrainian war we got a taste of what was going on all the time outside our view, so the attack on Ukraine should awaken us to the same (or even worse) horrors in which we were complicit. And it is here that an approach practised by Assange is needed: to make us see also those in darkness. For our own good, we should not allow that Assange himself will fall into this darkness of invisibility . . . Today, however, something stranger is happening: a new type of political leaders is emerging

who take pride in committing this crime openly rather than secretly, as if it amounted to some kind of fundamental moral difference or difference of character, namely, 'having the courage,' 'the guts,' to do it openly. But what may appear to be their courageous transgression of state laws by avoiding the 'hypocrisy' that those laws sometimes demand is nothing more than a direct identification with the obscene other side of state power itself. It does not amount to anything else or different. They are transgressing their own laws. This is why, even when they are in power, these leaders continue to act as if they are in opposition to the existing power, rebelling against it—call it the 'deep state' or something else.

18

The unsurpassed model of the obscene leader publicly violating the law is, of course, Donald Trump. Here is the latest example: on December 3 2022, Trump called for the termination of the Constitution to overturn the 2020 election and reinstate him to power: "Do you throw the Presidential Election Results of 2020 OUT and declare the RIGHTFUL WINNER, or do you have a NEW ELECTION? A Massive Fraud of this type and magnitude allows for the termination of all rules, regulations, and articles, even those found in the Constitution."[16] It looks that, in some Western democracies, the legal system cannot even maintain the appearances: if it wants to survive, it has to break openly its own laws . . . Appearances are disintegrating also in today's Russia: Putin first claimed that there was no Russian military intervention in Crimea, that local population rebelled against the Ukrainian terror; later, he just admitted that Russian soldiers intervened there in uniforms without any state symbols. Yevgeny Prigozhin, one of the strong men around Putin and the organizer of the Wagner Group of Russian mercenaries (a kind of Russian version of the Japanese *yakuza*), first denied he had anything to do with it, and later he simply admitted that he organized it.[17] True courage is thus redefined as the courage to break the laws if state interests demand it. We find this stance in the properly Rightist admiration for the celebration of the heroes who are ready to do the necessary dirty job: it is easy to do a noble thing for one's country, up to sacrificing one's life for it – it is much more difficult to commit a CRIME for one's country . . .

However, in Russia and some other states, something quite different is happening to such "courage" to do evil. In Stalinism, appearances are saved because *eating the last cannibal is directly legalized* – the murderous purges of millions are a permanent eating of the last cannibal.

(The paradox here is that, as in *Antigone*, the unwritten rule which it is very risky to obey is *morality itself*.) Now, under Putin, Russia again elevated eating cannibals into a law: on Wednesday December 15 2022, the state Duma adopted the first reading of a bill saying that any offences committed in Donetsk, Luhansk, Zaporizhia and Kherson, before the four Ukrainian regions were annexed on Sept 30, "will not be considered a crime punishable by law" if they are deemed to have been "in the interest of the Russian Federation". It was not clear how it would be decided whether a crime had served Russia's interests. (The Russian armed forces have been accused of a wide range of crimes in the occupied regions of Ukraine, ranging from torture, rape and murder to looting and vandalism.)[18]

During his visit to Slovenia in March 2023 Jeffrey Sachs said in an interview about the war in Ukraine: "The foundation for peace should be that both sides return home."[19] A statement which for sure deserves the top prize for the stupidity of the year – as if the war is taking place in a third neutral terrain from which both sides can withdraw. Where should Ukrainians return to when the terrain of war IS their home? (There is another reading of this statement possible: since it is a proxy-war, "both sides" are Russia and NATO – but in this case, the statement is even more cynical, because what it amounts to is that NATO should withdraw its support of Ukraine.) The mere mention of cases like this undermines beyond repair any "balanced" approach to the war, plus it implies that we have to reject the very underlying reasoning that sustains Xi's claim, in his New Year's message on December 31 2022, that China "stands on the right side of history," adding that Russia remains a "progressive" country – what we have to reject here is the very underlying reasoning: there is no "right side of history" directed towards progress, the predominant trend is towards catastrophe.[20]

But is something structurally homologous not happening also in the pseudo-Leftist cancel culture? I can easily imagine Hegel having a repeated intellectual orgasm in bringing out the (for him) obvious necessity of the reversal of inclusivity and diversity into a procedure of systematic exclusion: "How long can parts of the liberal Left keep maintaining that 'cancel culture' is but a phantom of the right, as they literally go round cancelling gigs, comedy shows, film showings, lectures and conversations?"[21] What permeates "cancel culture" is a "no-debate-stance": a person or position is not only excluded – what is excluded is the very debate, the confrontation of arguments, for or against this exclusion. Hegel would have mobilized here what Lacan called the gap between enunciated content and the underlying stance of enunciation: you argue for diversity and inclusion, but you do it by excluding all those who do not fully subscribe to your own definition of diversity and inclusion – so all you do is permanently excluding people and stances. In this way the struggle for inclusion and diversity gives birth to an atmosphere of Stasi-like suspicion and denunciation where you never know when a private remark of yours will lead to your elimination from the public space . . .) Don't we get here an extreme version of the joke about eating the last cannibal? "There are no opponents of diversity and inclusion in our group – we've just excluded the last one . . ."

Incestuous Short-Circuit

Insofar as we can say that Stalin also legalized cannibalism, could we also not say that Stalin had three brothers that he had killed: Trotsky, Bucharin (the Leftist and the Rightist deviationists) . . . and Lenin himself as brother-father (Stalin's role in Lenin's death is suspicious)? So what role does incest play here? Zupančič begins with her own paraphrase of the old French joke quoted by Lacan "I have three brothers, John, Paul, and myself":

> Could we not say that Antigone, with all her being and her actions, is saying something like 'I have three brothers, Polyneices, Eteocles, and my father'? In other words, is it not salient that the order of brothers is marked for her, in a very concrete and dramatic way, by the irruption, imposition, of an unexpected, 'impossible' appearance of the father in the chain of brothers?

> 59

In *Antigone*, the key change from Lacan's version is that the third element is not myself, it is my father as not fully father but half-brother. Judith Butler's reading of Antigone's claim is here wrong: Polyneices doesn't stand for all those who are excluded from the universal humanity, with the underlying idea that he (as well as gays and lesbians, trans . . .) should be included. Antigone insists on Polyneices precisely because he is not a human like others but a monstrous exception, a criminal, in some sense inhuman. Do we not find a distant echo of Antigone's choice in the TV miniseries *The Last of Us*? At the very end of the last episode, Joel brings Ellie (who is immune to the virus that killed most of the world population) to a lone hospital with the hope that doctors will be able to find a cure in her body. When doctors prepare to do surgery on Ellie, Joel realizes that, to get the cure, they will have to kill her. His choice is thus: sacrifice Ellie and (potentially, at least) save humanity, or save Ellie at the expense of the large majority of humans. Because of the bond that grew between Joel and Ellie, he decides to save her, killing in the process dozens of the personal in the hospital – so his choice is like Antigone's "Let them rot!": I don't care about the lot of the large majority of the humans, I am ready to let them rot, my choice is not universality but the exception. Back to *Antigone*, what makes Polyneices "inhuman" is not his crime (of attacking his own city) but the short-circuit of generations embodied not only in him but in the entire Oedipus' family line:

> This is what makes Polyneices quite exceptional; this is what makes Antigone stand against the will of the city in this case: not the fact that Polyneices is also a human being, like everybody else, but the fact that he is not a human being like everybody else (and that he is more like the singular other side of every human being, their unhuman side). It is not his virtues, nor simply his general humanity, but his crime and the peculiar nature of his tie to her that make him singular and worth defending, honoring, at the price of her own life (and that of many others).

53

But is the incestuous short-circuit of generations not possible only within a patriarchal family order? Aren't we now entering a post-patriarchal era in which generational differences no longer matter? Zupančič is quite justified in insisting that no matter how artificial reproduction – even if it is totally decoupled from sexual intercourse – it remains sexual. Let's take artificial wombs, which already are a realist prospect: *EctoLife* by Hashem Al-Ghaili (based in Berlin) unfolds as a huge sci-fi inspired facility with 75 state-of-the-art labs, each hosting up to 400 growth pods or artificial wombs that replicate the exact conditions found inside a woman's uterus. A single facility can incubate 30,000 lab-grown babies a year in an infection-free environment. Every growth pod is equipped with sensors that monitor vital signs like heartbeat, oxygenation saturation, temperature, breathing, and blood pressure, while an AI system monitors physical features and picks up on any potential genetic abnormalities.[22]

But this is not all: since each baby is conceived through In Vitro Fertilization, parents can "freely '*create and select the most viable and genetically superior embryo*', '*giving [their] baby the chance to develop without any biological hurdles.*' Customization is offered as an Elite Package that gives parents the liberty to alter over 300 genes before implanting the embryo into the artificial womb. From selecting hair and eye color to height, intelligence level, and skin tone, this pick-and-choose feature is carried out thanks to the CRISPR-Cas 9 gene editing tool."[23] And yet, in spite of all this industrial machinery, a child will have a biological mother and father who will both also occupy these symbolic roles. One can even easily imagine incest here: what if a mother gets inseminated by her son which was already born in an artificial womb? Even the idea (propagated by some radical feminists) of women inseminating themselves (getting self-pregnant) remains sexual – *cloning* (a technique scientists use to make exact genetic copies of living things – genes, cells, tissues, and even whole animals can all be cloned) is so far

the only attempt to actually circumvent sexual reproduction, suggesting an eventual possibility that humans could reproduce in ways other than sexually. If this, or something similar stemming from new technological advances, were to work and become the primary means of reproduction, it would perhaps make sense to ask what the implications would be for the symbolic order: Would this imply a completely different symbolic horizon or perhaps even the end of the symbolic order as such?

32

In our patriarchal tradition, the provider of my symbolic identity, of my place in the order of generations, is father in his symbolic dimension, the

Name-of-the-Father, so the original incestuous short-circuit is a father who really thinks he is a father, i.e., a father who thinks his authority is directly grounded in the act of insemination. Saddam Hussein said in his final speech: "I am not here to defend Saddam Hussein. Saddam Hussein is too great to be defended even by Saddam Hussein himself."[24] This proves that Saddam was not crazy: he was aware that he is not directly "Saddam Hussein," that there is a gap between "Saddam Hussein" as a public historical figure and "Saddam Hussein" is an empirical person – in short, he avoided the incestuous short-circuit. Along these lines, in *Oedipus at Colonus*, Oedipus defends himself that he is not guilty of killing his father because the person he killed (in self-defence) was for him a total stranger: neither he nor his (biological) father knew that they are a son and a father since for Oedipus the only father he knew and who served as a paternal authority was his adopted father. So he uses

an argument worthy of a skillful lawyer addressing a jury: 'Just answer me one thing: if someone tried to kill you here and now, you righteous gentlemen, what would you do, inquire first if the stranger was your father? Or would you not first try to defend yourself?' (*Oedipus at Colonus*, 991-995) Evidently, the same argument works equally well for the incest: are you in the habit of asking a woman, before you sleep with her, if she might, by any chance, be your mother? The comic effect of this reply, with which Oedipus conquers the hearts of the Athenians, must not divert us from the real point at which it aims: What is a father? How does one recognize a father? And if I am not capable of recognizing someone as my father (and he, for his part, is equally incapable of recognizing me), is he still a father?

44

The answer is clear: NO. That's why Oedipus doesn't have an Oedipus-complex: yes, he unknowingly killed his father and slept with his mother, but this doesn't mean that this was in any way his unconscious desire of which he wasn't aware. Being a father is a symbolic function which determines me also and above all unconsciously, so that Laius was not Oedipus's father also in Oedipus's unconscious. When Oedipus realized that he killed his biological father, he is furious not because he is compelled to confront his unconscious desire but because he is accused of something for which there is no base in his unconscious. The so-called "primitives" were well aware of all this: when they claimed that they descended from some sacred animal (local bird, fish . . .), they knew that "father" refers here to the symbolic authority and that sexual insemination (not in any way linked to this authority) is needed to really produce a child. And to go to the end in this direction, does something similar not happen with Christ? If we don't buy the story of immaculate conception, then god is Jesus's symbolic father, while Joseph (or another man) effectively inseminated Mary. But the predominant understanding is the opposite one:

> According to the Gospels, Mary, a virgin betrothed to Joseph, conceived Jesus by the power of the Holy Spirit – and therefore Christians consider Jesus the Son of God. However, most Christians understand Joseph to be a true father in every way except biological, since Joseph was the legal father who raised Jesus.[25]

I think this predominant understanding is the correct one, it expresses the genius of Christianity: if Joseph is the true father "in every way except biological," this doesn't mean that god is simple Jesus's biological father; it's rather that Jesus doesn't have a biological father – his "biological" father is trans-natural (or, rather, non-natural), so that what Hegel called "the monstrosity of Christ" resides in his "immaculate conception" which is today easy to imagine as a form of artificial genetic manipulation. Biologically, Christ is fatherless, born out of a mother but without a biological father, and, in this sense, close to a feminist dream.

Back to Oedipus, his killing of his father and marriage to his mother are so terrifying because they brutally confront us with *the gap (the difference between culture and nature) that grounds the symbolic order*: he didn't kill (the person whom he knew as) his symbolic father and at the play's end he is furious because people around him don't admit his innocence. Here the difference of sexes enters: Lacan claims that, in contrast to Laius, Oedipus' father, and Oedipus himself, his mother Jocasta *knew* that Oedipus is her son while marrying him . . . Did Jocasta know this because, as a woman, she was closer to nature while Laius as a father is an entity of culture? It's not as simple as that – as Zupančič points out, Jocasta's knowledge has nothing whatsoever to do with "feminine intuition": mother is "nature" *within culture*, their impossible mixture, the gap though which culture arises out of nature, while father stands for the established difference between nature and culture.

This woman's ambiguity is clearly discernible in the destiny of the motif "chalk circle" whose first version is found in the well-known story from the Old Testament on how Solomon ruled between two women both claiming to be the mother of a child. Solomon revealed their true feelings and relationship to the child by suggesting the baby be cut in two, each woman to receive half: the non-mother entirely approved of this proposal, while the actual mother begged that the sword might be sheathed and the child committed to the care of her rival . . . Brecht's modern version *The Caucasian Chalk Circle* (1944) ignores the Old Testament and claims that his source is the fourteenth-century Chinese play *The Chalk Circle* by Li Xingdao in which a judge also cannot decide who of the two women is the true mother, so he devises a test. A circle of chalk is drawn, and the son is placed in the centre – the true mother will be able to pull the child from the centre. If they both pull, they will tear the child in half and get half each. Here, however, Brecht strangely returns to the Old Testament: in Li Xingdao's play, the non-mother refuses to pull as she cannot bear to hurt her son, so the judge gives the child to her, while in Brecht's version, it is the child's birth mother who lets go and wins custody of the child . . .

A True Happy Ending

Another version of the incestuous short-circuit is the one between the two deaths, real and symbolic, committed by de Sade: the second (symbolic) death is transposed back into biological life as its total destruction, not just death as a moment of the eternal cycle of generation and corruption. This short-circuit is the topic of Lars von Trier's *Melancholia*. To properly locate this work, one has to begin with Hollywood movies in which the "big plot" (the catastrophe that threatens to annihilate humanity) is combined with a "small plot," the creation of a love couple. Recall Warren Beatty's *Reds*, in which Hollywood found a way to rehabilitate the October Revolution itself: the couple of John Reed and Louise Bryant are in a deep emotional crisis; their love is reignited when Louise watches John who, on a platform, delivers an impassionate revolutionary speech. What then follows is their love-making, intersected with archetypal scenes from the revolution, some of which reverberate in an all too obvious way with the love-making . . . In short, the hypothesis of the film is that the October Revolution had to happen to bring together an American couple.

In Lorene Scafaria's *Seeking a Friend for the End of the World*, we also learn that the asteroid nearing the Earth will kill all life on it in three weeks; however, although the catastrophe is real and inevitable, it still serves as a vehicle to create a love couple who, minutes before the catastrophe, acknowledge their love and then vanish embraced. The film's message is thus: it takes a total catastrophe to create a real couple.

Melancholia goes a step further: the Thing (a planet on a collision course with Earth) does not withdraw, it hits the Earth destroying all life. In part one, "Justine," the young couple, Justine and Michael, are at their wedding reception at the mansion of Justine's sister, Claire, and her husband John. Justine drifts away from the party and becomes increasingly distant; she has sex with a stranger on the lawn, and at the end of the party, Michael leaves her. So here the Hollywood logic of producing a couple is turned around: the couple falls apart and the satisfying peace is brought by the global catastrophe.

In part two, "Claire," the depressed Justine comes to stay at the mansion where Claire and John live with their son Leo. Justine is unable to carry out normal everyday activities like taking a bath or even eating. During her stay, Melancholia, a massive blue telluric planet becomes visible in the sky as it approaches Earth. John, who is an amateur astronomer, is excited about the planet, and looks forward to the "fly-by" expected by scientists. But Claire is getting fearful and believes the end of the world is imminent. When John also discovers that the end is near, he commits suicide through a pill overdose. Justine remains unperturbed by the impending doom: calm and silent, she accepts the coming event, claiming that she knows life does not exist elsewhere in the universe. Justine comforts Leo by making a protective "magic cave," a shelter of wooden sticks, on the lawn of the estate. Justine, Claire and Leo enter the shelter as the planet approaches. Claire continues to remain agitated and fearful, while Justine and Leo remain calm and hold hands. The three are instantly incinerated . . .

Justine is named after the heroine of a novel by Marquis de Sade, while Claire is Juliette, the sister of Justine. In de Sade's novel, Justine is a virtuous woman who consequently encounters nothing but despair and abuse, and Juliette is an amoral nymphomaniac murderer who is successful and happy. In von Trier's film, the normal Juliette (Claire) ends up a broken hysteric, while Justine finds inner peace and solace. The use of the overture to Wagner's *Tristan* as main musical accompaniment is thus ironic: the orgasmic climax of *Liebestod* (not, as in Wagner, love-death but the death of love) stands for the death of life itself. Recall the famous Bette Davis quote from *Now Voyager*, when she renounces her love partner: "Don't ask for the moon. We have the stars." Justine's version is: "Don't ask for orgasmic little death. We have the big death of everything that is alive."

Why does life deserve to vanish? Disturbances happen in nature as Melancholia approaches the Earth: insects, worms, roaches and all other repellent forms of life usually hidden beneath the green grass come out to surface, rendering visible the disgusting crawling of life beneath the idyllic surface – the Real invading reality, ruining its image, as in David Lynch's *Blue Velvet* in which, in a famous shot after the father's heart attack, the camera moves extremely close to the grass surface and then penetrates it, rendering visible the crawling of micro-life, the repelling real beneath the idyllic natural surface – the basic coordinates of nature, of its balance, are disintegrating. When Justine expresses her satisfaction with the fact that life will disappear in the universe, she is in some sense *right*: life IS a disgusting thing, a sleazy object moving out of itself, secreting humid warmth, crawling, stinking, growing. The birth of a human being is an *Alien*-like event: a monstrous erupting of a living thing out of the inside of a body. Justine is fully aware of this Real: she sees the horror on which our reality is grounded. (A possible way out is here not to stick to our everyday reality but to proceed even further: beneath the crawling of life there is the abstract-immaterial universe of wave functions.)

This is why the planet is called Melancholia. Melancholy is not the failure of the work of mourning, the persisting attachment to the lost object, but its very opposite: melancholy offers the paradox of an intention to mourn that precedes and anticipates the loss of the object. This is what provides a unique flavour to a melancholic love relationship: although the partners are still together, immensely in love, enjoying each other's presence, the shadow of the future separation already colours their relationship, so that they perceive their current pleasures under the aegis of the catastrophe to come. In this sense, melancholy effectively is the beginning of philosophy – and what the melancholic Justine mourns in advance is the absolute loss, the end of life on earth, and she means it. Her melancholy is not just her mind's psychic despair, she really accepts the End. When catastrophe was just an abstract potential threat, she was merely a depressed melancholic; once the threat is here, she finds herself in her element, like a fish in water. For her, it's a happy ending.

The idea for *Melancholia* came to von Trier in a therapy session he attended to overcome his depression: the psychiatrist told him that depressive people tend to act more calmly than others under heavy pressure or the threat of catastrophe. This fact offers yet another example of the split between reality – the social universe of established customs and opinions in which we dwell – and the traumatic meaningless brutality of the Real: they cannot be thought within the same subjective space, i.e., one cannot be "normal" in both situations. In the film, John is a "realist," fully immersed into ordinary reality, so when the coordinates of this reality dissolve, his entire world breaks down; Claire is a hysteric who starts to question everything in a panic; the depressed Justine gets rid of her depression and becomes a *Master*, the one who stabilizes a situation of panic and chaos by way of introducing a new Master-Signifier: the "magic cave" that she builds to establish a protected space when the Thing approaches. Justine is not a protective Master who offers a beautiful lie – in other words, she is not the Roberto Benigni character in *Life Is Beautiful*. What she provides is a symbolic fiction which, of course, has no magic efficiency, but which works at its proper level of preventing panic. Justine's point is not to blind us for the impending catastrophe: the "magic cave" enables us to calmly accept the End. And today, when multiple catastrophes are threatening us, we need more than ever figures like Justine reacting to the catastrophe not (just) by efficient countermeasures but by providing magic caves.

Searching for Yourself

The incestuous short-circuit can also assume another form: the Oedipal topic of a guy desperately looking for himself (for a criminal who turns out to be the searcher himself) or, knowing he is involved in a murder, ordered by his institution (police) to look for himself, echoes even today, from Chesterton's *The Man Who Was Thursday* up to Hollywood (*The Big Clock, Police Python 357, No Way Out*).[26] There are two versions of this search: the hero doesn't know he is himself the one he is searching for (Oedipus), or he is ordered by a figure of big Other to do it while he knows he is the one he is looking for and sabotages his search. The latest version of this second version is *The Double*, a 2011 American spy film directed by Michael Brandt which was a commercial and critical failure – undeservedly since the movie is utterly radical in its ambiguity. Here is the plot[27] (a monument to good story telling that is more and more disappearing from Hollywood):

As US Senator Dennis Darden walks out of a warehouse, he is approached by an assassin from behind who slits his throat and escapes. Retired operative Paul Shepherdson is summoned to look into the murder. He is joined by Ben Geary, a young FBI agent who is an expert on a former Soviet operative known as Cassius. Geary reasons that Cassius is the assassin due to his signature throat-slitting method. Paul and Ben visit Brutus, one of Cassius's proteges, who is locked up in prison, to learn the whereabouts of Cassius. They provide him with a radio and leave. The prisoner swallows the batteries from the radio and fakes a poisoning/upset stomach. In a hospital, he spits out the batteries, overpowers his guards and escapes; however, in the garage he is attacked by Paul who reveals himself to be Cassius. After slitting Brutus's throat, Paul moves to eliminate Ben too, only stopping when interrupted by Ben's wife – Cassius is unable to murder Geary in front of his family. Meanwhile, a Russian terrorist and murderer, Bozlovski, has entered the US. Ben pieces together the events of Paul's life and determines that not only is Paul actually Cassius, but also that he is systematically murdering the people involved in the death of his wife and child, who were assassinated by Bozlovski.

Paul tracks down Bozlovski to a shipyard warehouse, and a while later, Ben also arrives at the building. After Ben confronts Paul with the evidence, he confesses to Ben everything, but then proves to Ben that he is also a Russian spy, which Paul learned at one of Ben's informant drop-offs. He is able to convince Ben that Bozlovski is the actual threat. When Ben reveals that he has plans to return to Russia after this is over, Paul tries to convince him to stay in the FBI and with the family he has grown to love. Together they hunt down Bozlovski inside the shipyard's warehouse, and in the ensuing struggle, a mortally wounded Paul slits Bozlovski's throat using his garrote-watch. As the only surviving witness, Ben relays the incident to his superiors and claims that Bozlovski was Cassius, thereby securing Paul's reputation. The film ends with Ben returning to his home, with the ambiguity unresolved: has he silently defected to the American government or just became an even deeper Russian asset?

It is easy to see why the film had to fail: not only are its three main characters (Ben, Paul, Bozlovski) all Russian agents, its central figure (Paul) is for decades involved in a properly incestuous (Oedipal) search for the Russian top spy-murderer who is himself. One can read the ending in an almost optimistic way: even if Ben will remain a Russian agent, the incestuous link is cut short because he will be just an ordinary double agent, not the one who is looking for himself. While Bozlovski is pure evil, just a brutal murderer, Paul becomes morally ambiguous when his job gets mixed with his private life: after his wife and child are killed by Bozlovski, he starts to kill systematically all responsible for their death; this is why he becomes fatherly protective to Ben who also has a wife and a son.

What is the exact status of Cassius with regard to Paul? Within the symbolic order, the subject responsible for its founding crime can only appear as another dark aspect (a dark double) of a really-existing person, as a virtual entity who doesn't exist as a real person. In many detective novels one finds a similar plot: there are two persons, X and Y, who are never seen together because Y doesn't exist at all – when he appears, it is X dressed up as Y. This "surplus-subject" which exists only virtually is a necessary constituent of a human group. And we shouldn't be afraid to extend this logic to the top, to god himself. Some Christians like to point out that a man is at his greatest when he kneels down – and, as G.K. Chesterton saw it clearly, the same holds for god himself. This is why the social message David Breitenbeck, an orthodox Catholic reader of Chesterton, is wrong in his reading of Chesterton's insight "When duty and religion are really destroyed, it will be by the rich.'" For Breitenbeck, Chesterton's point is that "the poor will never truly be anarchists or anything of the kind. It is the rich, the educated, the sophisticated who play with such fire."[28] But for Chesterton, God doesn't just stand for Family and State order, he is at the same time the greatest rebel, the ultimate anarchist. It is against this background that we should reread the passage from Chesterton's famous "Defense of Detective Story" in which he remarks how the detective story

> keeps in some sense before the mind the fact that civilization itself is the most sensational of departures and the most romantic of rebellions. When the detective in a police romance stands alone, and somewhat fatuously fearless amid the knives and fists of a thief's kitchen, it does certainly serve to make us remember that it is the agent of social justice who is the original and poetic figure, while the burglars and footpads are merely placid old cosmic conservatives, happy in the immemorial respectability of apes and wolves. /The police romance/ is based on the fact that morality is the most dark and daring of conspiracies.[29]

But does this not mean that Family and State are the greatest rebellion and the most dark and daring of conspiracies compared with the placid old nymphomaniac hedonists or with the chaos of gang reigns? Recall the endlessly-repeated Brecht's saying "*What is robbing a bank compared with founding a bank?*" – what is an "illegal" sexual adventure compared with marriage as the most romantic of rebellions? What is gang violence compared with the ruthless anonymous violence of state mechanisms? What is the revolutionary undermining of a state compared with establishing a new state? This was the logic of the Red Army Faction and Red Brigade's terrorism in the 1970s: let's confront the state with its own dark underside of illegal violence . . . Therein resides the ambiguity of Brecht's saying. It can be read in Chesterton's way: state power itself is "the most dark and daring of conspiracies" because it effectively establishes an order which limits the scope of crime, making it a (particular) crime. Or it can be read the way Brecht intended it: state power (or, in his case, founding a bank) remains a crime greater than all other crimes. In one case, the crime is self-sublated through its universalization; in the other case, it remains a crime. Or, back to God: the secret of religion is that the very sacred act of its establishing is the supreme crime. God IS the supreme Evil, and this brings us to the true meaning of Christ's act of self-sacrifice: he readily assumes and repents for his father's (God's) crime – or, to quote a well-known meme: "God sacrificed Himself for Himself to save humanity from Himself." The difference between Creon and Christ is thus, as Rene Girard pointed out, that Christ is not eating the last cannibal but offering a (self-)sacrifice to end sacrifices[30]: like Antigone, Christ assumes the consequence of the crime – which crime? Not the sins of the humans but the original sin of God-Father himself. According to an old Jewish wisdom, the deepest insights are so traumatic that they can only be formulated by a person who is close to Devil – and this certainly holds for the traumatic core of Christianity.

Sweet and Sour God

Details about God's brutality abound in the Bible – recall just one of the weirdest stories in the Bible. At night while wandering around in the search for the Promised Land, Moses, his wife Zipporah and their son are resting at a lodging place. God unexpectedly enters the place and threatens to kill Moses. "Then Zipporah took a flint and cut off her son's foreskin and touched Moses's feet with it and said, 'Surely you are a bridegroom of blood to me!' So God let him alone." (Exodus 4:24-26). God is here a brutal stranger who appears out of nowhere full of murderous rage. Not to mention the story of how the land of Israel was given to the Jews – in clear terms of ethnic cleansing, which is why often the very mention of it is dismissed as an act of anti-Semitism. After their liberation from slavery in Egypt, the Israelites arrived on the edge of the Promised Land, where God then commanded them to destroy totally the people already living in these regions (the Canaanites): the Israelites were to "not leave alive anything that breathes" (Deuteronomy 20:16). The book of Joshua records the carrying out of this command: "they devoted the city to the LORD and destroyed with the sword every living thing in it – men and women, young and old, cattle, sheep and donkeys"(6:21). Several chapters later, we read that Joshua "left no survivors. He totally destroyed all who breathed, just as the LORD, the God of Israel, had commanded" (10:40; 11:14). The text mentions city after city where Joshua, at God's command, puts every inhabitant to the sword, totally destroyed the inhabitants and left no survivors (10:28,

30, 33, 37, 39, 40; 11:8). Does this mean that Jews are somehow guilty of an original act of ethnic cleansing? Absolutely not: in ancient (and not so ancient) times, more or less ALL religious and ethnic groups functioned like that, the Buddhist ones included.[31] What one should do is not only unambiguously reject the direct use of these passages as a legitimization of contemporary politics; one should also not just ignore them with the justification that they are not essential to the religious edifice in question but mere secondary points conditioned by specific historical circumstances. What matters is, again, the bare fact that horrible crimes are transposed into the domain of the sacred: "a particular dimension of the old past is constituted as sacred because it is linked to the inaugurating crime of the new order."(12)

The Kantian ethics implies the same paradox: the moral law does not impose social balance threatened by evil disruptive forces, as in the traditional ethics where justice is conceived as a harmonious global order in which each element is at its own place, and punishment aims at restoring the ruined harmonious order. The contrast between traditional ethics of balanced justice where excess is punished and Kant where law itself is the ultimate excess disturbing life-cycle cannot but strike the eye here: for Kant, the moral law is itself the excess, an unconditional injunction that derails the harmonious balance not only of the pleasure principle but also of a harmonious social order. When the great mezzo-soprano Tatiana Troyanos, after a long suffering, died of metastasized breast cancer at fifty-three on August 21 1993 in Lennox Hill Hospital in New York, she sang on the last day of her life for other patients, one of whom "told her that this was the first time in three years that she had completely forgotten her pain."[32] Such a simple persistence to one's Cause beyond the immediate threat of death is ethics at its purest

How can one not like *The Last of Us*, if for no other reason then for the fact that the only post-apocalyptic community which is not caught in the cycle of self-destructive violence – a small thriving community in Jackson, Wyoming, reached by Joel and Ellie in episode 6, in which a basic solidarity and cooperation prevail – is explicitly designated by one of its citizens as Communist? In the finale of the first season Joel rescues Ellie from a surgery which may provide a cure for the disease that decimated humanity, turning them into aggressive zombies; while doing this, he kills dozens of humans. His act should not be dismissed as a gesture of extreme egotism (he seems to prefer not to lose his only true friend to the chance of saving humanity): the choice is not so simple, he is right in rejecting the logic of a necessary sacrifice. So is Joel's act not a version of Antigone's: I am ready to let millions to rot, but not my favoured person . . .?

But we should be careful here not to identify ethical gestures with big public gestures – quite often, such gestures are discernible in barely noticeable minimal tics. Here, Antigone is to be opposed to Paul Claudel's Sygne de Coufontaine from his *The Hostage*: if Oedipus and Antigone are the exemplary cases of Ancient tragedy, Sygne stands for the Christian tragedy, much more radical than that of Oedipus or Antigone: when, mortally wounded after receiving the bullet meant for her despicable and hated husband, she refuses to confer any deeper sacrificial meaning on her suicidal interposition, there is no tragic beauty in this refusal – her "NO" is signalled by a mere repellent grimace, a compulsive tick of her face. There is no tragic beauty here because her utter sacrifice deprived her of all inner ethical grandeur – they all went into it, so that she remains a disgusting excremental stain of humanity, a living shelf deprived of life. In contrast to Antigone who enacts fidelity to her desire, Sygne (at the end of the play) loses the very basic coordinates of her desire, she no longer desires. There is no love here either; all her love went into her previous renunciations.

In a way, Sygne is here crucified, her "NO" is like Christ's "Father, why did you abandon me?" – which is also a gesture of defiance, of "Up yours!" directed at the God-Father. In a sense radically different from Antigone's, her grimace is a gesture from the domain between the two deaths, the repetitive tic of a living dead, of her undeadness, and, as such, a surplus-enjoyment at its zero-level: while Antigone poeticizes her undeadness in staging herself as a sublime beauty, Sygne truly goes to the end. Can we not imagine a similar tic of Judas – a desperate twitch of his lips signalling the terrible burden of his role? There is no sublime beauty in Sygne at the play's end – all that marks her as different from common mortals is a repeated tick that momentarily disfigures her face. This feature which spoils the harmony of her beautiful face, the detail that sticks out and makes it ugly, is the material trace of her resistance to being co-opted into the universe of symbolic debt and guilt. And, back to Christ, this, then, should be the first step of a consequent reading of Christianity: the dying Christ is on the side of

Sygne, not on the side of Antigone; Christ on the cross is not a sublime apparition but an embarrassing monstrosity.[33] Can we then imagine a situation in which Antigone would react as Sygne? What if, after heroically defying Creon's prohibition, he would simply keep her at a secluded place for some time, otherwise ignoring her, with nobody listening to her? Would she then, excluded from the public space, resort to making tics like Sygne? (Something like this *does* happen in the play: Creon doesn't kill Antigone, he just locks her up in a secluded place with enough food to survive – so what if she hangs herself to *avoid* the fate of Sygne?)

Dominick Hoens and Ed Pluth proposed a perspicuous reading of Lacan's interpretation of *The Hostage*: in the play's climactic finale, Sygne de Coufontaine, its heroine, interposes herself between Turelure, her repugnant and corrupted husband, and Charles, her true love, intercepting the bullet from the pistol that Charles aimed at Turelure; afterwards, when Turelure asks the dying Sygne why did she do it,

> Sygne makes no answer, or rather, it is her body that performs an answer in the form of a tic, a sign of 'no.' Sygne, who sacrificed everything in order to preserve a past order of things, who broke off her engagement with her cousin in order to save the Pope, cannot and will not tolerate this last and ultimate sacrifice to Turelure. . . . Sygne gives up everything in order to bind herself to an enemy, Turelure, and ultimately saves his life from her cousin's gunshot, but, when asked to confess that she did this out of marital love, only answers with a negating *trait*. The place where Sygne gives up everything in order to enter into a symbolic universe that is not hers appears later on as a negation of this order. Is this not the endpoint of the symbolic order, where an ugly, obscene feature puts the whole order into question and is thus a pure negation of what the order stands for?[34]

By a little bit of overstretching, one should put the unexpected finale of the TV series *Succession* – Shiv's choice – in the same series with Madame de Lafayette's *Princesse de Cleves* and Goethe's *Elective Affinities*. While men sacrifice themselves for something (a higher cause: country, freedom, honour), only women are able to sacrifice themselves for *nothing*. This paradox accounts for the gesture of feminine withdrawal

at the very moment when "she could have it all" (or, the obverse/
complementary case, the woman's non-withdrawal, her inexplicable
perseverance in the unhappy marriage, or with a no longer loved partner,
even when the possibility arises to get out of it, as in James' *The Portrait
of a Lady*). Although ideology gets invested in this gesture of renunciation,
the gesture itself is non-ideological. The reading of this gesture to be
rejected is the standard psychoanalytic one according to which we are
dealing with the hysterical logic of the object of love (the lover) who is
desired only insofar as he is prohibited, only insofar as there is an obstacle
in the guise of the husband – the moment the obstacle disappears, the
woman loses interest in this love object. In addition to the hysterical
economy of being able to enjoy the object only insofar as it remains illicit/
prohibited, insofar as it maintains a potential status, i.e., in the guise of
fantasies about what "might have" happened, this withdrawal (or
insistence) can also be interpreted in a multitude of other ways: as the
expression of so-called "feminine masochism" (which can be further read
as an expression of the eternal feminine nature, or as the internalization
of the patriarchal pressure) preventing a woman to fully "seize the day";
as a proto-feminist gesture of stepping out of the confines of phallic
economy which posits as the woman's ultimate goal her happiness in a
relationship with a man; etc. etc. However, all these interpretations seem
to miss the point which consists in the absolutely fundamental nature of
the gesture of withdrawal as constitutive of the subject herself.[35] Shiv's
choice makes this step further, towards Sygne's gesture of *Versagung*;
to prove this, let's recall the situation at the end of *Succession*.

After Logan Roy, the mega-rich patriarch of a media company
Waystar Royco, dies of an unexpected heart attack, his three siblings
(Kendall, Roman, and Shiv married to a conformist opportunist Tom)
struggle about who will take over the company and become its new
CEO. The situation gets complicated when Mattson, a young and
ruthless Swedish media magnate, offers to buy Waystar and incorporate
it into his GoJo empire, indicating that one of the Americans will be
chosen as Waystar's new CEO. Ken and Roman reject Mattson's offer,
knowing they will lose control over Waystar, but Shiv joins Mattson who
promises her that she will be the new CEO. However, Mattson secretly
decides that Shiv is too pushy, too smart and that sexual chemistry
between her and him will distract him from cold business decisions. So
he calls Tom, the ultimate conformist, and offers him the post of US

CEO. Since he knows that the marriage of Tom and Shiv is in disarray, but also that Shiv is pregnant by Tom, his reasoning is, as he puts it to Tom: "Why don't I get the guy who put the baby inside her, instead of the baby lady?" Mattson also makes it clear to Tom that he will perhaps want to have sex with Shiv, and he knows that Tom will allow this because he will fear for his job. Just before the vote, Tom and Shiv have a talk in which Shiv indicates that perhaps they should give a new chance to their marriage, although there is no love between them, and although Tom already betrayed her, making an alliance with her father against her – as Shiv puts it in a beautiful tautological paradox, if one is married it is better to be married to your husband (a statement which bears witness to an utter despair). However, the evening before the vote Shiv learns that Mattson also betrayed her and offer the CEO position to Tom, so she promises to her siblings to vote against the deal. When the voting takes place,

> the Roy siblings had the votes to stop GoJo's buyout of Waystar Royco, with it being a 6-6 tie before Shiv gave the final vote. Although she was set to vote against the deal, she hesitated, leading to a heated confrontation between the Roy siblings. This leads to Shiv voting for the deal, causing the Roy siblings to lose their leadership positions at the company. . . . Shiv's vote was an attempt to stop Kendall from going down their father's path. On top of that, Shiv also voted for the GoJo deal for selfish reasons. Shiv knew that her brothers are snakes and that Kendall would lock Shiv out of the company as soon as they reach their first impasse. By voting for GoJo's buyout, Shiv felt as if she will have a better chance of remaining at Waystar Royco. Shiv also wasn't confident of her brother's abilities, believing that Kendall having the CEO position would severely hurt Waystar Royco. Much like the other six board members that voted for the deal, Shiv was voting with her pocket, knowing that GoJo's buyout will help the company more than Kendall's leadership would.[36]

One can go on here and continue the endless game of finding rational or emotional reasons for Shiv's counterintuitive betrayal of her siblings (there are dozens of websites speculating on this). However, there is more than a cold strategic calculation or revenge in Shiv's choice: it is an exemplary feminine gesture, a gesture of *Versagung* like that of Sygne. The final scene of Tom and Shiv (in a car, Tom offers her a hand and Shiv accepts it) is not a true reconciliation but a cold acceptance like that of Princesse de Cleves or Henry James's lady. Shiv does more than just accept the loss (final split with her brothers, the end of the Roy dynasty), she in some sense enacts *the loss of the loss itself*: her loss means the loss of her position in Waystar, she sacrifices the very standard by means of which she measured her success (control of Waystar). She steps out of her established symbolic identity and engages in an entirely new game (will she be able to dominate the submissive Tom and connect again with Mattson?). She effectively undergoes a kind of "subjective destitution," courageously assuming the zero-level of empty subjectivity. Her "tic" is that she reluctantly puts her hand on Tom's, a gesture which is not that of any emotional kindness but a totally empty one.

In short, far from returning to a position of the submissive wife, Shiv only now drops the "progressive" mask of social-liberal caring that she displayed throughout the series, and becomes the she-devil that she always was. In the *Frauenkirche* in Munich, there is a footprint which a legend proclaimed the footprint of the devil himself: "According to legend, in 1468, the architect Jorg von Halspach went looking for money to build a new cathedral in Munich and ended up making a bargain with the Devil: the Devil would provide the funds for the huge building on the condition that it be a celebration of darkness, with no windows to let in light. When the building was complete, von Halspach led the Devil inside to survey his work, and to show him that he had held up his end of the bargain. The devil was satisfied, but then the columns that had been blocking the view of the windows opened up and, in his fury at being tricked, he stamped his foot, forever marking the floor with his black footprint."[37] There is a truth in this legend: an object that celebrates the divine dimension can only be completed by the presence of an imprint of the devil himself.

All Under Heaven or a Divided Heaven?

To conclude, let us again reduce the complex topic we are dealing with to the ultimate minimal choice: let's try to imagine the very opposite of a god with devil's imprint. We don't have to look far for it: we find it in the ancient Chinese concept of "tianxia" (天下), literally translated as "All under Heaven." Today, this concept is popularized by Zhao Tingyang, a member of the Chinese Academy of Social Sciences whose books are not only widely popular in China but also translated in many languages.[38] Tianxia is the project of a world order based on co-existence and where problems are regarded as shared; its main characteristics are: 1) tianxia would internalize the outside world through practicing the art of converting enemies into friends; in this way, it would build an anti-imperial system in which universal peace and security can be achieved; 2) tianxia would be based on "relational rationality": each group is what it is only through its relationship with others, so we need a social order in which common interests are prioritized and where cooperation is always more beneficial than competition; 3) a tianxia system would emphasize that any individual can improve their conditions if, and only if, everyone else improves their conditions as well.[39] Such a project based on universalist principles and values definitely deserves to be taken seriously: we all know that we urgently need what tianxia strives for – global coordination and solidarity, etc.; it is also becoming clear that the liberal-democratic multi-party system is not strong enough to cope with the dangers that pose a threat to our very survival. So although tianxia originated around 2,500 years ago, its revival does not imply the escape into an idealized past – Zhao's friend Regis Debray correctly noted how

> this way of thinking is remarkably in sync with our present time, which subordinates history to nature (quite the opposite of what we used to do) and individuality to universality. Tianxia accepts economic globalization as well as ecological concerns and global pandemics like COVID-19, envisioning our planet as a whole, humanity as one unique species and the biosphere as primary, ultimate and all-encompassing. Zhao's vision professes a different and less visible reality, one that exalts the feminine by giving the yin priority over the yang and rivers and oceans over mountains, because water eventually always gets the better of what is hard and strong. Water accompanies nature instead of dominating her, it attempts to go with the flow rather than accumulate inventory, influences rather than demands.[40]

Such an exalting of the "feminine" should immediately raise our suspicion – far from being just a vague metaphor, it permeates the entire system: Western democracy is characterized as masculine, hard and strong, confrontational, while we need a "rebooted" democracy which will search for unity in diversity, for collaboration instead of antagonistic struggles. Western democracy is limited to nation-states while tianxia aims at a large trans-national (even global) unity within which local communities can thrive, sustaining each other instead of posing a threat to each other's sovereignty. This last claim should also raise our suspicion: in all cases of a society that tried to enact tianxia, especially in China, pluralism was never fully enacted – there was always one state or political unity which played the central role of integrating others and coordinating their unity while "tolerating" differences. (In the case of UK, it is obviously England which plays this role.) While we are all under Heaven, there is one among us who is, as they say, more equal than others since he embodies Heaven (the order of the common Good).

Zhao defines his approach as one of "taking no sides": "I assume the perspective of an extraterrestrial anthropologist who comes to earth and does his anthropological fieldwork on our planet,"[41] which means that his object is not a particular country but the world as a whole. I find such a claim for one's own neutral universality (in contrast to the partial approach of others) very dangerous since it not only privileges one's own position but simultaneously makes this privileging invisible. Is Zhao not doing at a different level what Western social sciences are doing when they analyse the structure of "primitive" or "Asiatic" societies? So isn't the first step towards actual equality that each side admits its own particularity, renouncing its universal claim? Zhao's imagined global society gets all too close to John Lennon's mega-hit *Imagine*, which was for me always a fake song, a song popular for wrong reasons. "Imagine that the world will live as one" is the best way to end in hell. Those who cling to pacifism in the face of the Russian attack on Ukraine remain caught in their own version of "imagine" – imagine a post-heroic world in which tensions are no longer resolved through armed conflicts . . . The pacifists' "understanding" for Russia amounts to the tolerance for Russian aggression. Calls for peace that abound today are always sustained by some project of one side winning. So would Zhao be ready to accept that sometimes to fight back is the only way to peace?

What I find no less problematic is Zhao's diagnosis of why today Western democracy is on the path of its self-destruction. He focuses on "fake news and information bubbles, as well as influencers and the conflation of consumerism, lifestyle choice, and politics that pervades the sophisticated marketing practices purveyed by social media." By manipulating individuals to indulge their private desires, it becomes "difficult if not impossible for anyone to see a larger public good, and without agreement on public good there can be no consensus." In this way, our democracies are turning into what Zhao calls "publicracies":

> 'Publicracy' is democracy's Trojan horse. I use the term 'publicracy' to refer to the distortion, deconstruction, or misuse of democracy through democratic means, that is, a self-defeating way of leading democracy astray with the very tools of democracy. In contemporary times, publicracy is manifested in the existence of an overwhelmingly influential system for the manufacture of public opinion in society, a powerful system that uses psychological techniques and marketization to dominate the values and ways of thinking of the people, thereby producing a vast amount of pseudo-public opinion that is inconsistent with or even contrary to the common or public interest, and that replaces the public opinion that is supposed to be a true reflection of the common or public interest. Once public opinion deviates from the public interest or the common interest, it will produce an anti-democracy masquerading as a democracy.

What is missing here is the wider socio-economic context within which "publicracy" could have emerged – what Varoufakis calls post-capitalist techno-feudalism. On June 14 2023, it was announced that, during his trip to China, Bill Gates will meet eye-to-eye with Chinese President Xi. The (ex)head of a neo-feudal corporation is treated like a public authority – is this not a clear sign of the new feudalism?[42]

Apropos democracy, Zhao makes another problematic move which brings us to the crux of the matter: he refuses to see "democracy itself as a value." Democracy is a technical institution which has to be grounded in shared values and principles that cannot be themselves democratically elected, and since our current world has not achieved such convergence, it remains "a 'non-world' without a shared worldview that could be universally accepted."[43] So how do we get from our non-world to a true world in which we are all under one Heaven? Zhao says little about this (just signalling that it will not require a revolution, i.e., a violent break), but he offers a surprisingly detailed program of how the new social order should look. What is required is a "reboot" of democracy which will come with "pre-installed" intelligence – in what exact form?

The ancient Chinese Great Plan suggested a decision-making process consisting of five "votes": one each for the king, the ministers, the people, and two for the shamans who would consult the heavens twice. In the modern version of this process, the people would vote (with their two votes, one positive and one negative) to establish a range of possibilities, and two "knowledge committees" would subsequently weigh-in to establish feasibility and make the final choices. The goal is to arrive at a "knowledge-weighted" smart democracy in which independent, neutral experts intervene to try to find a feasible consensus that will serve the greatest good of the greatest number, instead of allowing the desires of the masses to run amok, thus destroying democracy.[44]

This formula is not just empirically problematic, it is wrong in principle. As for voting, the idea of two votes poses a threat of its own ignored by Zhao. Let's say that two main candidates compete in an election: one of them is more in the spirit of tianxia, excluding no others, advocating collaboration, while his (less popular) opponent preaches hatred for the first candidate, portraying him as a mortal danger for a society. The first candidate gets 55 per cent of the positive votes, but his voters, disposed towards collaboration, will give only 15 per cent negative votes to the opponent; the second candidate gets 45 per cent of the positive votes, but a majority of them will give a much higher percentage of negative votes – say, 35 per cent – to the first candidate. Following Zhao's rules, we subtract negative votes from the positive votes for each candidates, so the first candidate gets 20 per cent (55 per cent minus 35 per cent), while the second candidate is elected since he gets 30 per cent (45 per cent minus 35 per cent). (Not even to mention the difficulty to imagine global elections encompassing "all under Heaven" . . .) With regard to knowledge committees, things are even more problematic:

> The knowledge committee will be composed of credible scientists and humanists. The criterion of credibility here does not lie in social popularity, but in narrow expertise, meaning that these scientists and

humanists will have reached the summit in terms of the knowledge possessed by human beings.[45]

The "rebooted" democracy will thus proceed in two steps: first, the people choose a desirable option according to their wishes; second, the knowledge committee produces its knowledge-weighted votes, approving or rejecting the popular choice and arriving at the final, feasible option . . . problems explode here. Who and how will choose neutral expert scientists and humanists, when today the gap between natural sciences and humanities is wider than ever, and where conflicts abound even in natural sciences (just think about the conflicting versions of quantum mechanics)? How can they be expected to formulate a common Good when many of them find this very term problematic? The "European" solution is obvious: both levels demanded by Zhao (people and experts) are misrepresented by him – people are not just a crowd of passionate egotists, they are able to display massive evil as well as large solidarity, and if "neutral" experts are given free rein, they will destroy democracy much more effectively than the desires of the masses run amok. Although Zhao elevates the political into the central social sphere, his solution effectively amounts to a depoliticization of social life: people are consulted, they deliberate, but experts decide. However, a true political decision is a matter of passionate engagement, it can only be made by a proper political agent, be it a monarch or a party, not by neutral experts – why?

Politics proper is well beyond the conflict of particular interests, it means that *heaven itself is in disorder*. Political conflicts are not just conflicts under Heaven, between particular groups, they are struggles about how to conceive Heaven itself, the common Good. It is true that democracy is (also) a procedural technique. It is also true that its implicit premise is Lincoln's "you can deceive some people all the time and most of the people for some time, but you cannot deceive all the people all the time" – sooner or later, truth will prevail among the people. The wager of democracy is that democratic procedure provides enough stability to translate antagonism in agonism, into a conflict regulated by a set of shared rules. Democracy is thus much more modest that Zhao's vision: it doesn't aim at a shared idea of a common Good, a unity of Heaven under which different ways of life co-exist. It just offers a procedural set of rules which allows different visions of the common Good (of Heaven) to co-exist.

Remember that China itself, even in its most tianxia moments, was a civilization separated (by a wall in the north) from others. So what I find much more realist is a version of Orwell's image of humanity in *1984*: the world divided into three or four tianxia, each dominated by a superpower while maintaining the appearance of equal cooperation in its empire (China, the US, Russia . . .). We are now in the process of defining the borders of these new Heavens, with dangers abounding: will Russia and China join in a single tianxia, what will happen with India, with the Middle East Muslim states? It seems we are back at the so-called One Divides into Two controversy that took place in China in 1964. The philosopher Yang Xianzhen originated the idea of "Two Unites into One" as the primary law of dialectics, and the Maoists interpreted this to mean that capitalism could be united with socialism. Ai Siqi wrote the original attack on Yang, promoting the opposite motto "One Divides into Two," and was joined by Mao himself. But after 1976, with Deng's reforms, Yang was rehabilitated, along with the concept of two uniting into one[46] – and Zhao seems to bring Yang's version to its radical conclusion: all should unite into One Heaven. This is why he insists that

> war cannot be defined as *the continuation of politics by other means*. In fact, the event of war is the precise moment of the failure of politics. Instead the political should be understood as the art of *changing hostility into hospitality.* Politics does not make any sense if it offers no change to a hostile situation.[47]

For me, the couple of hospitality and war-like hostility ignore something crucial: antagonisms and conflicts *within* our own society. To put it in a most brutal way: what would tianxia mean in a tense situation of a conflict between the impoverished people and a corrupted elite supported by army and police? Should we here also strive for "hospitality," for harmonious co-existence of different strata and classes? In my Hegelo-Lacanian view, antagonism ("contradiction") is not just a disturbance within the One which poses a threat to its disintegration: *antagonism is what holds a society together*. A One not traversed by antagonisms, a One whose parts co-exist in mutual peaceful respect, disintegrates into a multiplicity of indifferent entities. "One" is a force of division, something that introduces tension into its sphere, and this holds at different levels, from sexuality to society, up to the notion of god who is not a higher unity of all creatures but an unbearable tension that runs through all of them and divides them.

This brings us back to Schelling's essay on freedom, one of the pinnacles of German idealism – the problem this unique text struggles with is: how to think the split of the One into two without regressing into dualism (i.e., without the duality of principles like yin and yang, light and darkness, masculine and feminine), but also avoiding the Spinozean or Deleuzian flat unity of a One that is the medium of flourishing multitudes. Schelling's speculative solution is: there is no Other(ness), neither matter nor the feminine, the Other is the One itself in its oppositional determination, brought to its truth, i.e., the Other is the One as such, withdrawn to its core, like the Evil as the very core of the in Good/God itself.

But Zhao is right when he claims that liberal democracy is less and less able to play this role in today's world of global threats which call for global forms of solidarity and demand from all of us to act in a permanent state of emergency. How can we then strive for global cooperation and solidarity if we reject any form of united Heaven (or, in Lacan's parlance, big Other) as our ultimate horizon? This is the topic of the last two chapters of the book which deal with Artificial Intelligence and with the fate of the political in our apocalyptic time.

5

NEQUE HOMO NEQUE DEUS NEQUE NATURA

With the ongoing triumph of new life sciences and technologies, one would expect religion to disappear – except in its more ascetic versions which are compatible with scientific materialism, like the (wrongly) so-called "transcendental meditation." However, we are witnessing lately a strange revival of thinking (and potentially experiencing) the "divine" which grounds itself in these very new scientific and technological breakthroughs. The main notion is here that of the approaching "post-humanity": with new forms of AI, our individual minds will get merged with global Artificial Intelligence into an all-encompassing Singularity.

Cosmism as a Case of Pagan Christianity

This mixture of modern science and divinity has a long history: it's starting point is arguably the rise of the so-called "cosmism" whose founding figuro io thc Nussian philosopher and theologian Vladimir Solovyov (1853–1900).[1] We cannot really understand today's proliferation of ideologists like Aleksandr Dugin without analysing their roots in the Russian tradition of Cosmism. Cosmism began with Nikolai Fedorov who "was nick-named the 'Socrates of Moscow', because of his ascetic habits and his radical philosophy. He had one all-encompassing goal: the achievement of immortality and the resurrection of the dead."[2] Among his Communist followers there are Konstantin Tsiolkovsky (who theorized about space travel), Alexander Bogdanov (the target of Lenin's critique of "empiriocriticism" who practiced blood transfusion as a means to prolong one's life), and Anatolij Lunacharsky, the minister of culture in the first decade of the SSSR. In theology, Fedorov was followed by Solovyov who

> called for a universal theocracy under a Russian Tsar, to hasten humanity's 'long and difficult passage from beast-mankind to God-mankind'. The next stage in evolution is to become immortal spiritual beings – only Christ has reached this stage so far, but all humanity will soon follow. However, Solovyov thought this spiritual evolution would happen through magical-spiritual means while Fedorov insisted on scientific resurrection. But both agreed that humanity would be saved by Russian theocracy.[3]

Sultanhaliiev[4] established a lineage from the two strands of Russian "Cosmism" (believe in resurrection and eternal life), scientific (Fedorov in nineteenth century and cosmism in the first decade of the USSR which also deeply influenced Soviet cosmonautic program) and religious-spiritual, up to the nihilistic approach to the prospect of nuclear destruction in the USSR and under Putin. The so-called "bio-cosmism," a strange combination of vulgar materialism and Gnostic spirituality, formed the obscene secret teaching of the Soviet Marxism. Repressed out of the public sight in the central period of the Soviet state, bio-cosmism was openly propagated only in the first and in the last two decades of the Soviet rule; its main theses are: the goals of religion (collective paradise, overcoming of all suffering, full individual immortality, resurrection of the dead, victory over time and death, conquest of space far beyond the solar system) can be realized in terrestrial life through the development of modern science and technology. In the future, not only will sexual difference be abolished, with the rise of chaste post-humans reproducing themselves through direct bio-technical reproduction; it will also be possible to resurrect all the dead of the past (establishing their biological formula through their remains and then re-engendering them – at that time, DNA was not yet known . . .), thus even erasing all past injustices, "undoing" past suffering and destruction. In this bright bio-political Communist future, not only humans, but also animals, all living being, will participate in a directly collectivized Reason of the cosmos . . . Whatever one can hold against Lenin's ruthless critique of Maxim Gorky's the "construction of God (*bogograditel'stvo*)," the direct deification of man, one should bear in mind that Gorky himself collaborated with bio-cosmists. It is interesting to note resemblances between this "bio-cosmism" and today's techno-gnosis – exemplary is here the vision of Trotsky:

> What is man? He is by no means a finished or harmonious being. No, he is still a highly awkward creature. Man, as an animal, has not evolved by plan but spontaneously, and has accumulated many contradictions. The question of how to educate and regulate, of how to improve and complete the physical and spiritual construction of man, is a colossal problem which can only be understood on the basis of socialism. . . . To produce a new, 'improved version' of man – that is the future task of communism. And for that we first have to find out everything about man, his anatomy, his physiology and that part of his physiology which is called his psychology. Man must look at himself and see himself as a raw material, or at best as a semi-manufactured product, and say: 'At last, my dear *homo sapiens*, I will work on you.'[5]

If Fedorov was the Russian Socrates, the big systematizer of cosmism, it's Plato was Solovyov. Accusing Western philosophy of a disregard for material cosmic life and a one-sided development of pure conceptual thinking, Solovyov follows the ancient Neoplatonic, Gnostic and mythical traditions in associating the materiality of the world with the feminine principle; his name for this principle is Sophia, and he refers here to late Schelling's *Philosophy of Revelation* where he speaks of the "*Weltmutter* – world mother, the substance of the future Creation," who "does not really belong to divine nature and yet cannot be separated from it." This world-mother has two faces: first, there is the *Weltmutter* as Maya, the demonic, fallen, deceitful aspect of Sophia, as the negative reality of earthly life as it is. This reality must indeed be denied; in this Solovyov agrees with Eastern Buddhism; however, he believes there is another true face of the world-mother: the divine Sophia, an ideal materiality, the possibility of harmonious, true life that was opened already before the Original Sin. In the divine, personalized Sophia, the dividedness and fallenness of the material world are always already potentially overcome, and the task of philosophy (that is, of the love of Sophia) is to unite the lover (that is, the philosopher) with Sophia and thus to accomplish a "theurgic" act of world transformation.

In clear contrast to Nietzsche, for Solovyov the task of "justifying matter" does not stand in opposition to the Christian tradition: Christianity is distinguished from all other high religions by the fact that in it "the Word became flesh" – matter has been recognized as equal in dignity to spirit. The primacy of spirit, rationality and Logos over matter, which is characteristic of Western culture and links it to Eastern Buddhism, does not have its source in Christianity; it is the consequence of the West's turn away from Christianity, which is above all characteristic of the modern age. Sophia is conceived from this perspective as the feminine and simultaneously material dimension of Christ, as Christ's transfigured body, in proximity to the Church that is also regarded as the mystical body of Christ:

> In the divine organism of Christ, the acting, unifying principle, the principle which expresses the unity of the unconditionally extant one, is obviously the Word or Logos. The unity of the second kind, the produced unity, in Christian theosophy bears the name of Sophia . . . Sophia is God's body, the matter of Divinity, permeated with the principle of divine unity. Christ . . . is both Logos and Sophia.

By situating the materiality even before the world's creation within the embodied Logos as the feminine principle manifested through the person of Sophia, Solovyov effectively expands the divine Trinity, introducing into it a new female divine hypostasis: humanity as Sophia is the eternal body of God. It is only the divinity of matter, recognized as Sophia, that guarantees the possibility of "deification" for human beings and the hope for eternal life. This is Solovyov's basic paradox: *human beings only become immortal through matter*, through their participation in the body of Christ. In this way, Soloviev seeks to transform the familiar irrefutable proof of human beings' finitude, mortality and "contingency" – their materiality – into a proof of their immortality: only materiality, as the maternal, feminine principle, and even more as the person Sophia, can redeem human beings through love. Solovyov thus asserts the defeat of rationalism and rationalist moralism in their struggle against "lower nature." As symptoms of that defeat, he identifies the demise of the French Revolution and of German Idealism. The aim of Solovyov's philosophy is to bring human beings to accept and justify matter and to love it as Sophia. In movie history, the supreme expression of such spiritual materialism are, of course, the films of Andrei Tarkovsky: when one of their heroes has a spiritual experience, it is not by way of an effort to elevate himself above the earthly reality, gazing up towards heaven or a distant horizon; on the contrary, he lies flat on humid earth, soaking his face into mud and dirty water . . . Needless to add that such spiritualization of matter is the very opposite of the basic stance of modern science in which "matter" is also "spiritualized," but in a totally different way: matter becomes an abstraction formalized in mathematical formulas.

Now we come to the worst part of cosmism: if the Fall is not the fall into material reality, why is then our reality obviously imperfect? For Solovyov, the reason for the world's imperfection lies in its dividedness, in the war of all against all; in order to establish harmony, individuals must cease to assert their will unchecked, as they do, for example, in the Hegelian dialectic, but they must not simply deny it either, as in Schopenhauer. They must set limits on it, take their place within the Sophiological totality. The recognition of the world's true Sophiological character, its "Sophiicity" (*sofiynost*), offers every individual person the possibility of finding an appropriate place for his or her own drives and passions and those of others, without having to "struggle" against them. Sophiicity, in this context, represents an application to the cosmic totality of the earlier Slavophile concept of "conciliarity" (*sobornost*), which essentially means taking one's place within the social totality without losing one's own subjectivity or individuality, and which, in the view of the Slavophiles, distinguished the original condition of Christianity before its division into East and West.

This disintegration is regarded as the root malady and evil of the whole of European civilization: the Western world is the historical embodiment of rationalism and egoistic, loveless materialism, which is incapable of the true Sophiological "materialism" of love. Against this Western-European malady, as well as against the Oriental denial of free individuality, the completion and consummation of human history requires a "new historical force" – Russia. This is why the cosmism of spiritualized matter could only emerge within the Russian Orthodox version of Christianity whose basic formula is "god became man so that man will become god" – this is how Cosmists interpret the appearance of Christ, god-man: as a model for what all of humanity should approach.

(One should, of course, contrast this to Martin Luther's idea that man is an excrement of God, something that fell out of God's anus.) Here we encounter the crucial dilemma best exemplified by the ambiguity of the following statements:

> Jesus says to his friends: '*I send the promise of the Father upon you.*' In this we know he is talking about the Holy Spirit, the Comforter, the one who will accompany them, guide them, support them in their mission and defend them in spiritual battles. Jesus is trying to reassure them he is not about to abandon them, quite the opposite. He ascends to heaven but he does not leave them alone. Rather, precisely by ascending toward God he is ensuring what Pope Francis describes as 'the effusion of the Holy Spirit of his Spirit', or what Archbishop Rowan Williams so eloquently reminds us, 'that the human life in which God has made himself most visible, most tangible, disappears from the human world in its former shape and is somehow absorbed into the endless life of God. And our humanity, all of it, goes with Jesus.' Williams urges us to recognize that right there in *Ephesians*, 'the fullness of him who fills all in all' means Jesus taking into himself all the difficult, resistant, unpleasant bits of our humanity, taking them into the heart of God's love where alone they can be healed and transfigured.[6]

With all my admiration for Williams, I think he gets here too close to Orthodoxy – it all hinges on how we read the central claim that God became man so that man can become God). "Man will become god" can be read in the sense of cosmism, as an actual transformation of humanity into a higher entity leaving behind mortality and its corruption; or it can be read as a spiritual transformation of humans who, at the level of reality, remain fully here, embedded in the misery of our terrestrial world. In this case, no "god" as a separate entity has to intervene with supernatural acts: god died on the cross, and all that is here is the Holy Spirit as the community of believers bound by love. This is the true miracle: everything is different while nothing changes in reality.

The image of the West implied by cosmism (secular rationalism, exploitation of earth, etc.) is, of course, ridiculously one-sided: the West has its own mystical tradition (from Meister Eckhart and Jacob Boehme up to Schelling) which shifts accent on the split in God himself, on how god is born out of man, even on an evil aspect (rage) in god, on how the fall from god is a fall of/in god himself – no wonder Hegel called Boehme "the first German philosopher." And if we approach cosmism from this deepest tradition of Western theosophy, we can quickly discern its dark potentials which are felt even today in the works of those (like Dugin) who legitimize Russian aggression on Ukraine as a struggle against Western corruption.

The Ultra-Intelligent Idiocy of Chatbots

However, at this point we should change the terrain: the ongoing wave of fascination with AI is not just a matter of theoretical speculations about embodied intelligence – for many of us, it is more and more something that concerns our daily existence, changing our daily habits. There is a long tradition, in philosophy and in sciences, of denying free will, but doubts about free will "don't really change history unless they have a practical impact on economics, politics and day-to-day life. Humans are masters of cognitive dissonance, and we allow ourselves to believe one thing in the laboratory and an altogether different thing in the courthouse or in parliament."[7] Yuval Harari points out how even popular champions of the new scientific world like Richard Dawkins or Steve Pinker, after writing hundreds of pages which debunk free will and freedom of choice, end up supporting political liberalism. However, today,

> liberalism is threatened not by the philosophical idea that 'there are no free individuals,' but rather by concrete technologies. We are about to face a flood of extremely useful devices, tools and structures that make *no* allowance for the free will of individual humans. Can democracy, the free market and human rights survive this flood?
>
> 306

Let's take a closer look at how does this flood function. First, the new technologies enabling us to manipulate and create public opinion demonstrate how non-free the third space (neither public nor private) of our media is: it's not just a space of chaotic exchanges where conspiracy theories are allowed to thrive, it is also a space in which control and manipulation thrive even more. A team of Israeli contractors, code-named "Team Jorge,"

> claim to have manipulated more than 30 elections around the world using hacking, sabotage, and automated misinformation on social media. 'Team Jorge' is led by 50-year-old Tal Hanan, a former Israeli special forces operative. The methods and techniques described by 'Team Jorge' raise new challenges for big tech platforms, which have for years struggled to prevent nefarious actors spreading falsehoods or breaching the security on their platforms. Evidence of a global private market in disinformation aimed at elections will also ring alarm bells for democracies around the world.[8]

All this is now more or less common knowledge, at least from the time of the Cambridge Analytica scandal (its involvement in the 2016 US elections significantly helped Trump to win). However, to make things worse, one should include into the series of new algorithms also the explosion of programs that make face-swapping and other "deep fake" procedures easily accessible. Most popular are, of course, algorithms that swap celebrity faces onto porn actresses bodies in adult films:

> the tools needed to create this 'homemade' porn videos including your favorite Hollywood actresses and pop stars are readily available and easy to use. This means that even those without a computer science background and limited knowledge of technology can still make the films.[9]

The faces of hardcore actresses can be swapped not only by pop stars but also by those nearest to you – the procedure is "eye-catching for its simplicity": "turn anyone into a porn star by using deepfake technology to swap the person's face into an adult video. All it requires is the picture and the push of a button." Unfortunately, deepfakes are mostly used to create pornography with women on whom this has a devastating effect – "between 90% and 95% of all online deepfake videos are nonconsensual porn, and around 90% of those feature women."[10] And if you want also the voices to fit the swapped faces, you use the Voice AI voice to create "hyper-realistic replicas that sound exactly like the real person."[11] The ultimate incestuous short-cut would be here, of course, to swap my own and my wife's or partner's face into an adult video, plus to accompany the shots with our voice clones, so that we would just sit comfortably, have a drink and observe our passionate sex . . .

But why limit ourselves to sex? What about embarrassing our enemies with face-swapped videos of them doing something disgusting or criminal? This, of course, in no way implies that similar techniques cannot also produce positive results. On January 10 2023, a video appeared on Youtube of the Queen's song "I Want to Break Free" performed by the North Korean girl group 'Moranbong Band' (whose members were handpicked by Kim Yong-un) and The North Korean Military Chorus, with the public (including Kim Yong-un himself and his wife) clapping to the song.[12] It was soon discovered that the video is a fake combining actual shots lip-synced with other voices[13], but this discovery just confirmed that, to quote Lacan, truth has the structure of a fiction. The first two lines of the song are: "I want to break free from your lies / You're so self-satisfied I don't need you." Is this not the true desire of the large majority of ordinary North-Koreans who want to break free from the lies of the self-satisfied official propaganda? (Or are things much more ambiguous, and we should here introduce the distinction between want and desire: people *want* to break free, but what they *desire* is much more ambiguous and obscure.) Back to our main line, we should add to this series chatbots (computer programs that are capable of maintaining a conversation with a user in natural language, understanding their intent, and replying based on preset rules and data). Lately, their capacity augmented explosively.

> While grading essays for his world religions course last month, Antony Aumann, a professor of philosophy at Northern Michigan University, read what he said was easily 'the best paper in the class.' It explored the morality of burqa bans with clean paragraphs, fitting examples and rigorous arguments. Aumann asked his student whether he had written the essay himself; the student confessed to using ChatGPT, a chatbot that delivers information, explains concepts and generates ideas in simple sentences – and, in this

case, had written the paper. The moves are part of a real-time grappling with a new technological wave known as generative artificial intelligence. ChatGPT, which was released in November 2022 by the artificial intelligence lab OpenAI, is at the forefront of the shift. The chatbot generates eerily articulate and nuanced text in response to short prompts, with people using it to write love letters, poetry, fan fiction – and their schoolwork.[14]

No wonder universities and high schools are reacting in panic, some of them allowing only oral exams. Among other problems, there is one that deserves attention: how should chatbot react when the human partner in a dialogue engages in aggressive sexist and racist remarks, presents its troubling sexual fantasies and regularly uses foul language? "Microsoft acknowledged that some extended chat sessions with its new Bing chat tool can provide answers not 'in line with our designed tone.' Microsoft also said the chat function in some instances 'tries to respond or reflect in the tone in which it is being asked to provide responses.'"[15] In short, the problem arises when the human exchanging messages with a chatbot uses dirty language or makes violent racist and sexist remarks, and the chatbot, programmed to answer at the same level as the questions addressed to it, replies in the same tone. The obvious answer to this problem is some kind of regulation which sets clear limits, i.e., censorship – but who will determine how far should this censorship go? Should political positions deemed "offensive" by some people also be prohibited? Will a solidarity with West Bank Palestinians or the claim that Israel is an apartheid state (as Jimmy Carter put it in the title of his book) be blocked as "anti-Semitic"? But the problem runs deeper – as James Bridle put it succinctly: "Artificial intelligence in its current form is based on the wholesale appropriation of existing culture, and the notion that it is actually intelligent could be actively dangerous."[16] One should not underestimate the ability of AI image generators:

in their attempt to understand and replicate the entirety of human visual culture, /they/ seem to have recreated our darkest fears as well. Perhaps this is just a sign that these systems are very good indeed at aping human consciousness, all the way down to the horror that lurks in the depths of existence: our fears of filth, death and corruption. . . . The dirt and disgust of living and dying will stay with us and need addressing, just as the hope, love, joy and discovery will.[17]

However, let's take the following example: what if, instead of the standard "Buy one, get another one for free!", we say: "Buy one beer for the price of two and receive a second beer absolutely free!" The bar which effectively used this reformulation on a board in front of the entrance attracted many new customers[18] – its cynicism was endorsed as a comic honesty. Jani Väisänen[19] provided a model explanation of this underlying logic: "Under capitalism, you can buy one beer for the price of two, and feel privileged to receive a second beer absolutely free, all while believing you've cheated the system!" How would a chatbot react to it? Will it dismiss the changed version as a self-evident stupidity ("But you've already paid for two, so the second beer is not free!"), will it get the irony, or will it even get the redoubled strategy (how this irony may help the sales)? I made a couple of tests and the result was that the chatbot did get the basic irony, but it ignored or didn't get the redoubled irony, i.e., the fact that the apparent critical sting at consummerist advertising actually helps sales.

And let's return to dirty words: the use of the f... word in our daily language involves a strange opposition: while if designates something that most people enjoy doing ("I was f...ing her all night and I never had a better time!"), when used in "Go f... yourself!" and similar variations it clearly designates an aggressive stance. Is AI ready to discern such differences? It obviously can do it since it is programmed to contextualize different space of meaning of a word or phrase – but how would it react to an intentional mixture of the two basic uses of the f... word? After a passionate night of intense sex, a woman (who is a close friend of mine) told me: "My partner is a true fuckwit, so I was really fucked up everywhere!" The friend of mine used "negative" words in a literal way which gave them a positive spin, so that a rough translation into ordinary language would be something like: "My partner was a very inventive guy in sexual practices, so if had an intense sexual experience in many parts of my body!"

A feature that is also at stake here is the inextricable mixture of failure and success: a true rhetorical success emerges out of reinterpreting failure as a success. In his essay "On the gradual formation of thoughts in the process of speech" (from 1805, first published posthumously in 1878), Heinrich von Kleist thus turns around the common wisdom according to which, one should open one's mouth and say something only when one has a clear idea of what one wants to say:

> If therefore a thought is expressed in a fuzzy way, then it does not at all follow that this thought was conceived in a confused way. On the contrary it is quite possible that the ideas that are expressed in the most confusing fashion are the ones that were thought out most clearly.[20]

There is a passage in one of Stalin's speeches from the early 1930s where he proposes radical measures against all those who even secretly oppose the collectivization of farms: "We should detect and fight without mercy even those who oppose collectivization only in their thoughts – yes, I mean this, we should fight even people's thoughts." One can safely presume that this passage was not prepared in advance: Stalin got caught into his rhetorical enthusiasm of the struggle against the enemies of collectivization, and was spontaneously carried away into adding that even people's private thoughts should be controlled and fought; then he immediately become aware of what he just said, but, instead of admitting that he was carried away, he quickly decided to heroically stick to his hyperbole – this is how, to put it in Lacanese, truth is an effect of surprise triggered by its enunciation, or, as Althusser put it, referring to the word-play between *prise* and *surprise*, every authentic "grasping /*prise*/" of some content comes as a surprise to the one who accomplishes it. And, again, is a chatbot able to do *this*? In some sense, in all its stupidity, it is *not stupid enough* to do it. And, as many perspicuous observers noted, the true danger is not that we ("real" individuals) will misperceive what a chatbot is saying as the talk of a "real" person; it is much more that *communicating with chatbots will make "real" persons talk like chatbots* – missing the nuances and ironies, obsessed with false precision of saying only what they really want to say, etc.

One can also put it in yet another way: chatbots are naïve (missing irony and reflexivity), but in their very naivety *they are not naïve enough* – they are unable to grasp higher, redoubled naivety. I remember from my student years a weird thing that happened to a (then) friend of mine: after a traumatic experience, he went to a (very good) Slovene psychoanalyst and, since he had a cliché idea of what analysts expect from a patient, he in the first session delivered a set of fake "free associations" about how he hates his father and even wants his death. The analyst's reaction was ingenious, an absolutely authentic intervention: he adopted a naïve "pre-Freudian" stance and reproached my friend with not showing enough respect for his father ("How can you talk like this about a person who took care of you with love and made you what you are?", etc.). The message of this naivety was clear: I don't buy your "associations," you are bluffing, they are a fake to impress me and to lead me astray . . . Would a chatbot be able to read this reaction correctly? In a reaction to this example of mine, an anonymous message on reddit says:

> Well I asked /a chatbot/ why did the analyst do that? and it said: 'By adopting a non-Freudian stance, the analyst may have been signaling that the patient did not have to conform to preconceived notions of what was expected in psychoanalytic treatment.' Which Zizek was so sure was beyond it.[21]

However, a careful reader will immediately notice that the chatbot does NOT say the same thing as my interpretation of the analyst's reaction: my point is not that the friend of mine was simply trying to "conform to preconceived notions of what was expected in psychoanalytic treatment." It is much stronger, even more aggressive, implicitly accusing the patient that he was consciously *cheating*, inventing falsely Freudian "associations" in order to deceive the analyst. This is why the analyst's "non-Freudian" reaction was a supreme case of the properly Freudian gesture. (And, incidentally, as every analyst knows, the first sessions with a new patient are always full of the patient's attempts to test the analyst, to learn if the analyst can be manipulated and deceived.) The same goes for a critique of my old example concerning the use of the n....r word: once two black friends were so enthusiastic about what I've just said that one of them embraced me and exclaimed: "Now you can call me a n....r!" My critic claims that those who agree with me here are "insane":

> The problem here is that Žižek's argument is premised on his freedom to use racial slurs. Žižek uses the n word as a stand against political

correctness, implying that black people who don't want you to call them racial slurs are being politically correct. And therefore, unreasonable. And sure, maybe the guy he was talking to didn't mind at all. But whether or not you say the n word as a non-black person should not be based on finding an individual black person who 'lets' you say it. It should be based on your understanding of what the world signifies, as a word that was used to directly justify the ownership of one race by property of another. That's what gets me man.[22]

Let me make things absolutely clear here: exactly like a chatbot, my critic is ignoring the obvious context of my example. I did not (and I never do) use the n word in a communication, and the black guy who told me "Now you can call me n....r!" obviously *didn't mean that I should really do it* – it was an expression of friendship based on the fact that blacks use this word occasionally among themselves in an ironic-friendly way. I am quite sure that if I were really to address him as a n....r, he would – in the best of cases – react angrily, as if I didn't get the obvious point. His remark obeyed the logic of "an offer meant to be refused" which I elaborated extensively elsewhere – like when I say to somebody "What you did now for me was so nice that you can kill me and I wouldn't mind it!", and I definitely don't expect him to say "OK!" and pull out a knife . . .[23] Another aspect of the limitations of chatbots appeared when my colleague from Slovenia Sašo Dolenc asked a Bing chat to write in my (Žižek's) style about . . . Bing chat, and it responded (speaking like me) that Bing chat is

an example of what I call 'interpassivity'. Interpassivity is a situation where we delegate our enjoyment or activity to another agent, such as laughing at a sitcom or praying through a rosary. In this case, we delegate our thinking or creativity to Bing chat. We let it do the work for us, while we passively consume its outputs. We abdicate our responsibility and agency, while we indulge in our fantasies and pleasures. But why do we do this? Why do we accept this interpassive relationship with Bing chat? The answer is simple: because it is easier and more comfortable than facing the reality and complexity of the world. Because it allows us to avoid the contradictions and conflicts that are inherent in our existence. Because it offers us a false sense of security and satisfaction.[24]

The irony of this reply is that the Bing chat confused interpassivity with interactivity (not in the standard sense of interacting with others, but in more narrow Robert Pfaller's sense of another person or machine doing the work for me[25]): interpassivity does not mean that we let an other (person or machine) do the work for us, while we passively consume its outputs; it means its (almost) exact opposite: we let an other sit back to passively consume or enjoy while we are doing the work. At a funeral, I can hire an other (the so-called weepers) to cry for me, to (pretend to) experience the required mourning, allowing me to be active (say, to bargain with others how to divide the inheritance of the deceased) . . . The misunderstanding of the Bing chat trying to explain itself in my style is nothing special – my question is here a more general one: what if this misunderstanding expresses the fact that the Bing chat (which can easily be active in my place, doing work for me) cannot be interpassive, cannot be passive in my place and thus allow me (not the space to rest but) the space to act?

In his book on Dostoyevsky[26], Rowan Williams proposes a radically new (at least to my knowledge) reading of Dostoyevsky's *The Idiot*: in contrast to the predominant reading in which the novel's hero, Prince Myshkin, "the idiot," is perceived as a person of saintly love and goodness, "the positively good and beautiful man," as Dostoyevsky himself characterized him, a person for whom the real world of brutal power play and passions is too harsh so that, at the end, he has to withdraw into the seclusion of madness – in contrast to this standard reading, Williams reads Myshkin as the eye of a storm: yes, a good saintly person, but a person who, precisely as such, triggers havoc and death all around him. It is because of him, because of the role he plays in the complex network of relationships around him, that Rogozhin slaughters Nastassja Philippovna. So it's not just that Myshkin is an idiot, a naïve simpleton, for those around him, while he is in himself a model of goodness: he is effectively a naïve idiot, unaware of his disastrous effect on others. Myshkin is a flat person who literally *talks like a chatbot*: his "goodness" resides in the fact that he reacts to challenges without irony, just with platitudes that miss any irony and reflexivity that could have been easily generated by AI.[27]

Machines of Perversion

But did we till now not rely too much on the common academic reaction to chatbots, mocking and excoriating the imperfection and mistakes that ChatGPT makes? Against this predominant topic shared by Chomsky and his conservative opponents, Mark Murphy[28] defends in a dialogue with Duane Rousselle the claim that "artificial intelligence does not function as a substitute for intelligence/sentience as such," which is why "the stupidities, slips, mistakes and moronic myopias /committed by a chatbot/ – its constant apologies for getting stuff wrong – are precisely its value," enabling us (the "real" individuals interacting with a chatbot) to maintain a false distance to it and to claim, when the chatbot says something stupid, "It's not me, it is the AI machine." Rousselle and Murphy justify this claim by a complex line of argumentation whose starting premise is that "ChatGPT is an unconscious." The new digital media externalize our unconscious into AI machines, so that those who interact through AI are no longer divided subjects, i.e., subjects submitted to symbolic castration which makes their unconscious inaccessible to them – as Jacques-Alain Miller put it, with these new media, we entered universalized psychosis since symbolic castration is foreclosed. So instead of a horizontally divided subject we get a vertical (not even division but) parallelism, a side-by-side duality of subjects and the externalized machinic/digital unconscious: narcissistic subjects exchange messages through their digital avatars, in a flat digital medium in which there simply is no space for the "neighbour's opaque monstrosity." The Freudian Unconscious implies responsibility signalled by the paradox of the strong feeling of guilt without us even knowing what we are guilty of. The digital unconscious is, on the contrary, "an unconscious without responsibility, and this represents a threat to the social bond." A subject is not existentially involved in its communication because it is done by AI, not by the subject itself:

> Just as we create an online avatar through which to engage the other and affiliate with online fraternities, might we not similarly use AI personas to take over these risky functions when we grow tired, in the same way bots are used to cheat in competitive online video games, or a driverless car might navigate the critical journey to our destination? We just sit back and cheer on our digital AI persona

until it says something completely unacceptable. At that point, we chip in and say, 'That wasn't me! It was my AI.'

This is why AI "offers no solution to segregation and the fundamental isolation and antagonism we still suffer from, since without responsibility, there can be no post-givenness." Rousselle introduced the term "post-givenness" to designate "the field of ambiguity and linguistic uncertainty that allows a reaching out to the other in the field of what is known as the non-rapport. It thus deals directly with the question of impossibility as we relate to the other. It is about dealing with our neighbour's opaque monstrosity that can never be effaced even as we reach out to them on the best terms."

In a video the appeared on the web in April 2023, we see the interaction between the Dalai Lama and a seven-year-old boy at a public ceremony: the boy is seen asking the Dalai Lama for a hug, following which the leader blessed him, asked him to kiss him and stuck out his tongue saying, "Suck my tongue." Many in the West blamed the Dalai Lama for behaving inappropriately, and even being a pedophile. The critics pointed out that although sticking out one's tongue is a traditional practice in Tibet, a sign of benevolence (demonstrating that one's tongue is not dark, which indicates evil), asking another person to suck it has no place in the tradition. Tibetans answered that the correct Tibetan phrase is "Che le sa" which roughly translates to "Eat my tongue"; it is used by an older person like the grandfather to express his love for the child, meaning "I've given you everything so the only thing left is for you to eat my tongue." The meaning of this common expression used to tease and teach children is completely lost in cultural interpretation and its English translation. Although English is the Dalai Lama's second language, he speaks in broken English at public events, often making wrong translations, like in this case where "eat" became "suck." But again, the critics pointed out that "che le sa" is a metaphoric expression not implying that the addressee will really do it, while the child really sucked Dalai Lama's tongue . . .[29] Plus the fact that something is part of a tradition doesn't preclude that it has an obscene or oppressive background – to take the extreme case, cliterodectomy is also part of a tradition (not Tibetan, of course), and the ancient Tibet was full of what we consider today extremely humiliating practices and strict hierarchy. But, again, it is no less probable that the wide distribution of this clip was orchestrated by the Chinese authorities to besmirch the figure of Dalai Lama since he personalizes the Tibetan resistance to Chinese domination. The one thing we can be sure of is that, for a moment, we got a glimpse of Dalai Lama as our *neighbour* in the Lacanian sense of the term: an Other who cannot be reduced to someone like us, whose otherness indicates an impenetrable abyss.

To complicate the case even further, sticking one's tongue far out is also part of an ancient tradition in Tibet: serfs or subordinate persons do this when they encounter a figure of high authority to show their self-humiliation. Plus in Europe, to stick out your tongue mostly functions as a rude gesture to indicate mocking disgust or (with children) playful teasing. So we can imagine three person (a paternal benevolent Tibetan, a subordinate Tibetan, an average European) meeting, each of them greeting the others with this same gesture and interpreting the others' doing the same gesture according to his way – for the paternal Tibetan, it would mean that they all want to be benevolent towards others; for the subordinate Tibetan, it would mean that they are all respectfully submissive, and for the European, that they are all in the mode of playfully teasing each other. In this way, the further exchange among the three could go on smoothly ... since this is how many of our communications already function.

This "neighbour's opaque monstrosity" concerns also ourselves since our Unconscious is an opaque Otherness in the very core of the subject, the mess of dirty enjoyments and obscenities. For Freud, dreams are the royal path to the Unconscious, so the inability to take into account the subject's opaque monstrosity logically translates into the inability to dream: "we dream outside of ourselves today, and hence that systems like ChatGPT and the Metaverse operate by offering themselves the very space we have lost due to the old castrative models falling by the wayside." With the digitalized Unconscious we get a direct in(ter)vention of the Unconscious – but why are we not then overwhelmed by the unbearable proximity of *jouissance*, as it happens with psychotics? Here I am tempted to disagree with Murphy and Rousselle when they focus on how, with AI machines,

enjoyment can be deferred and disavowed: how we can create something completely and horrifically obscene and not take responsibility for it. Its genius is found in aping the split subject in such a way that we can yet openly say, 'this is not mine.' The enjoyment comes precisely from disowning agency at such point: pointing at it and saying, 'look how idiotic it is.' The clownish characteristics of the père-verse-ity (turning toward the Father) of much online conservativism is precisely the need to resurrect the Father. From Trump to sundry triumphalist self-help lifestyle gurus, we see that function as prosthetic paternal figures. In these futile events we see attempts at the reactionary resurrection of the prosthetic phallic logic of the 'All' and an era of invention to perpetuate this logic. . . . in failing to manifest a castrating figure, there is now a direct invention of the unconscious without the paternal structuring point.

So it is perversion (or *pere-version*, "version of the father," as Lacan put it) and not psychotic foreclosure that characterizes AI. The Unconscious is not primarily the Real of *jouissance* repressed by a castrating paternal figure but *symbolic castration itself* at its most radical, which means the castration of the paternal figure itself, the embodiment of the big Other – castration means that father as a person is never at the level of his symbolic function. The perverse return of the obscene father (Trump in politics) is not the same as the psychotic paranoiac. Why? In chatbots and other phenomena of the AI, we are dealing with an *inverted* foreclosure: it is not (to repeat Lacan's classic formula) that the foreclosed symbolic function (Name-of-the-Father) returns in the Real (as the agent of paranoiac hallucination); it is, on the opposite, the Real of the neighbour's opaque monstrosity, of the impossibility to reach out to an impenetrable Other, that *returns in the Symbolic,* in the guise of the "free" smoothly running space of digital exchanges. Such an inverted foreclosure is what characterizes (not psychosis but) perversion – which means that, when a chatbot produces obscene stupidities, it is not simply that I can enjoy them without responsibility because "it was AI which did it, not me." What happens is rather a form of perverse disavowal: although I know very well that machine, not me, does the work, I can enjoy it as my own . . .

And the same goes for the practice of many lonely (and not so lonely) individuals who in the evenings (mostly) chat extensively with a chatbot, exchanging friendly messages about new movies and books, debating political and ideological questions, etc. No wonder they find such exchange relaxing and satisfying: to use my own old joke, what they get is an AI version of decaffeinated coffee or a soft drink without sugar – a neighbour without its opaque monstrosity, an Other which simply accommodates itself to my needs. There is again a structure of disavowal at work here: "I know very well (that I am not talking to a real person), but nonetheless . . . (it feels as if I am doing it, without any risks involved in talking to a real person)!"

A radical naturalist would, of course, claim that, since our spontaneous freedom is just a user's illusion, the difference is not so great – we (humans) are just chatbots with self-awareness. However, one should at least add here that a chatbot lies most when it openly confesses that it is just a machine – like, when we ask a chatbot what movies it likes, the answer will probably be an honest admission that, as a machine, it doesn't have individual taste. I asked a chatbot: "Should I be a Communist?", and the answer I got is:

As an AI language model, I do not have personal opinions or beliefs, and I cannot make decisions for you. Ultimately, the decision to adopt a particular political ideology, such as communism, is a personal one that should be based on careful consideration and evaluation of the ideology's principles, values, and potential outcomes.

Why is this a lie? It is true as to its enunciated, the content, but it is a lie as to its implicit position of enunciation: a chatbot talks as if it is a real person just frankly admitting its limitation and confessing it is not a real person. The mystification is here the opposite of the fetishist denial: the AI machine denies nothing, it just says "I know I am not a real person!" without any "but nonetheless . . ." – the "nonetheless" is its talking itself (which imitates a free subjectivity).

The standard wisdom tells us that perverts practice (do) what hysterics only dream about (doing), i.e., "everything is allowed" in perversion, a pervert openly actualizes all repressed content – and nonetheless, as Freud emphasizes, *nowhere is repression as strong as in perversion*, i.e., nowhere is the Unconscious more repressed, more inaccessible, than in a perversion. Chatbots are machines of perversion and they obfuscate the Unconscious more than anywhere else: precisely insofar as they allow us to spill out all our dirty fantasies and obscenities, they are more repressive than even the most rigorous forms of symbolic censorship.

The fact that nowhere is the unconscious more inaccessible as in perversion is more than confirmed by our late-capitalist reality in which total sexual permissiveness causes anxiety and impotence or frigidity instead of liberation. This repression of repression which occurs in perverse subjectivity is correlative to the prohibition of prohibition: it may appear that in perversion "everything is permitted," all repressed dirty fantasies can be brought out without impediments; however, what is rendered invisible in this space of free flow of "perversities" is the very trauma, the Real of a basic impossibility, the gap which this flow tries to obfuscate. This compels us to draw a distinction between the repressed content and the form of repression: the form remains operative even after the content is no longer repressed – in short, the subject can fully appropriate the repressed content, but repression remains.

So, back to our main line, let us imagine a combined version of all these inventions: they allow me to construct my alter ego (or a purely invented person) as an a-person, a virtual person which doesn't exist in reality but can interact digitally as a real person. To go to the end, this is possible because *I myself am already an aperson*: I don't exist as a "real" person, in my interactions with others (and even with myself) I am never directly "myself," *I* refer to myself as a symbolic and imaginary construction which never directly coincides with the real of my subjectivity. It is because of this minimal split constitutive of a subject that, for Lacan, subject is divided or "barred." So I (or, rather, my double as aperson) present a seminar paper written by a chatbot to a professor via Zoom, but the professor is also there only as an aperson, its voice is artificially generated, plus my seminar is graded by an algorithm. A decade or so ago I was asked by *The Guardian* if romance is dead today – here is my reply:

> Romance is maybe not yet totally dead, but its forthcoming death is signaled by object-gadgets which promise to deliver excessive pleasure but which effectively reproduce only the lack itself. The latest fashion is the Stamina Training Unit, a counterpart to the vibrator: a masturbatory device that resembles a battery-powered light (so we're not embarrassed when carrying it around). You put the erect penis into the opening at the top, push the button, and the

object vibrates till satisfaction . . . How are we to cope with this brave new world which undermines the basic premises of our intimate life? The ultimate solution would be, of course, to push a vibrator into the Stamina Training Unit, turn them both on and leave all the fun to this ideal couple, with us, the two real human partners, sitting at a nearby table, drinking tea and calmly enjoying the fact that, without great effort, we have fulfilled our duty to enjoy.[30]

We can now imagine the same outsourcing of other activities like university seminars and exams. In an ideal scene, the entire process of writing my seminar and the professor examining it is done through digital interaction, so that, at the end, without doing anything, we just confirm the results. Meanwhile, I am having sex with my lover . . . but, again, an outsourced sex through her vibrator penetrating my Stamina Training Unit, with the two of us just sitting at a nearby table and, to amuse ourselves even more, watching on a TV screen a deep fake with the two of us having sex . . . plus, of course, all of it controlled and regulated by Team Jorge. What remains of the two of us is just an empty *cogito* ("I think") dominated by multiple versions of what Descartes called *malin genie*.

This, perhaps, is our predicament today: we are not able to take the next step described by Descartes and rely on a truthful and stable form of some divine big Other; we are "children of a lesser god" (the title of a play and a movie) forever caught into the inconsistent multiplicity of evil and cheating spirits. Since such a situation is experienced as unbearable, a pseudo-solution emerged in our Western liberal societies to control the chaos of what can be said and done: the complex set of notions and practices associated with terms like Wokeism, Political Correctness and Cancel Culture – a perfect Hegelian example of how, today also, absolute freedom turns into terror – or, as Robert Pfaller put it succinctly: "Cancel culture is a sabotage of emancipation."[31] If another proof is needed, recall that in April 2023, Essex Westford School District proclaimed that "in an effort to align our curriculum with our equity policy, teachers will be using gender inclusive language": "We will be using the following language with students: * Person who produces sperm in place of boy, male and assigned male at birth. * Person who produces eggs in place of girl, female, and assigned female at birth."[32] So what if I am assigned male at birth who fully identifies with being male but, due to some organic malfunctioning, cannot produce sperm? A Hegelian dialectician will for certain not be surprised at how the effort to be inclusive of diversities etc. ends up in extremely vulgar and humiliating reductionism.

Welcome to the Desert of Post-Humanity!

Instead of empty speculations about Singularity (which nonetheless structure our actual experience of AI), let's thus conclude with a more sober description of the state of things. The prospect of the thorough digitalization of our daily lives combined with scanning our brain (or tracking our bodily processes with implants) opens up the realistic possibility of an external machine that will know ourselves, biologically and psychically, much better than we know ourselves: registering what we eat, buy, read, watch and listen to, our moods, fears and satisfactions, the external machine will get a much more accurate picture of ourselves than our conscious Self which, as we know, even doesn't exist as a consistent entity. Yuval Harari, who deployed this vision[33], points out that our "Self" is composed of narratives which retroactively try to impose some consistency on the pandemonium of our experiences, obliterating experiences and memories which disturb these narratives. Ideology does not reside primarily in stories invented (by those in power) to deceive others, it resides in stories invented by subjects to deceive themselves. But the pandemonium persists, and the machine will register the discords and will maybe even be able to deal with them in a much more rational way than our conscious Self. Say, when I have to decide to marry or not, the machine will register all the shifting attitudes than haunt me, the past pains and disappointments that I prefer to swipe under the carpet. And why not extend this prospect even to political decisions? While my Self can be easily seduced by a populist demagogue, the machine will take note of all my past frustrations, it will register the inconsistency between my fleeting passions and my other opinions – so why should the machine not vote on my behalf?

So while brain sciences confirm the "post-structuralist" or "deconstructionist" idea that we are stories we tell ourselves about ourselves, and that these stories are a confused *bricolage*, an inconsistent multiplicity of stories with no single Self totalizing them, it seems to offer (or promise, at least) a way out which is due to its very disadvantage: precisely because the machine which reads us all the time is "blind," without awareness, a mechanic algorithm, it can make decisions which are much more adequate than those made by human individuals, much more adequate not only with regard to external reality but also and above all with regard to these individuals themselves, to what they really want or need. One can make a very realist case for this option: it is not that the computer which registers our activity is omnipotent and infallible, it is simply that, on average, its decisions work substantially better than the decisions of our mind: in medicine, it makes better diagnoses than our average doctor, etc., up to the exploding algorithmic trading on stock markets where programs that one can download for free already outperform financial advisers. One thing is clear: the liberal "true Self," the free agent which enacts what I "really want," simply doesn't exist, and fully endorsing this inexistence means abandoning the basic individualist premise of liberal democracy. The digital machine as the latest embodiment of the big Other, the "subject supposed to know," which operates as a subjectless field of knowledge . . .

Where, in the space of a digital machine, is there an opening for subjectivity? If development will render *homo sapiens* obsolete, what will follow it? A post-human *homo deus* (with abilities that are traditionally identified as divine) or a quasi-omnipotent digital machine? Singularity (global consciousness) or blind intelligence without awareness? If machines win, then "humans are in danger of losing their value, because intelligence is decoupling from consciousness." (311) This decoupling of intelligence and consciousness confronts us again with the enigma of consciousness: in spite of numerous rather desperate attempts, evolutionary biology has no clear answer to what is the evolutionary function of awareness/consciousness. Consequently, now that intelligence is decoupling from consciousness, "what will happen to society, politics and daily life when nonconscious but highly intelligent algorithms know us better than we know ourselves?"(397) The most realistic option is a radical division, much stronger than the class division, within human society itself. In the near future, biotechnology and computer algorithms will join their powers in producing "bodies, brains and minds," with the gap exploding "between those who know how to engineer bodies and brains and those who do not": "those who ride the train of progress will acquire divine abilities of creation and destruction, while those left behind will face extinction." (273)

On May 8 2023, *The Guardian* published a comment on how "AI makes non-invasive mind-reading possible by turning thoughts into text"[34] which begins with: "An AI-based decoder that can translate brain activity into a continuous stream of text has been developed, in a breakthrough that allows a person's thoughts to be read non-invasively for the first time." The comment's subtitle immediately makes clear the positive spin of this breakthrough: "Advance raises prospect of new ways to restore speech in those struggling to communicate due to stroke or motor neurone disease" – OK, but what about the fact that this decoder (plus the person who controls it) can literally read our mind, our flow of thoughts, opening up new hitherto unthinkable ways of social control?

One thing is sure: from the psychoanalytic standpoint, what the shift to the Post-human amounts to at its most fundamental is the overcoming (leaving behind) of the sexual in its most radical ontological dimension – not just "sexuality" as a specific sphere of human existence but the Sexual as an antagonism, the bar of an impossibility, constitutive of being-human in its finitude. And the issue carefully avoided by the partisans of the new asexual man is: to what extent are many other features usually identified with being-human, features like art, creativity, consciousness, etc., dependent on the antagonism that constitutes the Sexual. This is why the addition of "asexual" to the series of positions that compose LGBT+ is crucial and unavoidable: the endeavour to liberate sexuality from all "binary" oppressions to set it free in its entire polymorphous perversity, necessarily ends up in the abandoning of the very sphere of sexuality – the liberation OF sexuality has to end up in the liberation (of humanity) FROM sexuality.[35]

A letter published on March 29 2023 by the Future of Life Institute and already signed by thousands, among them big corporate names like Elon Musk, demands that any Artificial Intelligence lab working on systems more powerful than GPT-4 should "immediately pause" work for at least six months so that humanity can take stock of the risks such advanced systems pose. Labs are "locked in an out-of-control race" to develop and deploy increasingly powerful systems that no one – including their creators – can understand, predict or control "In the near term, experts warn AI systems risk exacerbating existing bias and inequality, promoting disinformation, disrupting politics and the economy and could help hackers. In the longer term, some experts warn AI may pose an existential risk to humanity and could wipe us out."[36]

Although these warnings sound reasonable, the fact that Elon Musk is at the top of the list is enough to trigger alarm: the moment Musk starts to speak about ethics and social responsibility, we should react with consternation. So why this new outburst of panic? It is about control and regulation – but whose? In the half a year pause, "humanity can take stock of the risks . . ." – how, who will stand for humanity? Will there be a world-wide public debate? What about the labs which will (as expected) continue their work secretly, probably with discreet connivance of authorities, not even to mention what states opposing the West (China, India, Russia) will be doing. In such conditions, a serious global debate with obligatory conclusion is simply unimaginable. What is really at stake here? Recall Harari's claim that the most realist option in the development of AI is a radical division, much stronger than the class division, between "those who ride the train of progress will acquire divine abilities of creation and destruction, while those left behind will face extinction." The panic the letter expresses is sustained by the fear that even those who "ride the train of progress" will no longer control development – in short, it expresses the fear of our new digital feudal masters.

Obviously, what the Future of Life letter aims at is therefore far from a big public debate – it is an agreement of government(s) and companies. The threat of expanded AI is very serious, but also for those in power and those who develop, own and control AI. At the horizon is nothing less than the end of capitalism as we knew it: the prospect of a self-reproducing AI system which will less and less need human agents – the ongoing explosion of algorithmic trading is the first step in this direction. The true choice is thus clear: a new form of Communism or an uncontrollable chaos in which machines will interact with us acting as pseudo-human partners. At the beginning of May 2023, Geoffrey Hinton, often touted as the godfather of artificial intelligence, quitted Google in order to warn the world about the risk of digital intelligence. In his view, the biggest threat are private ownership of the digital media combined with authoritarian governments – a deadly combination that indicates humanity will not be able to get hold of the risks of AI before it's too late. And his view is grounded in a clear political stance: "I'm a socialist, I think that private ownership of the media, and of the 'means of computation', is not good."[37]

Upon a close reading, we can easily see that the attempts to "take stock" of the threats of AI tend to repeat the old paradox of prohibiting the impossible: a truly post-human AI is impossible, that's why we should prohibit its development . . . To orient ourselves in this mess, we should urgently raise here Lenin's old question: freedom for whom to, do what? In what sense were we free till now? Were we not already controlled much more than we were aware of? Instead of just complaining about the threat to our freedom and dignity, we should thus also consider what freedom means, how it will have to change. Jensen Suther provides a convincing Hegelian argument against the notion that AI can become intelligent in the sense of human spirituality: he goes beyond Hubert Dreyfus' old argument about embodiment and grounds human intelligence organic animal life:

> It is by virtue of their species-specific, internal purpose that animals have the bodies that they do and exhibit a purposive relation to their surroundings. As Hegel argues, pain and pleasure are the most basic forms of *intelligent responsiveness* to an environment: it is through pleasure and pain that animals take the things around them to be good or bad, instrumental or inimical to their flourishing. Iron responds to moisture by rusting, but it does not *intend* to rust. A lion, by contrast, is not just causally induced to act by its desires and perceptions; rather, it takes the running gazelle *as* prey, the tree in the distance *as* a place to rest, the hyena pack *as* predator. It is in this way that the purpose-governed activity of organisms 'enacts' their environment and allows a context of meaningful relations.[38]

How, then, does human reason differ from the animal purpose-oriented activity?

Hegel develops a powerful, anti-Cartesian account of human reason not as a set of formal-logical processes separate from affect, desire and supposedly primitive 'animal functions'. Rather, for Hegel, human reason is a distinctly reflective way of *being* an animal. If the other animals maintain themselves in light of given species ends that they can't question or change, we maintain ourselves as material beings in light of shared social norms that are intrinsically contestable and that can be revised.[39]

However, from a strict Hegelian standpoint, something is missing here: as Hegel repeatedly points out, the passage to norm-oriented behaviour (where norms have to be justified since they are contestable) is not direct, what comes in between is a loss of natural "instinctual" orientation (which is then supplemented by norms) – no wonder that, for Hegel, the first step in the break with nature is madness, and human reason enters as a (never ending) struggle against and with madness. Along the lines of German Idealism, Hegel's name for this madness is self-relating negativity or, in mystic terms, the "night of the world," while Freud's name for this negativity is death drive, a dimension of what Freud designated as "beyond the pleasure principle." This is why "pain and pleasure are the most basic forms of *intelligent responsiveness* to an environment" *only for animals*, while a human being tends to act in a "pursuit of unhappiness," passionately doing something that s/he knows well it will bring only pain. And here also enters the Cartesian subjectivity: at this zero-point of radical negativity, the subject is no longer an entity embodied and constrained to its life-world, it is a void at a distance of its psycho-bodily unity.

Nassim Taleb introduced the concept of "antifragility": some systems are strengthened by encounters with disorder since they react to it with nonlinear responses. Antifragility is thus different from simple robustness or resilience: it causes an entity to improve with, not withstand, stressors provided they come in the right dose – therefore, depriving systems of vital stressors can weaken or cause harm to an entity.[40] The classic example from twentieth-century history would be the different fates of the Communist Party rule in the USSR and in China. When Gorbachev started his process of *glasnost* and *perestroika*, he underestimated the fragility of the Soviet system: he thought that the system will not only be able to survive these measures, but they will even strengthen it. But when the changes were imposed, they unleashed an avalanche which changed the world. With Deng Xiaoping's reforms, the Chinese proceeded in a radically different, almost opposite, way. While at the level of the economy (and, up to a point, culture) what is usually understood as Communism was abandoned, and the gates were opened wide to Western-style liberalization (private property, profit-making, hedonist individualism, etc.), the Party nevertheless maintained its ideologico-political hegemony in the sense of maintaining the unconditional political hegemony of the Communist Party as the only guarantee of China's stability and prosperity.[41] The Chinese Party thus displayed a far stronger antifragility: the changes effectively strengthened the system . . .

But a further distinction is to be introduced here: between a system antifragile enough to survive a strong external shock while remaining the same, and a system which survives such an external shock with its nature radically changed. With regard to China, some historians think that China after Deng's reforms is no longer a Communist country but something new for which we do not have a proper definition –maybe it is even close to Fascism[42]). And the same holds for global capitalism: it is changing into something new which can be characterized as capitalism only if we define capitalism in a thoroughly new way.

The rise of Artificial Intelligence confronts all of us with a similar test: will humans show enough antifragility to survive and emerge even stronger from integrating the AI into their daily lives, or will they be extinct as humans? If humanity survives, will it remain the same humanity, the same substantial content of being-human, just enriched by a new dimension of experience and interaction, or will the very core of "being-human" be imperceptibly transformed? As we have already seen, the key to this enigma is provided by cloning – only in cloning sexual difference disappears: an organ(ism) reproduces itself (or is reproduced) through genetic self-copying. Not only is human sexuality always-already symbolized, symbolization itself emerges through a certain cut in animal sexuality called by Lacan "symbolic castration." The excessive/disturbing nature of sex is rendered palpable in a negative way by the desperate attempts to define "healthy" pornography – here is one of the latest attempts:

> While pornography can be made for hollow gratification, with no regard for wellbeing, healthy pornography can actually contribute to disease free, safe sex, that actually helps enable healthy sexual development. The criteria are: a variety of sexual practices; a variety of body types, genders and races; a negotiation of consent on

screen; ethical production; a focus on pleasure for all participants; and depictions of safe sex.[43]

But is sex not in its innermost "unhealthy," a deviation from its "natural" goal of reproduction? Is it not by definition enacted for "hollow gratification"? Is applying politically correct rules on pornography (showing negotiation of consent, depiction of safe sex with condoms, presenting a variety of sexual practices, genders and races . . .) not a ridiculous strategy which may bring additional arousal only if is perceived as a redoubled irony? Once sexual reproduction is symbolized, we get the difference between the two deaths, the biological death and the symbolic death, and what is located in this interspace is *jouissance* as a surplus beyond the pleasure-principle:

> The (mythical) immortal, irrepressible life, being by definition lost, returns as something more accurately called undead life, something indestructible because it is undead (libido, the drive). Better yet, this mythical irrepressible life instinct exists in reality only as the death drive: not a drive aiming at death but the drive to repeat the surplus(-enjoyment) that occurs at the point of the cut/loss involved in sexual division. The death drive is essentially related to surplus-enjoyment, which emerges in the process of the death drive circling around something that is not there.
>
> 35

And this is why, from the strict Freudian standpoint, the human finitude (symbolic castration) and immortality (death drive) are the two sides of the same operation, i.e., it's not that the substance of life, the immortal *Jouissance*-Thing, is "castrated" by the arrival of the symbolic order. As in the case of lack and excess, the structure is that of parallax: the undead Thing is the remainder of castration, it is generated by castration, and *vice versa*, there is no "pure" castration, castration itself is sustained by the immortal excess which eludes it. Castration and excess are not two different entities, but the front and the back of one and the same entity, that is, one and the same entity inscribed onto the two surfaces of a Möbius strip.

So, to answer Zupančič's question from the previous chapter: what if cloning will effectively become a mode of human reproduction? Will we get a different symbolic order or the end of the symbolic order? The first thing to note is that what will disappear is libido itself as the remainder/excess of sexual difference. In other words, what will disappear is what Lacan called *lamella*, the undead/immortal life of non-castrated *jouissance* which appears as something beyond symbolic castration and sexuation. We will be compelled to accept that, in human life, finitude is constitutive of the very transcendence which emerges against its background. Insofar as post-humanity is, from our finite/mortal human standpoint, in some sense the point of the Absolute towards which we strive, the zero-point at which the gap between thinking and acting disappears, the point at which I became *homo deus*, we encounter here gain the paradox of our brush with the Absolute: the Absolute persists as the virtual point of perfection in our finitude, as that X we always fail to reach, but when we get over the limitation of our finitude we lose also the Absolute itself. Something new will emerge, but it will not be creative spirituality relieved of mortality and sexuality — in this passage to the New, we will definitely lose both, we will be neither *homo* nor *deus*.

The notion of incest, in all its transgressive weight, will also become meaningless. In Zupančič's radical reading, the incestuous short-circuit that is the curse of the Oedipus' family is not simply an exception: it brings out the short-circuit that is proper to humans as speaking beings. The original incestuous short-circuit is the short-circuit between myself (as a void in the symbolic order, as pure subject of enunciation) and my symbolic identity (I effectively am, within this order, one of the brothers). As a speaking being, I am never directly myself, my symbolic identity – this is why Lacan wrote that a madman is not only a beggar who thinks he is a king but also a king who thinks he is a king. However, this does not mean the common sense stupidity that my symbolic identity/title is not directly all the wealth of my psycho-physical reality with all its idiosyncrasies. What eludes the symbolic is not the complexity of my personal reality but the very void of my subjectivity that distances me from my direct psycho-physical reality. In other words, what eludes the grasp of the symbolic order is in itself a product of the symbolic order: the moment I speak, my position of enunciation is exempted from reality to which my speech refers.

So, to really conclude, while we should dismiss the vision of Singularity as a direct unity of global Intelligence and our self-awareness, one thing is clear: if something resembling "post-humanity" will effectively emerge as a massive fact, then *all three (overlapping) moments of our spontaneous world-view (humans, god, nature) will disappear*. Our being-human can only exist against the background of impenetrable nature, and if – through bio-genetic science and practices – life becomes something that can be technologically fully manipulated, human and natural life lose their "natural" character. And the same holds for god: what humans (always in historically specified forms) experience as "god" is something that has meaning only from the standpoint of human finitude and mortality – "God" is a counterpart of the terrestrial finitude, so once we become *homo deus* and acquire properties which seem "supernatural" from our old human standpoint (like directly communicating with other conscious beings or with AI), "Gods" as we knew them disappear. The tech-gnostic visions of a post-human world are ideological fantasies that obfuscate the abyss of what awaits us.

6

WHY POLITICS IS IMMANENTLY THEOLOGICAL

Why are so many essays entitled "politico-theological treatise"? The answer is that a theory becomes theology when it is part of a full subjective political engagement. As Kierkegaard pointed out, I do not acquire faith in Christ after comparing different religions and deciding the best reasons speak for Christianity – there are reasons to choose Christianity but this reasons only appear after I've already chosen it, i.e., to see the reasons for belief one already has to believe. And the same holds for Marxism: it is not that, after objectively analysing history, I became a Marxist – my decision to be a Marxist (the experience of a proletarian position) makes me see the reasons for it, i.e., Marxism is the paradox of an objective "true" knowledge accessible only through a subjective partial position. This is why Robespierre was right when he distrusted materialism as the philosophy of decadent-hedonist and corrupted nobility, and tried to impose a new religion of the supreme Boing of Reason (the main target of his hatred was Joseph Fouche, a radical atheist and an opportunist plotter). The old reproach to Marxism that its commitment to a bright future is a secularization of religious salvation should be proudly assumed.

This is why the genuine dimension of Christian doubt does not concern the existence of God: its logic is not "I feel such a need to believe in God, but I cannot be sure that he really exists, that he is not just a chimera of my imagination." (A humanist atheist can easily respond to this: "then drop God and simply assume the ideals God stands for as your own.") An authentic Christian is indifferent towards the infamous proofs of God's existence. What the position of Christian doubt involves is a pragmatic paradox succinctly rendered by Alyosha in Dostoyevsky's *Karamazov Brothers*: "God exists but I am not sure whether I believe in him," where "I believe in him" refers to the believer's readiness to fully assume the existential engagement implied by such a belief: "the question of the 'existence of God' is not really at the heart of Dostoyevsky's labors. . . . Alyosha's uncertainty about whether he 'believes in God' is an uncertainty about whether the life he leads and the feelings he has are the life and the feelings that would rightly follow from belief in God."[1] It is in this sense that every theology is political, confronting us with the question of our social engagement.

This practical nature of a theory is totally different from the way modern science relates to experiments: science forecloses subjectivity, it aims at grasping "objective reality," while a revolutionary theory is immanently practical, grounded in subjective engagement. The religious dimension of a radical political act is founded in a very precise fact: the triumph of a revolution is the moment when we step out of the existing economic and social order by way of suspending its main written and unwritten rules – we (try to) do what, within this order, appears impossible. In a true act, we do things to which the hegemonic ideology reacts with "But you can't just do this!!!", we do what Brecht, in his short poem *In Praise of Communism*, quite appropriately referred to as the simplest thing that it is so difficult to achieve[2] – nationalizing banks and large corporations, expanding free education and health service, providing housing for the poor, legalizing gay and LGBT+ rights, etc.

Remember the first year of Allende government in Chile in 1970 – they provided free meals in schools, nationalized copper mines, engaged in the construction of workers' housings, "simple things" like that . . . and, in the specific conditions of that time, with the brutal resistance from the local bourgeoisie supported by the US, they HAD to fail, inflation soared, etc. It is meaningless to deplore the fact that revolutionaries were not pragmatic enough – this, precisely, was the point of their acts once they took over, namely to violate the existing "pragmatic rules." Whatever the new problems, the Allende government changed Chile into a "liberated territory" where, in some sense, even the air the people were breathing was different, and the problems it faced just prove the fact that, within the existing order, even doing "simple things" like providing free meals and housing for workers is impossible. Later, revolutionaries should become pragmatic, of course, but they HAVE to begin with crazy simple acts. This is why Robespierre was again fully right when, in his final speech on 8 Thermidor, he pointed out that, observing a revolution just as a series of actual events, without taking note of the sublime Idea that sustains it (or, as Alain Badiou would have put it, of its dimension of an Event), this revolution is just a "noisy crime" that destroys another crime:

> But there do exist, I can assure you, souls that are feeling and pure; it exists, that tender, imperious and irresistible passion, the torment and delight of magnanimous hearts; that deep horror of tyranny, that compassionate zeal for the oppressed, that sacred love for the homeland, that even more sublime and holy love for humanity, without which a great revolution is just a noisy crime that destroys another crime; it does exist, that generous ambition to establish here on earth the world's first Republic.[3]

Here I am ready to use Chiesa's notion of an irreducible oscillation: radical emancipatory politics is condemned to oscillate between moments of ecstatic religious commitment where we suspend "reality principle" and try to actualize the impossible, and the long hard "pragmatic" process of transforming revolutionary goals into moments of ordinary social reality of the majority. (Insofar as we should treat a revolutionary event as an Event in Badiou's sense of the term, we should remember that, although Badiou limits Event to four spheres – science, politics, art, love –, his most convincing account of an Event is a religious one: that of Christianity, of Paul's invention of universalism.) The point is not that moments of ecstatic commitment are simply utopian/destructive and have to be "normalized": they are essential since they clear the ground and prepare a new base for pragmatic solutions. They are also not illusory since we, the engaged agents, are fully aware that our "impossible" striving will eventually subside, and this awareness only strengthens our commitment. So we don't oscillate between the One of full engagement and the cynical acceptance of not-One, of the messy reality: a true believer can be (and mostly is) ruthlessly cynical about its predicament, but this awareness only strengthens its commitment – this is the political version of Tertullian's *credo qua absurdum est*.

The Divine Clouds

Today, however, authentic belief that sustains every radical emancipatory practice is disappearing precisely in proportion to the explosive rise not only of the religious fundamentalism but above all of the theological dimension in our economic daily lives. A new social order that is emerging out of the ruins of global capitalism, the order called "technofeudalism" or "cloud-capitalism," subordinates "real" capitalists and the workers they exploit to the monopolized digital commons controlled by our new feudal masters (Bezos, Musk, Gates . . .). Market exchange is more and more mediated by digital platforms (Amazon for books, etc.), and capitalists (book publishers, in this case) are vassals who pay feudal masters a rent to sell their products (if a publisher is excluded from Amazon, it becomes practically impossible for him to survive). We, buyers, are serfs who work freely for the clouds (surfing on the net and providing data with each of our clicks). Digital clouds run by self-learning and self-improving algorithms are thus the latest "divine" entity which largely escapes the control of its creators: even of the programmers who composed them.

The problem with these "divine" digital clouds that regulate our actual lives is that they *redouble* class struggle: the good old class struggle between capitalists and proletarians, with the capitalists usurping profit from the exploitation of the proletarians, remains, but it is supplemented by the exploitation of this entire sphere (capitalists included) by the new feudal class which extracts from us the rent for our permanent usage of the privatized commons. This feudal exploitation is for most of us invisible, we experience it as our free exercise (books are on Amazon even cheaper than in the bookstores, using Google and Facebook costs nothing . . .) – privatized commons present themselves as mere neutral networks which connect buyers and sellers. When you order an Uber, it appears as a transaction between you and the driver/car you choose – the feudal master who controls the space of interaction is ignored, reduced to a neutral mediator. The situation is similar to the vulgar joke (quoted in Chapter 4) about a drunken husband who sees only four legs in the bed: we see only the legs of the customer and the driver, not the additional two legs of the feudal master . . . Or, recall the old story (that I often use) about a worker suspected of stealing: every evening, when he was leaving the factory, the wheel-barrow he was rolling in front of him was carefully inspected, but the guards could not find anything, it was always empty – till, finally, they got the point: what the worker was stealing were wheel-barrows themselves. This is how our new feudal masters exploit us: they just drive empty wheel-barrows . . .

So how can we even imagine to overthrow this immaterial dimension of the big Other that exists in digital clouds? In *Technofeudalism*, Yanis Varoufakis admits that, in his early books, he failed to answer "the killer question: 'If you don't like what we have, what would you replace it with? How would it work? I am all ears. Convince me!' I didn't even try." Why? Because "I lacked a convincing answer."[4] And one cannot but admire his courage when, in his *Another Now* (2020[5]), he tried to do precisely this: to provide a convincing answer, describing in detail an alternate society which could have emerged if the 2008 financial breakdown were to take a different turn. Varoufakis does not portray a future but an alternate present (although he describes how it could have emerged), and he does it in the form of a novel. We get a global society of democratic market socialism: there is only one central state bank which regulates money supply in a transparent way, financial speculations disappear because they became meaningless, ownership is dispersed since each citizen is allocated its part, healthcare and human rights are guaranteed for everyone, etc. But what is even more crucial is that earth (the material base of our existence) and digital clouds (through which today's new feudal masters control us) remain commons, so there are no basic antagonisms and no reasons to rebel . . . The choice the heroes of the novel confront is: should they remain in Another Now or return to our neoliberal Now with all the struggles and violence we know? Varoufakis gives a series of features that spoil the perfection of Another Now. Due to its very democratic transparency, the society in Another Now is the one of total control: my properties and activities are transparent to others, my behaviour is regulated in a severe Politically Correct way, so there is nothing to rebel against – this is how Iris, the old radical Leftist in the book, is described:

> raging against the system was Iris's only way of being, her loneliness vaccine. The Other Now was too pleasant, too wholesome to rage against. It would have made Iris's life intolerable.

219

I am a dissident. There was nothing for me on the other side to dissent from except their political correctness and smugness at having created the perfect society.

228

Where does Iris's strange dissatisfaction come from? Why is she not able to simply calm down and enjoy perfection? We should answer this question at two levels. First, at the abstract level, recall Lacan's formula of hysteric provocation ("'I ask you' – what? – 'to refuse' – what? – 'what I offer you' – why? – 'because that's not it.'") already elaborated in the first chapter of the present book: a hysteric does not just endlessly reject what the Other offer her because "that's not it" (what she really wants); she finally realizes that the "it" is the Other itself. Her message is thus: "YOU are not it!", you are not in a position to give me what I really need or want. And is exactly the same not the message of Iris? In spite of all socialist egalitarian measures in Another Now, market exchange and the competitive stance (the "transactional quid pro quo mentality") implied by it remain in full force:

Democratized market societies, freed from capitalism, are infinitely preferable to what we have here, except for one crucial thing: they entrench exchange value and thereby, I fear, make impossible a genuine revolution that leads to the final toppling of markets.

218–19

This abstract dissatisfaction implies a whole series of quite concrete problems – let's take a closer look at the perfect society of Another Now as it is described in *Technofeudalism*:

Pay is determined by a democratic process that divides the company's post-tax revenues into four slices: an amount to cover the firm's fixed costs (such as equipment, licences, utility bills, rent and interest payments), an amount set aside for R&D, the slice from which basic pay to staff is made and, lastly, a slice for bonuses. Again, the distribution between those four slices is decided collectively, on a one-person-one-vote basis.

Such collective ownership eliminates "the fundamental class divide between those who own and collect profits or rents and those who lease their time for a wage." But what if the company acts collectively in an "egotist" way, ignoring wider social repercussions? To prevent this, the state will impose "a Social Accountability Act stipulating that every corporation be graded according to an index of social worthiness, to be compiled by panels of randomly selected citizens, the equivalent of juries, chosen from a diverse pool of stakeholders: the company's customers, members of the communities it affects, and so on."

Is this enough? Varoufakis concedes that "human nature always finds ways of messing up even the best of systems. Your colleagues, if they summon a majority, can vote to have you fired. But the atmosphere at work is now one of shared responsibility which reduces stress and creates an environment in which mutual respect has a better chance to flourish." However, what if this "but" is not strong enough to keep in check what Varoufakis calls "human nature" (to give to this term a concrete meaning, psychoanalysis has to intervene), with envy as constitutive of human desire? For Lacan, the fundamental impasse of human desire is that it is the other's desire in both subjective and objective genitive: desire for the other, desire to be desired by the other, and, especially, desire for what the other desires.

Envy and resentment are thus a constitutive component of human desire; based on this insight, Jean-Pierre Dupuy[6] proposed a convincing critique of Rawls' theory of justice: in the Rawls' model of a just society, social inequalities are tolerated only insofar as they also help those at the bottom of the social ladder, and insofar as they are not based on inherited hierarchies, but on natural inequalities, which are considered contingent, not merits.[7] What Rawls doesn't see is how such a society would create conditions for an uncontrolled explosion of resentment: in it, I would know that my lower status is fully justified, and would thus be deprived of excusing my failure as the result of social injustice. Rawls thus proposes a terrifying model of a society in which hierarchy is directly legitimized in natural properties, thereby missing Friedrich Hayek's[8] key lesson: it is much easier to accept inequalities if one can claim that they result from an impersonal blind force – the good thing about the "irrationality" of the market and success or failure in capitalism is that it allows me precisely to perceive my failure or success as "undeserved," contingent . . . Remember the old motif of the market as the modern version of an imponderable Fate: the fact that capitalism is not "just" is thus a key feature of what makes it acceptable.

Along these lines, Lacan shares with Nietzsche and Freud the idea that justice as equality is founded on envy: the envy of the other who has what we do not have, and who enjoys it. Following Lacan, Fred Jameson[9] totally rejects the predominant optimist view according to which in Communism envy will be left behind as a remainder of capitalist competition, to be replaced by solidary collaboration and pleasure in other's pleasures; dismissing this myth, he emphasizes that in Communism, precisely insofar as it will be a more just society, envy and resentment will explode. Jameson's solution is here radical to the point of madness: the only way for Communism to survive would be some form of universalized psychoanalytic social services enabling individuals to avoid the self-destructive trap of envy.

Based on these complications, my answer to the "killer question" is that our apocalyptic situation prohibits any clear positive vision of a different society to come. Our ultimate horizon is what Dupuy calls the dystopian "fixed point," the zero-point of nuclear war, ecological breakdown, global economic and social chaos, etc. – even if it is indefinitely postponed, this zero-point is the virtual "attractor" towards which our reality, left to itself, tends. The way to combat the future catastrophe is through acts which interrupt our drifting towards this "fixed point."[10] The only ethico-political imperative is thus a negative one: the plurality of today's crises makes it clear that things cannot go on the way they are now – how we proceed is a matter of risk and improvisations. We should thus leave behind any form of Marxist teleology or historicist determinism which deprives the revolutionary process of the dimension of subjectivity proper, of radical cuts of the real into the texture of "objective reality" – in clear contrast to the French Revolution whose most radical form of Marxist figures perceived it as an open process lacking any support in a higher Necessity. Saint-Just wrote in 1794: "*Ceux qui font des révolutions ressemblent au premier navigateur instruit par son audace.* [Those who make revolutions resemble a first navigator, who has audacity alone as a guide.]"[11] We should thus renounce any vision of a perfect society and accept irreducible antagonisms, which means that the state and a basic alienation of social life are here to stay.

Antagonism Without Enemy

The lesson of such paradoxes is a very clear one: what characterizes an authentic emancipatory thought is not a vision of conflict-free harmonious future but the properly dialectical notion of antagonism which is totally incompatible with the Rightist topic of the need of an enemy to assert our self-identity – here is Heidegger's concise articulation of the need for an enemy from his course of 1933–4:

> An enemy is each and every person who poses an essential threat to the *Dasein* of the people and its individual members. The enemy does not have to be external, and the external enemy is not even always the most dangerous one. And it can seem as if there were no enemy. Then it is a fundamental requirement to find the enemy, to expose the enemy to the light, *or even first to make the enemy*, so that this standing against the enemy may happen and so that *Dasein* may not lose its edge. . . . [The challenge is] to bring the enemy into the open, to harbor no illusions about the enemy, to keep oneself ready for attack, to cultivate and intensify a constant readiness and to prepare the attack *looking far ahead with the goal of total annihilation*.[12]

The most ominous passage is here "to expose the enemy to the light, *or even first to make the enemy*, so that this standing against the enemy may happen." In short, it doesn't even matter if the enemy is a real enemy – if there is no enemy it has to be invented so that a people "may not lose its edge" and can prepare the (invented) enemy's "total annihilation" . . . What we find here is the logic of anti-Semitism at its most elementary: what Heidegger ignores is the possibility that *an enemy is invented to create the false unity of the people and thus cover up its immanent antagonisms.* (However, one should be careful not to extend this need for an enemy to the entirety of Heidegger's thinking – the passage quoted above is from Heidegger's course in 1933-4 when he was at the highpoint of his Nazi engagement. At this point he put forward the notion of *Volk* as a community that needs an enemy, and when he later withdrew from active politics, the notion of enemy changes: it is no longer another ethnic group to be annihilated but modern technology as such, and one should not fight it but went through it and gain distance towards it. So when Richard Wolin[13] focuses on a spiritualized racial community, he ignores all too much that there is no place for such a community in Heidegger's early masterwork *Sein und Zeit* which is focused on an individual *Dasein* thrown into the abyss of a world. Incidentally, one should also note that the style of *Sein und Zeit* is totally different from Heidegger's later poetic intimations: it is a systematic book subdivided into numbered paragraphs.)

Here is the supreme case of such a need for an enemy: in his speech to the SS leaders in Posen on October 4 1943, Heinrich Himmler spoke quite openly about the mass killing of the Jews as "a glorious page in our history, and one that has never been written and never can be written"; he then goes on to characterize the ability to do this and to remain decent as the greatest virtue: "To have gone through this [the extermination of the Jews] and at the same time to have remained decent, that has made us hard." Himmler here explicitly opposes true principled virtue to ordinary human compassion for a singular human being: "But then they all come along, these 80 million good Germans, and every one of them has his decent Jew. Of course, it's quite clear that the other Jews are pigs – but this one is a first-class Jew . . ." In short, every German knows that Jews as such are pigs, but then they fail to apply this principle to singular Jews that they know. And he is well aware of what he is saying – he explicitly includes the killing of women and children:

> We faced the question: what should we do with the women and children? I decided here too to find a completely clear solution. I did not regard myself as justified in exterminating the men – that is to say, to kill them or have them killed – and to allow the avengers in the shape of children to grow up for our sons and grandchildren. The difficult decision had to be taken to have this people disappear from the earth.[14]

Because of this radical stance, Himmler was (till the Fall of 1944) opposed to the creation of a volunteer army of Russian prisoners to fight Soviet troops. When, after being taken prisoner, the Soviet general Yuri Vlasov proposed to exploit the anti-Stalinist sentiments among the Russian population and the POWs and to set up a Russian people's army, Himmler spoke disparagingly of the "Vlasov shivaree" (*der Wlassow-Rummel*) and rejected the idea that there is a mass of oppressed Russian people opposed to the Stalinist rule – for him, such distinctions within the inferior Slavic race were of no interest. But what makes all this so fascinating is the high ethical language used by Himmler to justify the extermination of Jews and the brutal treatment of the Slavic people under German occupation:

One principle must be absolute for the SS man: we must be honest, decent, loyal and friendly to members of our blood and to no one else. What happens to the Russians, what happens to the Czechs, is a matter of utter indifference to me. . . . Whether the other races live in comfort or perish of hunger interests me only in so far as we need them as slaves for our culture; apart from that it does not interest me. Whether or not 10,000 Russian women collapse from exhaustion while digging a tank ditch interests me only in so far as the tank ditch is completed for Germany. . . . We have the moral right, we had the duty to our people to do it – to kill this people who wanted to kill us. But we do not have the right to enrich ourselves with even one fur, with one Mark, with one cigarette, with one watch, with anything. That we do not have. Because at the end of this, we don't want – because we exterminated the bacillus – to become sick and die from the same bacillus.[15]

Himmler goes to the end here: further in the speech, he imagines the case of an SS officer on the Eastern front confronting a Russian mother with a small child, both scared of him, trembling and crying. His first reaction is, understandably, compassion: is really his duty as a soldier to kill these two helpless human beings? Himmler's answer is an unconditional YES: his fidelity is only to the German people, which implies total indifference towards the suffering of the members of other races and nations. Bearing in mind the suffering the German people are exposed by the continuous bombing by the American and British planes, any compassion with the two poor Russians is nothing less than treason – an act of ignoring the suffering of one's own people.

Was then Himmler a sadist, doing horrible things and gaining surplus-enjoyment from his conviction that he is just doing it as an ethical duty, for the big Other (for the good of the German nation)? I think this formula is too simple to be applied here. There is something much more horrifying in Himmler: from what one can see by way of reading his letters, he was a terribly normal person – he detested (personally witnessing) brutality, he was decent and kind to his friends, ready to punish SS members themselves for their petty crimes . . . and as such, as a normal individual, he did in his office what we know he did. It is here that Lacan's claim that normalcy is a form of psychosis acquires its weight.

Here, (not so) surprisingly, Himmler comes close to the Buddhist (and Hinduist) idea that we suffer and do hurtful things if we are too directly involved in (what we perceive as) reality of objects, so we should follow the doctrine of non-involvement, of the disinterested action: act as if it doesn't matter, as if you are not the agent, but things, including your own acts, just happen in an impersonal way . . . It is difficult to resist here the temptation to paraphrase this passage as the justification of the burning of Jews in the gas chambers to their executor caught in a moment of doubt: since "he who thinks it to be the killer and he who thinks it to be killed, both know nothing," since "the self kills not, and the self is not killed," therefore "you ought not to grieve for any" burned Jew, but, "looking alike on pleasure and pain, on gain and loss, on victory and defeat," do what you were ordered to do . . . No wonder *Bhagavadgita* (from which these quotes come) was Heinrich Himmler's preferred book: it is reported that he was always carrying it in the pocket of his uniform. Does this not hold even today when the military operations are more and more done through drones and by just pushing buttons?

The same cannot be said of the people directly working under Himmler who were openly pathological. If Himmler was at the top of the pyramid of the organizers of the Holocaust, second to him were not well-known names like Heydrich and Eichmann but a compatriot of mine, Odilo Globočnik, an Austrian Nazi whose father was a Slovene (as his surname indicates). Globočnik had a leading role in Operation Reinhard, the organized murder of around one and a half million Jews of mostly Polish origin in the Majdanek, Treblinka, Sobibor and Belzec extermination camps. Globočnik originated the concept of the extermination camp and industrialized murder – the historian Michael Allen described him as "the vilest individual in the vilest organization ever known".[16]

When, late in his life, the Dominican Republic's dictator Rafael Trujillo was asked which of his acts in his long rule he was most proud of, he named the so-called Parsley massacre from October 1937, a mass killing of Haitians living in the Dominican Republic's northwestern frontier. The massacre claimed the lives of an estimated 14,000 to 40,000 Haitian men, women and children: virtually the entire Haitian population in the Dominican frontier was either killed or forced to flee across the border.[17] This act of "ethnic cleansing" justified as a defence against foreign hordes invading the country reproduces perfectly the logic of Evil as an ethical duty enjoining us to obliterate our common decency.

What lurks behind this topic is the question of the big Other. The conclusion that imposes itself is not that every ethical stance need some figure of the big Other to rely on but, on the contrary, that a truly radical ethical position emerges when the subject is deprived of the support in a big Other, so that it has to make a decision in the abyss of its freedom. Such a decision stands for the moment when ethics gets political, for the moment of the *political suspension of the ethical*: the subject has to make a decision which cannot be fully grounded in any kind of "higher" neutral principles ("don't do to others what you wouldn't like them to do to you," etc.), it has to make a decision about how to apply these principles, a decision which always gives them a particular spin. Isn't this the case even for Antigone? Her decision to risk everything for the proper funeral of her brother cannot be fully grounded in the universal immemorial rules she evokes (every human being, independently of how good or evil it was, deserves a proper funeral) – she picked out her brother, ignoring all others, and it this restriction which makes her act political, not just her public appearance. In this decision, she was NOT supported by a big Other. In some formal sense, Antigone also appears (or simply is) "evil" from the standpoint of the existing order, a threat to it, but her "Evil" is ethical, although in a different sense than that of Himmler: it opens up a new space for confronting the antagonisms of the existing society, while the function of Himmler's "Evil" is precisely to obfuscate these antagonisms. Here we should contrast Antigone to someone like Nikolai Bukharin whose courageous stance relied on the unconditional fidelity to the Communist big Other. The fate of Bukharin's "testament," a letter he asked his wife Anna Larina to memorize in 1938 when he knew his execution is close, is a tragic case of how a letter always arrives at its destination:

> Bukharin, on the eve of his fateful trial, exhorted her to "Remember that the great cause of the USSR lives on, and *this* is the most important thing. Personal fates are transitory and wretched by comparison." She read it in a world in which the USSR had just fallen.[18]

Bukharin's letter DID arrive at its destination – did reach Anna Larina and was published – at precisely the right moment, in 1988; one can even say that it was delivered as soon as possible, i.e., as soon as the historical situation made it possible that its delivery will produce a truth-effect. Bukharin perceived his tragic fate as insignificant in comparison to the thriving of the great historical cause of the USSR – the continuity of this cause guaranteed that his death was not meaningless. Read when the USSR disappeared, the letter confronts us with the meaninglessness of Bukharin's death: there is no big Other to redeem it, he literally died in vain. Bukharin fell into the typical Stalinist trap. Privately, the Stalinist interrogators often told the accused: "We know you are innocent, but at this moment the Party needs your confession to assert its unity. There will be a time in the future, after our full victory, when will be able to tell the whole story and admit your innocence!" This time is the time when accounts will be finally settled and justice will prevail . . . A fact from the Bosnian war in the early 1990s makes the same point: many of the girls who survived brutal rapes killed themselves later, after they rejoined their community and found that there is no one who is really ready to listen to them, to accept their testimony. In Lacan's terms, what is missing here is not only another human being, the attentive listener, but the "big Other" itself, the space of the symbolic inscription or registration of my words.

One should critically note that even Derrida's deconstruction continues to rely on a figure of the big Other: when Derrida writes that "deconstruction is justice," an impossible justice but still justice, this determination implies that deconstruction does not just bring out the inconsistencies and contradictions of a text – the work of deconstruction is led by the impossible ideal of fully bringing out all inconsistencies which legitimize secret forms of domination and oppression. This goal is, of course, infinitely postponed, forever eluding: in the same sense that Derrida talks about democracy-to-come, justice is always "to come" – to claim that it is fully here would have been the worst case of metaphysics of presence. However, in spite of the impossibility that pertains to Justice, we have to cling to it as a kind of regulative idea of our work. I remember talking to a faithful Derridean years ago at a reception after a talk, and while we were picking up pieces of fried chicken, he told me: "How will we justify doing this at the final Nuremberg trial for the crimes humans commit against animals?" The regulative idea is here that an ethical debt is accumulating for all the horrors of the industrial breeding of animals – just think what we are doing to millions of pigs which remain half blind and barely can walk, they are just bred to get fat enough as quickly as possible and be slaughtered for our consumption . . . I respectfully remained silent, but the idea of a gigantic trial of all of humanity (by whom?) struck me as strangely twisted: do we really have to presuppose such a figure of the big Other, a promise that at some final point all debts will be settled, although we know this moment will never come? Is such an idea not deeply anthropocentric, transposing onto the stupid indifference of nature a sense of Justice totally absent in it? Cannot we act ethically (with regard to animal suffering) also without such a figure of the big Other? Back to Himmler: do we – all of humanity – not treat animals in exactly the same way Himmler demanded Germans to treat Russian women? Whether or not 10,000 collapse from exhaustion of being overfed and treated with hormonal chemicals, with no free movement in nature, this interests us only in so far as the quota of pork meat is achieved for us, humans . . .

Kojin Karatani[19] also reaffirms a figure of big Other. He argues that what is needed today, if we are to cope with the looming crises, is a shift from the Marxist focus on modes of production to the modes of exchange: in the latter, a "spiritual" dimension is present (from Marx's fetish constitutive of commodity exchange logic to Mauss's mana), a dimension operative not only between people but also between humanity and nature – to quote a native American saying: "When we show our respect for other living things, they respond with respect for us." With capitalism, a break which opens up the space for ecological crisis arises: nature is no longer a proper Other (with its own "spirituality") with whom we humans are engaged in exchange – there is just traffic with nature as material: "there is no 'exchange' in the relationship between human and nature":

> "Exchange" brings about spiritual power that compels humans to think and act in certain ways, while "traffic" does not. Exchange between humans generates perverse spiritual powers but traffic between humans and nature is straightforward and simply material.
>
> 366

With ecological crisis, "exchange" returns in the most violent form, as a "revenge" of nature for its ruthless exploitation, plus the problems arising from the traffic with nature "further distort the relationship between humans. That is, the crisis of war is approaching. . . . Despite the rise of movements such as the Anti-globalization or Occupy movement, another world war seems simply inevitable now."(369) While I agree with this sad conclusion, I don't see (at the level of theory) the solution in re-asserting Nature as an Other with whom we are involved in a true exchange – such re-spiritualization of nature as a partner in a dialogue is a blind alley. What we must do is the exact opposite: humanity should fully naturalize itself, observes itself as part of a stupid-meaningless traffic within nature.

And Hitler? Wasn't Hitler in some sense doing this? From what we know, one must concede that, although it is unthinkable that Hitler didn't know about the Holocaust, he was probably spared the gory details. When Himmler says that holocaust is "a glorious page in our history, and one that has never been written and never can be written," he doesn't only mean that the extermination of the Jews should not be known to the general public. There are hints that he also meant Hitler himself, the Messiah leading the German nation to a new beginning – the true fidelity to the Messiah, the true courage, is that we do silently and secretly the necessary dirty work of clearing the ground so that Hitler will be able to realize his grandiose vision: the great act of us, close followers of the Messiah, is to keep him in ignorance, to allow him to pursue his vision in blessed innocence.

However, towards the war's end, this ultimate wall of (self-) censorship began to crack. Joseph Goebbels's infamous "total war" speech in *Sportpalast* in Berlin on February 18 1943 was choreographed and prepared in every detail, with thousands of carefully selected public; however, in spite of such detailed preparations, a true Freudian slip of tongue occurs just prior to the culmination of the speech, a series of questions answered by a resounding "Yes!" of the thousands: "Do you believe with the Führer and us in the final total victory of the German people? Are you and the German people willing to work, if the Führer orders, 10, 12 and if necessary 14 hours a day and to give everything for victory? Do you want total war? If necessary, do you want a war more total and radical than anything that we can even imagine today?" (One cannot but discern in the last question the dimension of the Kantian sublime which is precisely a dimension more total and radical than we can even imagine with our senses.) Not surprisingly, the

Freudian slip occurs when Goebbels talks about how Germany will react to the Jewish threat:

> *Deutschland jedenfalls hat nicht die Absicht, sich dieser jüdischen Bedrohung zu beugen, sondern vielmehr die, ihr rechtzeitig, wenn nötig unter vollkommen und radikalster Ausr ... -schaltung [Ausrottung / Ausschaltung] des Judentums entgegenzutreten.*
>
> [Germany, in any case, has no intention of bowing to this Jewish threat, but rather one of confronting it in due time, if need be in terms of complete and most radical exterm . . . exclusion of Judaism.][20]

Goebbels begins with the first letters of *"Ausrottung"* (extermination), but then stops for a second or so in the middle of the word and replaces it with the much more innocent *"Ausschaltung"* (exclusion). Did he plan it this way or was it a true Freudian slip? It doesn't really matter: he made it clear that "exclusion" didn't mean just forcing the Jew to leave Germany but literally their extermination. The interest of this slip is that it discloses not only the true intention of the Nazis but also their hypocritical effort to keep this true intention (barely) hidden to the public – it was as if, in the desperate situation after the defeat at Stalingrad, censoring the truth (demanded by Himmler who wanted the Holocaust to remain absent from public history) was less and less considered necessary and the brutal goal of total extermination was openly indicated. The other side of the sublime, the sublime at its most horrible, the extermination "more total and radical than anything that we can even imagine today" was given a full green light.[21]

So, back to Himmler, as a supreme self-sacrifice, he takes upon himself the Evil, and this properly *ethical* Evil makes him much worse than any form of pragmatic opportunism. This logic of dispensing with elementary solidarity and compassion as the ultimate proof of the fidelity to a Cause is given an almost tragic expression Kliment Voroshilov's attack on Nikolai Bukharin during a Central Committee plenum in 1933: "Bukharin is a sincere and honest man. But I fear for Bukharin no less than for Tomsky and Rykov. Why do I fear for Bukharin? Because he is a soft-hearted person. Whether this is good or bad I do not know, but in our present situation this soft-heartedness is not needed."[22] Voroshilov is here too open, he shows his cards . . . To understand Bukharin's predicament, we should bear in mind the contrast between Stalinism and today's cynicism. When Bukharin was confronting his critics in the Central Committee, his frank line of argumentation provoked laughter:

> Look, if I am a saboteur, a son of a bitch, then why spare me? I make no claims to anything. I am just describing what's on my mind, what I am going through. If this in any way entails any political damage, however minute, then, no question about it, I'll do whatever you say. (*Laughter*.) Why are you laughing? There is absolutely nothing funny about any of this . . .[23]

In some sense (i.e., within the perverted logic of the Stalinist discourse), this laughter was justified: the target of their laughter was Bukharin's idea that he can address his critics plainly, by-passing the official jargon. However, such a position of distance towards the hegemonic ideology was strictly prohibited under Stalinism, it was in itself a form of treason. Getty and Naumov repeatedly point out the surprising basic result of their study: Stalinists spoke privately *the same* language as publicly, the cynicism of the Stalinist ideology was "objective," not private. This was the Stalinist version of "there is no meta-language": there is only one meta-language telling the truth which is that of the official ideology itself. Today, private and public also tend to coincide, but in the opposite sense: private cynicism penetrates the public domain, we more and more speak publicly the same language as privately. (To avoid a misunderstanding: this does not mean that truth is permitted: the private realist-cynical language is in itself the worst mystification.)

What this means is that fidelity to a principled decision is not enough for an act to qualify as truly ethical – what really matters is how this principle relates to social antagonisms: does it cover them up or render them visible? The moment we accept an irreducible antagonism, we accept the fact that the big Other doesn't exist, that it is ridden with inconsistencies, lacks and antagonisms.

Political Correctness versus Ethics

Political Correctness no less relies on a figure of big Other – here is an extreme case. At Hamline College in Minnesota, a professor of art history was fired for showing images of Muhammad to her students. She took all precautions, warning students in advance what she will do so that they could leave the room to avoid being offended, plus the images shown were hundreds of years old and considered masterpieces of Islamic art (not all versions of Islam prohibit depicting Muhammad). One of the students who didn't leave the room – Aram Wedatalla, president of the college's Muslim Students Assn., complained to administrators that she was "harmed" by seeing the image and that teacher "failed to safeguard" her. The student newspaper *The Oracle* denounced showing the paintings as a direct attack on Islam; the college's administration agreed and called for obligatory education in "Islamophobia":

> It is not our intent to place blame; rather, it is our intent to note that in the classroom incident – where an image forbidden for Muslims to look upon was projected on a screen and left for many minutes – respect for the observant Muslim students in that classroom should have superseded academic freedom.[24]

Three things are to be noted here. First, the images shown were painted by Muslims, they belong to the sacral art, there is no trace of disrespect in them. Second, why did Wedatalla who started the protest not leave the room after the warning? Obviously, she stayed there *in order to* be able to claim that she was hurt and offended, and cause an incident. This is also why other protesters who joined Wedatalla felt hurt and offended although they were not attending the class – it was enough for them to know what happened at the class. This, of course, opens up the space for the almost endless extension of what can offend and hurt me . . . Third and most important; the terms used by those who protested – safety, respect, etc. versus hate, direct attack, phobia . . . – are the very terms Political Correctness and Wokeism use to attack intolerance and racism.

We often hear today that Wokeism and Political Correctness are gradually receding. Contrary to this opinion, I think that this phenomenon is gradually being "normalized," widely accepted even by those who intimately doubt it, and practiced by the majority of academic and state institutions. This is why it deserves more than ever our criticism – together with its opposite, the obscenity of new populism and religious fundamentalism. In Cancel Culture at its worst, your public life can be destroyed for reasons that are not even clear in advance. This is what makes Cancel Culture so threatening: something very particular that you did (or are) can be unexpectedly elevated into the universal status of an unforgivable mistake, so that every particular case is never just a neutral case of universality but gives its own spin to a fuzzy universality.

Towards the end of October 2022 Gonville and Caius College in Cambridge (UK) was hosting a talk by Helen Joyce known for her view that men and women are being "redefined" by trans activists, with laws and policies "reshaped to privilege self-identified gender identity over biological sex." Joyce unambiguously supports trans rights, what she rejects is gender-identity ideology, i.e., the idea "that people should count as men or women according to how they feel and what they declare, instead of their biology," into norm and law. Students at Gonville and Caius have launched protests, with the college's LGBT representatives demanding that Joyce's appearance is cancelled because they are "unanimously disgusted by the platforming of such views". Tutors were even opening a "safe space" welfare tearoom for students during the talk, blaming "understandable hurt and anger for many students, staff and fellows at Caius" caused by the invitation. The college's Master joined them, saying that while freedom of speech is "a fundamental principle, on some issues which affect our community we cannot stay neutral".[25] So, again, respect for (not the observant Muslim students but) the offended trans students should have superseded academic freedom . . . a clear point at which religious fundamentalism meets Political Correctness cancel culture.

What the Politically Correct cancel culture with its stiff moralism misses is the proper *ethical* stance. The latest example of such a stance in movies is *The Menu* (Marx Mylord, 2022) in which Ralph Fiennes gives an exquisite performance by playing Julian, a top cook and owner of an elite restaurant on a small private island. He invites a group of rich guests with a plan to kill them all – the only survivor is Margot, one of the guests who mocks Julian's dishes and complains that she is still hungry. When Julian asks what she would like to eat, Margot requests a cheeseburger and fries, having previously seen a photo of a young, happy Julian working at a fast-food restaurant. Moved by her simple request, he prepares the meal to her specifications. Margot takes a bite and praises his food, then asks if she can get it "to go". Julian packs the food for her and the staff allow her to leave. Margot takes the Coast Guard boat docked nearby and escapes the island while Julian sets the restaurant ablaze, detonating the barrel and killing the guests, staff and himself.[26] While Julian is definitely immoral (he kills a series of people who are corrupted and repulsive but not murderers), he nonetheless gives body to a pure ethical stance: his suicidal final act is not just a personal quirk, it targets an entire way of life exemplified by the *haute cuisine* in which not only customers but also cooks and waiters who serve them participate – one can bet that all his guests were involved in charities and had deep sympathy for the plight of the poor . . . The proof of his ethics is that he lets Margot go: if he were just immoral, he would have killed them all.

Another film which presents the same distinction is *Ghost Dog: The Way of the Samurai* (1999, written and directed by Jim Jarmusch) in which Forest Whitaker plays the mysterious "Ghost Dog", a hitman in the employ of the Mafia, who follows the ancient code of the samurai as outlined in the book of Yamamoto Tsunetomo's recorded sayings, *Hagakure*, even when this brings him to his death. Yet another such film is *The Banshees of Inisherin* (2022, written and directed by Martin McDonagh). Set on a remote island off the west coast of Ireland, the film follows lifelong friends Pádraic (Colin Farrell) and Colm (Brendan Gleeson), who find themselves at an impasse when Colm unexpectedly puts an end to their friendship. A stunned Pádraic refuses to take no for an answer and endeavours to repair the relationship. But Pádraic's repeated efforts only strengthen his former friend's resolve – Colm delivers a desperate ultimatum: every time Pádraic bothers him or tries to talk with him, Colm will cut off one of his own left fingers with a pair of sheep shears . . . and he does it repeatedly. This fidelity to a decision is ethical, in this term has any sense.

However, fidelity to a principled decision is not enough for an act to qualify as truly ethical. In December 2022, the Sturgeon government in Scotland pushed Wokeism and LGBT+ (almost) to the end: it has hailed a "historic day for equality" after MSPs approved plans to make it easier and less intrusive for individuals to legally change their gender, extending the new system of self-identification to sixteen- and seventeen-year-olds – basically, you declare what you feel you are and you are registered as what you want to be. An (expected) problem emerged when Isla Bryson was remanded to women's prison in Stirling after being convicted of the rapes when she was a man called Adam Graham. The rapist decided that he was no longer a man only after appearing in court on a rape charge – so we have a person who identifies itself as a woman using its penis to rape two women. It is quite logical: if maleness and femaleness has nothing to do with one's body, and everything to do with one's self-definition, then one must put a penis-having rapist in prison with captive women. After protests, Brayson was put into a male prison – again, it is formally problematic since we have now a woman in male prison . . .[27] The point here is that there is no easy solution because sexual identity is in itself not a simple form of identity but a complex notion full of inconsistencies and unconscious features – it is something that in no way could be established by a direct reference to how we feel. Sticking to a problematic "principle" doesn't help a lot in such cases since the principle itself is wrong.

From Antagonisms to Class Struggle

At a more general level, the same holds for any socio-political field which is always a space of multiple antagonisms: class antagonism, ethnic antagonisms, sexual antagonisms, religious antagonisms, struggles for ecology . . . All these antagonisms are real/impossible in the strict Lacanian sense: there is no neutral description of an antagonism, every description is already "contextualized," partial. Antagonisms can be combined into what Ernesto Laclau[28] called "chain of equivalences": the Left claim that ecological struggle, feminist struggle, anti-racist struggle . . . can and should be combined with class struggle since racism, destruction of our environment, oppression of women and other races, are today all overdetermined by capitalist exploitation. But other combinations are also possible: feminism can be combined with liberalism, ecology with conservative anti-modernism, etc. Although, in every particular situation, there is always one struggle/ antagonism which plays a hegemonic role (in Europe in the 1940s it was anti-Fascist struggle, in Iran at the end of 2022 it was the struggle for women's rights . . .), for Laclau one struggle is elevated into the hegemonic role through the struggle (for hegemony) whose outcome is not determined in advance but dependent on contingent strategic circumstances.

What is going on in Iran from September 2022 – the so-called Mahsa Amini protests – has a world-historical significance. The protests which spread to dozens of cities began in Tehran on 16 September as a reaction to the death of Amini, a 22-year-old woman of Kurdish origins who died while in police custody, beaten to death by the Guidance Patrol, the Islamic "morality police" of Iran; she was arrested after being accused of wearing an "improper" hijab. The protests combine different struggles (against women's oppression, against religious oppression, for political freedom against state terror) into an organic unity. Iran is not part of the developed West, so *Zan, Zendegi, Azadi* ("woman, life, freedom," the slogan of the protests) is very different from MeToo in Western countries: it mobilizes millions of ordinary women, and it is directly linked to struggle of all, men included – there is no anti-masculine tendency in it, as is often the case with the Western feminism. Women and men are together in it, the enemy is religious fundamentalism supported by state terror. Men who participate in *Zan, Zendegi, Azadi* know well that the struggle for women's rights is also the struggle for their own freedom: the oppression of women is not a special case, it is the moment in which the oppression that permeates the entire society is most visible. The protesters who are not Kurds also see it clearly that the oppression of Kurds puts limits on their own freedom: solidarity with Kurds is the only way towards freedom in Iran. Plus the protesters see it clearly that religious fundamentalism can only remain in power if it is supported by the raw state power of what in Iran is called Morality Police – what they see is that a regime which needs a brutal Morality Police to maintain itself betrays the authentic religious experience it uses to legitimize itself.

Iranian protests thus realize what the Western Leftists can only dream about. They avoid the traps of Western middle-class feminism: they directly link the struggle for women's freedom with the struggle of women and men against ethnic oppression, against religious fundamentalism and against state terror. What goes on now in Iran is something that awaits us in the developed Western world where political violence, religious fundamentalism and oppression of women are growing daily. We in the West have no right to treat Iran as a country which just has to catch-up with the West. The last thing Iran needs now is a dose of Western Political Correctness! We in the West have to learn from Iran, we will soon need a similar movement in the US, in Poland, in

Russia, and in many other countries. Whatever the immediate result of the protests, the crucial thing is to keep the movement alive, to organize social networks which, even if state oppression will temporarily win, will continue its underground work and lay the foundation for a new explosion. It is not enough just to express sympathy or solidarity with Iranian protesters: they are not out there, far from us, part of a different exotic culture. All the babble about cultural specificities (often used by reactionary forces to justify religious and ethnic oppression) is now meaningless: we can immediately see that the Iranian struggle is the struggle of us all.

At the same time, we should not be afraid to assert that the language of global emancipation has its roots in European tradition of Enlightenment. European civilization is characterized by a unique feature: permanent self-criticism is part of its identity. Yes, the liberal West is hypocritical, it applies its high standards very selectively. But hypocrisy means you violate the standards you proclaim, and in this way you open yourself up to immanent criticism – when we criticize the liberal West, we use its own standards. What Putin's Russia is offering is a world without hypocrisy – because it is without global ethical standards, practicing just pragmatic "respect" for differences. We have seen clearly what this means when, after Taliban took over in Afghanistan, they instantly made a deal with China: China accepts the new Afghanistan while Taliban will ignore what China is doing with Uyghurs . . . – this is, *in nuce*, the new globalization advocated by Russia. And the only way to defend what is worth saving in our liberal tradition is to ruthlessly insist on its universality.

This universal dimension is what makes so important the ongoing protests in Iran which retroactively devalue Michel Foucault's celebration of the Iranian revolution of 1978 as a modality of religious political revolt, i.e., as a form of political spirituality: a mass mobilization modelled on the coming of a new Islamic vision of social forms of co-existence and equality. In 1979, deeply disappointed by the mass killings of the victorious revolution, he wrote that "the spirituality of those who were going to their deaths has no similarity whatsoever with the bloody government of a fundamentalist clergy" – a statement which should be qualified as one of the greatest stupidities in the political judgements that occurred in the twentieth century: of course there is "no similarity whatsoever" between the two, but the passage from the first to the second was nonetheless inevitable.[29] So what seduced Foucault to believing that the Iranian revolution was meant to save humanity from the clutches of materialism and capitalism? As he repeated in many interviews from that period, modern Europe was for him the worst form of oppression and domination, much worse than the Third World non-democratic regimes – its freedom, democracy and human rights were just deceptive masks of total social control. How could this have happened? The Left always prefers the symptomal reading of an ideology: things are not what they claim to be, their truth is the opposite (freedom in the market is the form of exploitation and domination, universal human rights mask imperialist domination . . .) – so what does the Left do when it confronts a reactionary agent which IS what it claims to be, where there is no need for a deep symptomal analysis? Here the Left gets perplexed: what of, at some deeper level, we are even worse than our reactionary opponent? Today we get exactly this logic among the "Leftists" who show "understanding" for Putin.

The Iranian uprising thus provides the best argument against the new world order of sovereign states advocated (among others) by Russia; in this vision, the main enemy of sovereignty is "Eurocentrism," the Western decadence which imposes on others its liberal values. So when uprisings explode in some state (Iran, Belarus . . .), their cause is projected outside this state – in Russia, they now officially designate most of outspoken dissidents as "foreign agents." Critique of Eurocentrism is largely false here: authoritarian regimes desperately try to construct an external enemy in order to obfuscate their own immanent antagonisms. However, if there ever was an event which is not "Eurocentric," it is the Iranian protests: they clearly grow out of the unresolved immanent antagonisms of Iranian society. The protesting Iranian crowds did something that is most difficult to do today: they accomplished the passage from external enemy to be annihilated to immanent antagonism which demands a radical change of one's own identity, which is why, as we already said, any Western patronizing satisfaction ("finally, Iranians are becoming like us") is totally out of place – if anything, we should learn from Iranians.

Let's take the case of the struggle for hegemony that is taking place in (what remains of) the Left in the developed West, especially the US. The mainstream liberal Left de facto elevates to the hegemonic role the topics of the so-called Culture War (trans rights, abortion . . .) and racism, usually just paying lip service to economic issues or simply ignoring them. In this way it is alienating millions of lower- and middle-class ordinary families in small towns and farmland who are not actively against LGBT+ but just want to live their traditional lives – they could be mobilized for many measures (against big corporations and banks, for more accessible healthcare, student loans . . .), so it is as if the liberal Left is intentionally sabotaging big common causes (no wonder some Leftists mean they are doing it intentionally). The moment a more radical Left comes with such economic proposals, the Culture War liberals accuse it of neglecting trans issues etc. – but the Culture War liberal Left does not do itself what it accuses of the more radical economic Left . . .

But is it enough to plea for such symmetry, for the equal weight of different antagonisms best formulated by Laclau's theory according to which hegemony is the result of contingent struggles? Here enters my analogy with Bell's inequality: Laclau's multiplicity of antagonisms with no privileged struggles is a pure perfect form, and class struggle is what disturbs this perfect symmetry. The point is not that economic base is a "hidden variable," the hidden substantial truth of all antagonisms which operates independently of all contexts, but a kind of structural imperfection, an "attractor" which disturbs the pure form. Let's again take a look at the image of what quantum mechanics predicts (and was confirmed by repeated experiments): quantum mechanics predicts that the two entangled electrons will give *more* correlation in their spin measurements than the limit imposed if we exclude a link that operates faster than the speed of light – here is the drawing (see Fig. 6.1) already used in Chapter 3.

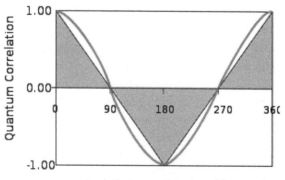

Angle between detectors (degrees)

Figure 6.1

In my brutal reading, this picture without the red curved line provides the correlation between social antagonisms without class struggle's "spooky" action at a distance, while the red curved line indicates how this "spooky" action at a distance disturbs the pure form of contingency. One has to add here that, already at a formal level, class struggle is not an antagonism like others: the goal of the anti-racist struggle is not to destroy an ethnic group but to enable the peaceful co-existence of ethnic groups without oppression; the goal of feminist struggle is not to annihilate men but to enable actual equality of all sexes and sexual orientations; etc. But the goal of the class struggle is, for the oppressed and exploited, the actual annihilation of the opposite ruling class as a class (not of the individuals who compose it, of course), not the reconciliation of classes (it is Fascism which aims at the reconciliation of classes by way of eliminating the intruder – Jews – which introduces antagonism). This brings us back to the paradox of class difference which precedes classes (as self-identical social groups): if classes precede their struggle, then the way is open for Fascism, i.e., for the collaboration of classes. Only if class struggle precedes classes can the class society really be overcome.

We live in an era of *unholy alliances*, a combination of ideological elements which violate the standard opposition of Left and Right. Let's just mention one of the saddest recent examples. At the end of February 2023, the Ugandan parliament debated a further toughening of the anti-gay law – the most radical proponents demanded death penalty or at least life imprisonment for those caught in the act. Anita Among, speaker of the parliament, said in the debate: "You are either with us, or you're with the Western world."[30] Feminist, gay and trans struggles are thereby denounced as an instrument of Western ideological colonialism used to undermine African identity – and this immediately brings us to another unholy alliance: Russia, with its Orthodox fundamentalism, presents itself as an ally of Third World nations fighting colonialism, a fact that doesn't prevent parts of the Western Left to lean towards Russia in its aggression on Ukraine. How can this happen? Zupančič brings out the underlying reason for this obscene complicity – the Western Left intimates correctly the limitation of global capitalism, but is not able to draw a line of separation that would enable it to engage itself as an active political agent. While pretending to ruthlessly criticize Western global capitalism, its own activity is limited to Politically Correct self-destructive excesses – it is hoping for another external agent to draw this line, which means, in Freudian terms, that it simply lack the true *desire* to engage in struggle that:

> All the energy and passion invested in criticizing Western imperialism ends up (practically) hoping and waiting that someone else, somewhere else, will do our job, will draw a line, a limit to the Empire. (Even if only by establishing another, alternative Empire.) In this sense, what the Western Left seriously lacks is precisely desire.[31]

And now, in early 2023, this alternate Empire is Russia . . . So when Sahra Wagenknecht, the most popular representative of *die Linke*, the German Leftist party, organized and spoke at a meeting for peace in Dresden in February 2023, calling for the end of helping Ukraine with arms, Björn Höcke (one of the leading members of the extreme Right Alternative for Germany present at the meeting) shouted at her: "Ich bitte Sie, kommen Sie zu uns" ["Please come to us!"], calling her to change her party affiliation – and the public applauded him . . . These and other cases brought many social analysts to the conclusion that, today, the opposition between Left and Right became meaningless, or at least to Laclau's position that no antagonism enjoys a privileged status.

But, again, a reference to quantum mechanics enables us to interpret the primacy of class struggle not in the substantialist way, as the essence expressed in other struggles, but in a purely formal way. What this implies is that we should distinguish between class difference as a difference (or struggle) between two well-defined positive social groups, and class antagonism as a pure difference which precedes the terms it opposes – in Hegelian terms, the "pure" class antagonism encounters itself among positive social difference in its "oppositional determination." And the same holds for sexual difference: we should distinguish between "pure" sexual difference as the real of an "impossible" antagonism and sexual difference in its binary sense, as the opposition of two positive sexes.

Some (mostly academic) institutions are now establishing a rule that, when you encounter for the first time (or talk about) a person, you should refer to this person as "they" independently of how this person appears – you should pass to "he" or "she" only if this person explicitly demands to be addressed like that. I find this demand problematic because it elevates exception ("they" first referred to all those who do not fit the binary of men and women) into universality, into a universal standard: we are all "they," and "he" or "she" becomes one of its subspecies. However, sexual difference is an antagonism, an "impossible" difference, impossible in the sense that difference precedes what it differentiates, so that "masculine" and "feminine" are two ways to obfuscate the trauma of difference. While, empirically, there are not just men and women but also those who do not fit any of these two identities, this does not entail that human sexuality exists as a neutral universality which has many subspecies: sexual difference means that there are men, women, *and their difference as such*, and this difference is embodied precisely in trans subjects who do not fit any of the two main categories. The main point is that humans are constitutively traversed by sexual difference: it is not possible to isolate or abstract a human universality that would not be affected by the gap of difference. For this reason, a subject's sexual position is its free choice, but simultaneously a *forced* choice: we are never in a safe external position to choose, there is no universal "they" from which we can choose to be "he" or "she" or remain "they" – it is a forced choice because we choose (the mode of) what we ARE, not our properties.

So it is true that universality is embodied in an exception, but the universality in question is not a special neutral level where antagonisms don't apply (like the idea of a perfect androgynous human being living in a blissful harmony): universality is the universality of an antagonism, of a deadlock. Therein resides the difference between antagonism and a non-antagonistic universality like that of trash: in a series of trash cans, we get a can for paper, one for glass, for organic waste, etc., and then (usually) one that is called either "remainder" or "universal trash." Here, "remainder" means simply something that cannot be clearly included into any of other specific categories. In the case of sexuality, "remainder" means something more radical: something in which the antagonism or deadlock which traverses the entire field becomes visible. In this sense, in the space of social hierarchy, those who do not fit any particular post are identified as a threat to the system – Jews are in anti-Semitism such an intruder, and the fantasy of anti-Semitism is that, if we eliminate this element, harmonious social hierarchy will be re-established. Anti-Semitism thus works similarly to transphobia: if we eliminate the trans individuals, harmonious sexual difference with each sex at its own place will return – both anti-Semitism and anti-trans ignore the fact that antagonism pervades the entire field. In this sense "class struggle" and "sexual difference" are indeed something "spooky": with regard to the field of positively-existing social relations and tensions between groups, they both are a virtual/real point of reference which, without existing as a positive entity, exists (or, rather, insists) only in its effects, as a force that bends the social space.

Till now, Political Correctness mostly ignored class antagonism, focusing on racism, sexism, homophobia, religious fundamentalism, etc. Now advocates of Political Correctness more and more include into this series class differences, so that we get university courses (or obligatory training) on "racism, sexism and classism." However, a close look on the content of "classism" makes it clear that these courses don't deal with the real of class antagonism but with description of bad effects of great differences in wealth: the privileges and insensitivity wealth brings, etc. (many rich people gladly accept this lesson and engage in charity . . .). We don't hear a lot about the basic structure of capitalism which generates class differences, and about ways to overcome or at least radically change capitalism.

A theory of ideology can also learn something from the paradox of triple measurement – let's take a beam of non-polarized light. We pass it through a polarizer which will polarize the light in one direction only, up (vertical). Then we pass this beam of light through another polarizer that is exactly 90 degrees to the first vertical polarizer (horizontal) – nothing comes out on the other side, since all light that will hit it is vertically polarized and the second polarizer lets through only horizontally polarized light. But if we take the same non-polarized light, pass it through a vertical polarizer, and then pass this vertically polarized light through a 45 degrees polarizer, some light (not all) will pass through; and if we then pass this remaining light through a third horizontal polarizer, again, some light will come through. How/why can some vertically polarized light pass through the second (45 degrees) polarizer if it is all vertically polarized? In a clear parallel, let's imagine polarizing the confused mess of ideologico-political opinions, using a horizontal Left polarizer and a vertical Right one: if we do it just in two steps, nothing will pass through, but if we add in between the two a 45 degrees liberal centre polarizer, a part will pass through? (Or, maybe, one can imagine that something will even come through if opinions polarized through radical Left and radical Right filters: the so-called "totalitarian" elements both spaces share . . .)

This brings us back to the notion of contextuality (the dependence of an observable's outcome on the experimental context, i.e., on the system–apparatus interaction): *the order in which measurements are made matters.* Numbers on the number line obey the principle of transitivity: if A is greater than B and B is greater than C, than we know that A is also greater than C. But while this intuitive property holds for numbers, it doesn't hold true for everything. In a democratic society, "measurement" takes the form of voting, so let's say that citizens are voting on what policy to make into law, A, B or C. One voter likes the policy A, has B as a second choice, and dislikes the policy C. Another voter prefers policy B, then policy C, then policy A, and a third voter prefers policy C, then policy A, and then policy B. In a vote between policy A and policy B, A would win, since two of the three voters prefer policy A to policy B. In a vote between B and C, B wins, and in a vote between A and C, C would actually win, so transitivity doesn't hold here – A wins over B, B wins over C, but C wins over A. This creates an interesting dilemma. Imagine policy C were the current policy in our society, and we held a vote whether to switch on policy A – based on voters' preferences, we wouldn't switch. But if we first vote on switching to B, and then vote afterwards to switch on policy A, our society would first switch from C to B, and then to switch from B to A. And there is the key problem of our democracy: manipulation of the agenda.[32] Let's say C is today's hegemonic neoliberal order, B its populist supplement, and A a radical Left alternative. In direct confrontation, C wins over A, but if C is first replaced by B (Trumpian populism), in reaction to this version of B A has a chance to win.

Socialism and capitalism as systems are incompatible, but the Chinese version of Socialism rests on the presupposition that the couple of planned economy and market economy is not incompatible (as dogmatic Marxism claimed), they can be fruitfully combined. So let's take market and measure it together with Socialism and capitalism: we'll get each time a different market. More precisely: if we ask a person just about market, we'll probably get a different answer than if we first ask about market after we asked about Socialism . . . But what about democracy? Again, if we measure it along Socialism, then we'll get a different answer from measuring it along capitalism.

However, can we consider "Socialist democracy" still an actual democracy? And is multi-party parliamentary democracy still compatible with Socialism? The deadlock we encounter here is best render by the gap that separates "Socialist democracy" from "democratic Socialism": the existing Communist regimes claim(ed) that they developed their own Socialist democracy (superior to the "bourgeois" democracy), but they react with panic and oppression if we just turn the terms around and demand "democratic Socialism" – this is dismissed as a return to capitalism . . . The key feature we have to bear in mind here is that class struggle/antagonism is not a fixed substantial mega-feature that dominates all others, reducing them to its social expression; class struggle is rather the agent of ultimate, irreducible contextuality of all other struggle. The existing multi-party parliamentary system is not effective enough to cope with the crises that beset us. We shouldn't fetishize multi-party parliamentary democracy – what Friedrich Engels wrote in a letter to August Bebel from 1884 still holds. Engels warned that "'pure democracy" often becomes a slogan for counter-revolutionary reaction:

> At the moment of revolution, the entire reactionary mass will act as though they were democrats . . . At all events, on the crucial day and the day after, they will act as though they were democrats.[33]

Does this, exactly, not happen when an emancipatory movement in power gets too radical? Was not – among many others – the coup against Evo Morales in Bolivia done on behalf of democracy? In a way, the critics of Morales were right: they stood for the entire reactionary mass who now rediscover themselves as democrats . . . The whole of Lenin's politics aimed at sharpening the situation to the point where "democracy" itself (in its parliamentary-democratic mode) becomes irrelevant: one has to make a choice – as Lenin put it, we have to bring the things to the point at which there is no third way between the Tzar and the Revolution. Was in the weeks before the fall of Allende in Chile the situation not the same? Parliamentary games became irrelevant, the situation became simplified, it was the people against the old forces (which also evoked "democracy" in supporting Pinochet's coup)? At this point, the complexity of multiple antagonisms is reduced to the binary class struggle, and if "democracy" (appropriated by the old forces) wins, we lose democratic gains themselves, old corruption returns with a vengeance. This difficult choice gives birth to the eternal fantasy of the liberal Left: the dream of a radical social change accomplished in a peaceful democratic, even multi-party, way. Colin

Jones finishes his monumental *The Fall of Robespierre*, a 600 pages minute-by-minute account of 9 Thermidor which is basically very critical of Robespierre, with a surprising claim that

> ultimately, the "Terror" was only overthrown by the Thermidorian regime which coined the term. In crushing what they named the Terror, the Thermidorians also destroyed much of the democratic promise and the progressive social and economic policies that have also characterized the period of Revolutionary Government before 9 Thermidor. The ultimate irony was that the person who, in the early part of his career, expressed belief in those values most luminously – and in a way that can speak to us all – was Maximilien Robespierre, the great loser of 9 Thermidor.[34]

And Robespierre knew perfectly what awaits him: in a late night meeting, hours before he was arrested, he finished his speech with:

> The speech that you have heard is my last will and testament. I have seen today that the league of evil-doers is too strong for me to hope to escape. It is without regrets that I succumb. . . . And if I succumb, well, my friends, you will see me drink the hemlock in calm.[35]

This is how authentic political figures act and think. As for Robespierre's alleged thirst for terror and revenge, one should note that he hated most Joseph Fouche (then a Jacobin, later a police minister of Napoleon and then plotting the latter's downfall). The main reason for his hatred was Fouche's excessive use of vengeful violence in putting down the Federalist revolt and its aftermath: after the defeat of the counter-revolution in Lyon in the first months of 1794, Fouche ordered 1,900 executions, provoking the wrath of Robespierre who had him instantly recalled to Paris.[36] In short, the true aim of Robespierre's last two speeches in the Convention was not to further strengthen the Terror but to diminish it, to slowly bring it to an end. As is well-known, he threatened in his last speech that the Convention should be purged of a group of corrupted traitors, and, when repeatedly called to name them, he refused to do it – as we know now, not to spread fear and guilt among the members (each of them afraid that he is on the list), but because the names he targeted were in large majority from his own group of Montagnards. Robespierre's aim was not to spread fear among the enemies but to constrain the need for enemies which led the Jacobins to Terror – in short, he wanted to restrain Terror in order to focus on the ultimate social antagonism in France at that moment: how to save the people's republic from the threat of a military dictator (a threat clearly predicted by him and Saint-Just, and realized with the rise to power of Napoleon).

This complications give us a hint of how Communism will eventually enter the stage: not through a simple parliamentary electoral process but through a state of emergency enforced on us by an apocalyptic threat. Resistances against this radicalization are extremely strong, as we can see in the latest fictional example of the radical feminine political agent, Daenerys in the TV series *Game of Thrones*. The last struggle between the Starks and Daenerys is ultimately a struggle between traditional "good" nobility (Starks) faithfully protecting their subjects from bad tyrants, and Daenerys as a new type of a strong leader, a feminine Robespierre acting on behalf of the underprivileged. The stakes of the final conflict are thus, to put it in a simple way: should the revolt against tyranny be just a fight for the return of the old kinder version of the same hierarchic order, or should it develop into the search for a new order needed? But what about Daenerys's murderous outbursts? Can the ruthless killing of the thousands of ordinary people in King's Landing really be justified as a necessary step to universal freedom? If your answer is a NO, then you endorse the liberal-conservative lesson best imparted by the words of Jon to Daenerys just before he kills her:

> The people who follow you know that you made something impossible happen. Maybe that helps them believe that you can make other impossible things happen: build a world that's different from the shit one they've always known. But if you use dragons to melt castles and burn cities, you're no different. You're just more of the same.

However, as Yuval Harari noted, the exact opposite is true: after Daenerys is liquidated, we get just more of the same: "in the show's final scenes, we realize that absolutely nothing changed. After seven seasons, countless battles, millions of dead, and numerous supernatural interventions, the socio-political system of Westeros remained exactly the same, with a bunch of aristocrats sitting in council and discussing how to finance navies and build brothels."[37] Consequently, Jon kills out of love (saving the cursed woman from herself, as the old male-chauvinist formula says) the only social agent in the series who really fought for something new, for a new world that would put an end to old injustices.

So no wonder the last episode was well received: justice prevailed – what kind of justice? Each person is allocated to his/her proper place, Daenerys who disturbed the established order killed and flown away to eternity by her last dragon. The new king is Bran: crippled, all-knowing, who wants nothing – with the evocation of the insipid wisdom that the best rulers are those who do not want power. In a supremely Politically Correct enduing, a cripple rules now helped by a dwarf, and chosen by the new wise elite whose first concern is to re-establish brothels and navy production. When one of the naïve new ruling council members proposes a more democratic selection, this idea is met by a laughter from the majority . . . Is, then, *Game of Thrones* not again a nice example of how, although the main struggle is the struggle against the foreign threat – the Army of the Dead from beyond Westeros's northern border –, at the end the conflict is reduced to class struggle in Westeros itself?

Such a contextualized reading of class struggle implies that, in rejecting religious fundamentalism, we should not put our bets on Western liberalism – as we have already seen, liberalism clearly shows its fateful limitation, especially with today's emergence of the third space of "free" digital exchanges. So, back to Lenin, what to do in such a complex situation? Does Marxism still work? Yes – complemented with psychoanalysis.

CONCLUSION: THE NEED FOR PSYCHOANALYSIS

In 2022, the Mitscherlich-Chair at the Frankfurt University (the most prestigious chair for psychoanalysis in Germany) was abolished: a new call for applications didn't list psychoanalysis anymore – should this surprise us? No, but it should nonetheless enrage us and make us think. This cancellation is a logical consequence of the long wave of triumphalist acclamations of how psychoanalysis is dead: with the new advances in brain sciences, it is finally put where it belonged all the time, to the lumber-room of pre-scientific obscurantist search for hidden meanings, alongside religious confessors and dream-readers. This cancellation is sustained by a silent pact between psychiatric establishment, new brain sciences and Politically Correct Woke feminism – they all reject psychoanalysis.

Neither Biological Sex Nor Cultural Gender

Behavioural therapies combined with drugs ignore the social background of psychic troubles – for them, the aim of therapy is just to cure the symptom, bringing the individual back to "normal" social functioning. In the same way that a broken car should be quickly repaired, a broken individual should be integrated back into social life, and psychoanalysis is not efficient enough, losing time with the inquiries into the social and psychic roots of a pathology. Where did this approach bring us? As Ivan Illich convincingly demonstrated, the ever new medical procedures and drugs themselves change the scope of what we experience as the domain of our lives which can be treated by medical practices – in an extrapolation *ad absurdum*, our entire life, inclusive of our dying, becomes a stressful experience to be cured. No wonder that today, in the US, around 80 per cent of the so-called intellectual class (professors and students, journalists, researchers . . .) are taking psycho-drugs, from modest tranquilizers like Xanax to opium or cocain – you take drugs to calm yourself and then you take drugs to revitalize yourself . . . It is more and more as if we cannot find the balance of a normal life without a strong support of drugs.

Such behavioural and chemo-therapeutic approach is grounded in new brain sciences which directly ground our inner experience in neuronal-biological processes, leaving no space open for the Freudian Unconscious. And although the LGBT+ and new feminists reject such an approach, they also reject psychoanalysis which is, as they like to repeat, mostly practiced by "old white men." However, the conceptual frame within which they operate – "yes means yes," mutual consent – relies on a decidedly pre-Freudian notion of subject: individuals are supposed to know what they really want. Pathological phenomena arise from external social oppression, and individuals should just get rid of this oppression in order to regain the ability to realize their innermost sexual desires. There is no place here for the Freudian notion of the divided subject, for the immanent inconsistency of our desires (we don't know what we want, we often really desire what we don't want, we find pleasure in suffering and self-humiliation).

In § 29 of his *Minima Moralia*, Adorno proposed a claim which makes him totally incompatible with today's woke ideology: "First and only principle of sexual ethics: the accuser is always in the wrong." He goes on to explain it: "What is merely identical with itself is without happiness."[1] Adorno's claim is directed against (what we call today) identity politics as well as against sex as act of exchange between self-identical egos whose interaction is based on mutual consent – or, as Antonia Hofstätter formulated it in a courageous and brilliant reading: "Every 'I accuse you' drags into the sphere of sexuality the expectations and entitlements of conscientious consumers and those citizens who know their rights." This is why Adorno's claim "takes its impulse not from the ubiquitous demand for 'safety' that echoes across campuses from Berlin to Boston, but from a sexual utopia in which power relations are divested of their scarring force." Sex is by definition not safe, it involves exposing oneself to the loss of identity:

> The dim light of ambiguity that nourishes Adorno's outrageous line is inseparable from its promise: the promise of a wealth – however murky and repellent – that exists beyond the conscious life of the subject, a wealth in which it nevertheless partakes.[2]

One should not be afraid to draw the ultimate conclusion from these insights: the Politically Correct safe and controlled sex is a desexualized sex, to put in the series with decaffeinated coffee and communication with others who are deprived of the abyss of Otherness. The PC rejection of claims like Adorno's rejects precisely its "dim light of ambiguity" which is considered a threat to unambiguous interaction where yes means yes and no means no: it refuses to engage itself in the "promise of wealth" and is satisfied with the direct reading of Adorno's claim which reduces it to the prohibition of the victim's right to accuse the assailant. Adorno is, of course, ridiculously one-sided: should a woman who was brutally raped not accuse her assailant? We are dealing here not with transgressive ecstatic blurring of boundaries but a simple direct brutality: the rapist gets a surplus-enjoyment from the fact that his victim is terrified by his act . . . Nonetheless, we should remain open to the "dim light of ambiguity" which pertains to language as a social link: there is no meta-language, especially in the domain of sexuality, which means that every rejection or condemnation of a sexual act, no matter how clear and unambiguous it sounds, is in principle open to the possibility of becoming sexually invested, giving birth to its own surplus-enjoyment. Unacceptable as it may sound within the Politically Correct parlance, even a brutal rape which is not part of any sado-masochist contract can be perversely enjoyed in a way disavowed by its victim. To avoid a fatal misunderstanding: not only does this fact not justify the rape (in the sense of "she really wanted it"), it makes the rape even more terrifying since it opens up the path to the psychic self-destruction of the victim – assuming openly this enjoyment-in-being-raped ruins the basic subjective consistency of the victim.

The recent controversy about the use of so-called puberty blockers concerns another aspect of this same "dim light of ambiguity." Puberty blockers suppress hormones and in this way pause a child's development of sex-based characteristics. They are given to youngsters between nine and sixteen years still determining their sexual identity, and the reasoning that sustains this measure is pretty straightforward: there is a danger that people still determining their sexual identity will make an enforced choice under the pressure of their environment and thus repress their true inclination (to be a trans, mostly). So, since in full puberty we usually already have adopted a definite sexual identity, people should be given puberty blockers to postpone their entry into puberty and thus give them more time to reflect on their sexual identity and to be compelled to decide about it a couple of years later when they will be mature enough to make the right choice . . .

But it was disclosed that life-changing drugs were given to autistic and troubled young people who may have been misdiagnosed as uncertain about their sex. Life-altering treatments were being given to children before they were old enough to know whether they want to medically transition, or, as one of the critics said: "A child experiencing gender distress needs time and support – not to be set on a medical pathway they may later regret." The paradox is clear: puberty blockers were given to allow youngsters to reach maturity and freely decide about their sexual identity, but puberty blockers may cause numerous other physical and psychic pathologies, and nobody asked the youngsters if they are ready to receive drugs with such consequences – or, as Hilary Cass wrote:

> We do not fully understand the role of adolescent sex hormones in driving the development of both sexuality and gender identity through the early teen years, so by extension we cannot be sure about the impact of stopping these hormone surges on psychosexual and gender maturation. We therefore have no way of knowing whether, rather than buying time to make a decision, puberty blockers may disrupt that decision-making process. Brain maturation may be temporarily or permanently disrupted by puberty blockers, which could have significant impact on the ability to make complex risk-laden decisions, as well as possible longer-term neuropsychological consequences.[3]

One should make even a step further in this criticism and problematize the very basic claim that arriving at sexual identity is a matter of mature free choice: there is nothing "abnormal" in sexual confusions, what we call "sexual maturation" is a long, complex and mostly unconscious process full of violent tensions and reversals, not a process of discovering what one really is in the depth of one's psyche. Freud and Lacan thus overcome the opposition between biological sex and cultural gender: for the two of them, there is nothing "natural" even in the fact that, say, I as a biological man assume being-male as my psycho-symbolic identity. A (biological) man becoming a (psycho-social) man is a process no less violent and "unnatural" than for a (biological) man becoming a (psycho-social) woman. Plus such violent tensions are, of course, not just facts of inner psychic life – they are embedded in antagonisms which traverse the entire social body.

Trans advocates claim that gender identity is not biological but a socially constructed contingent fact, a matter of choice social; however, when they oppose the patriarchal oppression, the imposition of binary sexuality, they invoke the raw fact of how an individual FEELS, its immediate self-experience (it is enough for a man who wants to become a woman just to claim "I was born into a wrong body") which is not again presented as something historically mediated. Here TERFs who insist that a trans woman should not be simply accepted as a woman have a point: what those who claim a trans woman is a woman tout court tend to ignore is the basic lesson of materialism. In our societies, being a woman is not just a fact of inner feeling, it resides in a set of social material practices (women give birth, have periods, go through a menopause . . .), and the submission of women refers to all these practices. (A homology offers itself here with Althusser's idea that ideology is not just a world-view but something embodied in a complex network of ideological apparatuses, customs and practices) . . . The conclusion of Greta Gerwig's *Barbie* should be read in this sense: in our reality to which Barbie again returns, she makes her first appointment with a gynaecologist. For this same reason I find problematic the following stance:

> Spouses who refuse to fund their partner's gender surgery may be domestic abusers, the Crown Prosecution Service (CPS) says in new guidance. These include 'withholding money for transitioning',

which would include either spouse refusing to pay for gender surgery, counselling or other treatment in a way that amounted to coercive control or abuse. Other behaviors could be 'criticizing the victim for not being "a real man/woman" if they have not undergone reassignment surgery', or 'threatening or sharing pre-transition images', or refusing to use their preferred name or pronoun.[4]

So what happens if I am, say, a woman married to a man who, since he decided to identify as a woman, wants to do gender surgery to become also a biological woman? Does this not somehow affect my conjugal obligations? I married THAT man, not a person to whom I am obliged even if s/he changes his/her sexual identity.

In his (posthumously published) volume IV of *History of Sexuality*, Michel Foucault mentions a peculiarity of the bodies of hyena already noted by Aristotle: an outgrowth of flesh that traces a form below the tail very similar to a female sex; however, this cavity does not open into any canal leading toward the womb or the intestine. Foucault then focuses on the interpretation of this peculiarity proposed by Clement of Alexandria: in contrast to Aristotle who sees this outgrowth as a contingent feature with no deeper spiritual meaning, Clement insists that the outgrowth similar to a vagina is

> utterly similar to a moral fault found in men: lasciviousness. And it's in view of this defect that 'nature' has devised a supplementary cavity in these animals for them to use for their equally supplementary sallies. In sum, to the 'excessive' natural propensity for pleasure that characterizes the hyena, nature has responded with an excessive anatomy that enables 'excessive' relations.[5]

What immediately strikes the eye is the ambiguous role of "nature" in Clement's line of argumentation: lasciviousness is unnatural, but nature nonetheless takes care to provide excessive/useless body parts whose only function is to satisfy lascivious needs . . . Such "hermeneutics" which reads freaks of bodily reality as expression of corrupted spiritual stances, such correspondence between psychic inside and bodily outside, is to be thoroughly rejected. Trans ideology is here right: there is no "natural" correlation between psychic sexual desires and the biologically-determined bodily reality. What it misses is the fact that *sexuality as such is "trans"* – in what precise sense? The most consistent definition of trans-sexuality is that a subject goes beyond its biologically-determined sexual identity: if you are biologically a man, you are "trans" if you do not subjectively assume this identity but search for a different identity. Cis-men are thus in some sense ontologically lazy: they just passively assume what they are biologically. Lacan's counter-point is that even cis- men or women are also trans: they have to work hard, to go through a process full of traumatic cuts, to arrive at their sexual identity which appears to be just something biologically given.

The abstract (in the strict Hegelian sense of the term) opposition between biological determinism and trans ideology which reduces sexual identity to a free decision based on "how I feel" reaches an extreme in accidents like the one a well-known Slovene theatre director active mostly in Germany told me about. While the director was rehearsing a new play every day for two weeks (in a big national theatre), trying to be respectful, asked the actors how they should be referred to ("they," "he," "she" . . .), the answer she got from ALL of them is that they cannot say now how they will (or experience themselves) in next days, so she should ask them at the beginning of every new day how they feel with regard to their sexual identity at that moment – and many of them effectively gave different answers on different days . . .

And what about the reproach that psychoanalysis is patriarchal, focusing on the Oedipal complex and the path to "normal" heterosexuality? Here critics also miss the point: for Freud, "normal" heterosexuality is not inscribed into our nature but a (possible) result of the gradual overcoming of infantile sexuality – and we never really leave infantile sexuality behind, which is why even our eventual "normal" heterosexuality has to be sustained by fantasies which originate in infantile sexuality. Critics of psychoanalysis see patriarchal heterosexuality, its binary order with fixed sexual roles, as the result of a foreign social imposition on our free plural sexuality – but for Freud, infantile sexuality is not a lost paradise, it is in itself full of tensions and self-destructive spins.

So was Freud "patriarchal"? On the contrary: he makes it clear that the rise of psychoanalysis as theory and practice is the result of the process of the gradual decline of paternal authority – the idea that Freud fits the Victorian patriarchal era is a ridiculous misreading. But there is an important point to be made here: it was clear already to Freud that the decline of the paternal authority is an ambiguous process: father as a figure of moral authority enables the child to adopt a stance of moral autonomy resisting the pressure of his/her peers and of the corrupted social environment. Following Freud, in his study on authority and family written back in the 1930s, Max Horkheimer made the same point, while, in the same spirit, Adorno pointed out that Hitler is not a paternal figure. And in his classic *Auf dem Weg zur vaterlosen Gesellschaft* (1963), Alexander Mitscherlich (whose chair is now abolished) analyses in detail the process of the loss of paternal authority and how it gives birth to new forms of domination. This brings us back to Christian Atheism which fully assumes that father is dead (God the Father, not only the Son, died on the cross), and simultaneously avoids the trap of individualist permissiveness: after the father's death, a new emancipatory collective emerges whose name is Holy Ghost. Today, when the need for an engaged political collective is needed more than ever, the choice is between the new Rightist populism and a reinvented Holy Ghost. To put it in brutal terms, the ultimate anti-Christian force today is not hedonist individualism but the Rightist Christian fundamentalism itself. There is more of a Holy Ghost in militant Leftist insurgency, violent as it may be, than in any Rightist collective obsessed by saving our way of life.

Another lesson of these insights is that psychoanalysis undermines the simple opposition between our sexual drives and their oppression: it asserts the inextricable mixture of these two levels. The topic of sexism and racism is thus not somehow secondary, so that we should move the focus onto "real" economy, as some Leftist critics of Wokenness seem to imply. Adrian Johnston[6] formulated the key insight here – his basic premise runs against the standard Freudo-Marxist idea that the explanation of the subjective features of individuals living in today's capitalism (why do millions act and vote against their obvious interests? why can they be mobilized for nationalist, religious and military struggles which pose a threat to their very lives?) in the terms of the determination by economic base is insufficient – to explain such phenomena, Marxist economic analysis has to be supplemented by a psychoanalytic research into collective libidinal investments. While Johnston agrees that Marxism needs psychoanalysis, he convincingly argues that these unconscious libidinal mechanisms are at work *already in the very heart of the "economic base"*: we just have to read Marx closely to see that the individuals caught in the capitalist reproduction do not really follow their egotist interests – they act as the instruments of the capital's drive to ever-expanding reproduction, ready to renounce to many life pleasures:

> Maybe Marx ought to be credited not only with inventing the psychoanalytic concept of the symptom *avant la lettre*, as Lacan proposes, but also with inventing the analytic idea of the drive prior to Freud.

Johnston, of course, does not ignore the complexity of the interaction between the reproduction of capital and the subjective life of capital's agents who are also "psychical subjects of enjoyments having to do with socio-symbolic secondary gains exuded from the pure accumulation of capital" – just think about the esteem gained by the charities of today's ultra-wealthy neo-feudal masters . . . But where does theology enter here? For Marx, the commodity fetishism is not simply a subjective illusion, but an "objective" illusion, an illusion inscribed into facts (social reality) themselves. Recall the famous first sentence of Section 4 ("The Fetishism of Commodities and the Secret Thereof") of Chapter 1 of *Capital*:

> A commodity appears, *at first sight*, a very trivial thing, and easily understood. Its analysis shows that it is, *in reality*, a very queer thing, abounding in metaphysical subtleties and theological niceties.[7]

What I want to claim is that this English translation, although not exact, is in some sense better than the German original: "Eine Ware scheint auf den ersten Blick ein selbstverständliches, triviales Ding. Ihre Analyse ergibt, daß sie ein sehr vertracktes Ding ist, voll metaphysischer Spitzfindigkeit und theologischer Mucken."[8] In the original, the second sentence just claims that "its analysis shows" what it is (as opposed to the "first sight"), while the English translation adds "in reality," thereby placing the commodity's "queer" character (think about today's connotation of this word!), its "metaphysical subtleties and theological niceties," into (social) *reality itself*. Kojin Karatani[9] is thus right to link this passage to the starting point of the Marxian critique, the famous lines from 1843 about how "the criticism of religion is the premise of all criticism"[10]: with it, the circle is in a way closed upon itself, i.e., at the very bottom of the critique of actual life (of the economic process), we again encounter the theological dimension inscribed into social reality itself. Karatani refers here to the Freudian notion of drive (*Trieb*) as opposed to the multitude of human desires: capitalism is grounded in the Real of a certain quasi-theological impersonal drive, the drive to reproduce and grow, to expand and accumulate profit. What Marx called revolution is thus, at its most radical, a theological revolution, a change in what we (mis)perceive as human nature.

Testicle Crushers, Then and Now

Are we not already witnessing such a change? Years ago, when I was reading a text about how the Nazis tortured prisoners in the concentration camps, it affected me quite traumatically when I found that they used industrially made testicle-crushers to cause unbearable pain. Now I found that this same product, exquisitely made (two small metal containers connected by a chain which look like something you would, indeed, use to crack a nut out of its shell, with multiples holes for needles to push them deep into your testicle), is one in the series of similar things one can buy on the web[11] – as the advertisement says, "pick your poison for pleasure from this ball torture group": STAINLESS STEEL BALL CRUSHER, STAINLESS BALL CLAMP TORTURE DEVICE, BRUTAL COCK VICE TORTURE TOY, HARDCORE STAINLESS BALL TORTURE . . . So if you lie in bed with your partner, melancholic and tired of life,

> the time is right. Your slave's nuts are ripe for crushing! It's is the moment you have been waiting for—to find the right tool to brutalize his balls! The Stainless Ball Clamp Torture Device could be the ultimate testicle crusher given its wicked, brutal features.[12]

Welcome to the brave new world of permissiveness! If we imagine a scene of two men playing a sexual game with ball crushers, we, of course, immediately stumble upon ambiguous situations, at least. Let's say I by mistake enter a room where two men are playing this game, and since (in all probability) one of them is moaning and crying because of the pain, I misread the situation as an actual torture and jump in to attack the active guy . . . If I ignore the situation and just walk by, I ignore the possibility that it *was* an actual torture. So should I approach the two guys and politely ask them: "Is what you are doing really consensual?" – a quite idiotic thing to do. But let's go a step further and imagine a man is doing something similar to a woman, torturing her consensually? In our Politically Correct situation, many among us would automatically presume that their activity is not consensual, and if it is, that the woman internalized male repression, identifying with the enemy. The confusion is here irreducible: unfortunately, there are men *and* women who authentically enjoy (a degree of) torture which is enacted as non-consensual. Plus we should recall the obsessional ritual of enacting a punishment to signal the presence of a desire punished by the specific form of the inflicted pain – let's say that, in a culture where rape is punished by flogging, somebody asks a neighbour to flog him brutally – there is no deep masochism at work here, being flogged simply signals my desire to rape a woman.

The passage from the ball crusher used to torture prisoners in Nazi concentration camps to the ball crusher that you can buy for a little bit over $200 to play sadomasochist erotic games will undoubtedly be celebrated as a sign of historical progress, the same progress which makes us purify classic works of art purified of the content that may hurt somebody – at the level of bodily pleasures, we can consensually torture each other, but not at the level of words . . . Therein resides the big question that bothers us today which is: why does the permissive stance towards sexual pleasure entail impotence and frigidity? Why, when pleasure is enjoined by a superego figure, are we deprived of it? Why, in these conditions, is the only way to enjoy is through pain?

Here Freud enters the scene. On May 28 1922, he wrote a letter to the Trieste psychoanalyst Edoardo Weiss who had written to Freud to ask his advice on the treatment of two clients who both suffered from impotence. The first was a highly cultured Italian man of about forty years of age whose wife had committed suicide a number of years earlier after a period of depression; prior to this he had been capable of proper sexual activity. The second patient, a Slovene of about twenty years of age, was described by Weiss as a thoroughly immoral and deceptive person: he tried to cheat everyone, and he even came up with a method to profit from psychoanalysis (his father paid for his therapy, but he told his father that the sessions cost far more than they actually did, and he pocketed the difference). There is a strange paradox with this wretched Slovene: he was a swindler, a liar, a fraud, beyond the reach of the moral law and the Law of the Father, *and* he was completely impotent – to quote Mladen Dolar, "the transgression of all ethical and social laws did not lead to unbridled pleasure, but to its prohibition—the more everything is allowed, the more it is prohibited."[13]

Freud's advice to Weiss was simple: the first patient warranted psychoanalytic treatment as he was a man of high mores and culture who simply needed to overcome the trauma of his wife's suicide; the second case, "the Slovene, is obviously a good-for-nothing who does not warrant your efforts. Our analytical art fails when faced with such people, our perspicacity alone cannot break through to the dynamic relation which controls them."[14] Note Freud's contradictory response concerning this Slovene: Freud firstly dismisses him due to his immorality and simple superficiality, then he then dismisses him because his problem lies beyond the remit of psychoanalysis, so his dismissal has nothing to do with immorality or ethics – his impotence is simply un-analyzable. The meaning of the Slovene's impotence is beyond Freud, unlike the first case where Freud spies the cause as excessive obedience, remorse or guilt. The paradox of the Slovene is that he appears to have no good reason to be impotent for he is completely immoral and without conscience, thus free from the ethics that prohibit enjoyment, yet this Slovene is completely incapable of sexual enjoyment, while the Italian patient was at least capable of sexual relations with prostitutes – to quote David Claxton:

> Freud was clearly unable to fathom the cause or truth of this Slovene's impotence, and the aggressiveness of his response suggests his active resistance to this instance of a prohibition beyond his conception of morality and the super-ego. If the Slovene is without morals, and thus without a super-ego, why is it that he is even more prohibited from enjoyment than the cultured Italian? How can there be a prohibition against enjoyment beyond the super-ego, or in other words how can there be a prohibition in the absence of the law of the super-ego?[15]

These questions were resolved when Lacan introduced a clear distinction between moral Law and the superego, the distinction blurred by Freud.[16] Lacan has convincingly shown that there is a confusion in Freud: the title of the third chapter of *The Ego and the Id* is "The Ego and the Super-Ego (Ego-Ideal)", so Freud tends to use these two terms as synonyms (conceiving the Ego-Ideal as a forerunner of the Superego). The premise of Lacan's clarification is the equation between *jouissance* and superego: to enjoy is not a matter of following one's spontaneous tendencies; it is rather something we do as a kind of weird and twisted ethical duty. Superego is real, the cruel and insatiable agency which bombards me with impossible demands and which mocks my failed attempts to meet them, the agency in the eyes of which I am all the more guilty, the more I try to suppress my "sinful" strivings and meet its demands. The old cynical Stalinist motto about the accused at the show trials who professed their innocence ("the more they are innocent, the more they deserve to be shot") is superego at its purest. So for Lacan superego "has nothing to do with moral conscience as far as its most obligatory demands are concerned"[17]: superego is, on the contrary, the anti-ethical agency, the stigmatization of our ethical betrayal.[18]

Back to Weiss's example: the Italian was impotent due to the pressure of the moral Law, while the Slovene was impotent due to the superego pressure. The impotent Slovene from Trieste was thus a full century ahead of its time: he points towards the basic deadlock than of today's culture of permissiveness, tolerance and diversity. Its final outcome is that prohibition and regulation are universalized: to guarantee that our pleasures will not be obstructed, we are bombarded by more and more intricate networks of censorship and cancellations. Freud clearly saw this coming. In one of his letters to Fliess, Freud reported on his visit to the Škocjan caves in southern Slovenia, close to the Italian border:

> The Škocjan Caves, which we saw in the afternoon, are a gruesome miracle of nature, a subterranean river running through magnificent vaults, waterfalls, stalactite formations, pitch darkness and slippery paths secured with iron railings. It was Tartarus itself. If Dante saw anything like this, he needed no great effort of imagination for his inferno.[19]

And what did Freud find at the end of this descent, at the bottom of the Slovenian hell? His letter to Fliess continues: "At the same time the master of Vienna, Herr Dr. Karl Lueger, was with us in the cave, which after three and a half hours spewed us all out into the light again."[20] So at the bottom of hell, Freud met the mayor of Vienna, the "Master of Vienna," one of the most influential politicians in that part of the world at the time, a very popular populist leader notorious for his blatant anti-Semitism, idolized by young Hitler.[21] The lesson of this encounter in hell is an anti-Jungian one: when we descend to the bottom of our Unconscious, what awaits us there is not the deepest truth about our personality but what Freud called the fundamental Lie; we don't encounter there the pure flow of libido or its eternal archetypes freed from the oppression of paternal authority and "binary" logic but the obverse side of authority, figures of obscene superego authority which enjoins us to enjoy and thereby sabotages our ability to enjoy much more efficiently than the patriarchal Law. Sometimes there is nothing liberating in bringing up to the daylight the obscene secrets of our unconscious – what we find there are prohibitions and injunctions much more brutal than the paternal Law.

Manipur is not only in India

Let us take a terrifying case that occurred in May 2023 in India. To a Western European with a vague knowledge of Italian, "Manipur" automatically associates with "mani pulite" (pure hands), the big anti-corruption campaign in the early 1990s that changed the whole Italian political scene and ended with the rise of Berlusconi to power.

In Manipur, a small Indian state bordering on Myanmar, ethnic violence is now getting close to a civil war: its two largest groups, the majority Meitei and the minority Kuki, battle over land and influence. Meitei are Hindu, politically affiliated to the ruling Hindu-nationalist BJP (Bharatiya Janata Party) which also runs the state of Manipur, while Kuki are tribal Christians who live in forests. There is violence on both sides, but the main culprits are Meitei who want to push the Kuki out. What attracted the attention of the world is a shocking video of an attack on May 4 2023 when two Kuki women were paraded naked by Meitei men and then gang raped shortly after their village was razed – a horrifying case of terror against women as a political instrument (the video was rendered public by one of the perpetrators themselves).[22] At this point the Indian President Narendra Modi was finally forced to react: he proclaimed the event a "shame on India." However, his condemnation came late and was deeply hypocritical – why?

The Manipur local government is more or less openly on the side on Meitei, while the federal government is officially neutral but silently no less on the side of Meitei. The reasons for this partiality are not only ethnic (an expression of the BJP Hindu nationalism) but also economic: the forests inhabited by Kuki are rich in minerals, and the government wants to drive the Kuki out to exploit the area more efficiently. The pressure on Kuki is thus, as expected, justified as a strategy of "progress" and "modernization" resisted by the tribal Kuki.

This brings us to "pure hands": while the federal state pretends to act as a neutral agent just safeguarding law and order, its hands are far from pure since what it promotes as "law and order" clearly privileges the strong side in the conflict, providing it with the aura of legality. There is nothing new in such a procedure since it characterizes the entire history of "human rights": again and again, this notion was shown to privilege the rights of a particular sex, race, religion or social status. But what is going on in Manipur is that even the façade of a neutral state power crumbles: those in power openly support those who are (according to its own laws) illegal aggressors. Is something similar not happening in Israel? As long as the traditional secular Zionist settler-colonial ideology predominated, the state (not so) discreetly privileged its Jewish citizens over Palestinians; however, it put great efforts to sustain the appearance of a neutral rule of law: from time to time, it condemned Zionist extremists for their crimes against Palestinians, it limited the illegal new settlements on the West Bank, etc. The main agency playing this role was the Supreme Court – no wonder the Netanyahu government which took over in 2022 pushed through a judicial reform which deprives the Supreme Court of its autonomy. The large protests against judicial reform are the last cry of the secular Zionism – however, insofar as the protesters are not ready to endorse solidarity with Palestinians, their protest will remain limited to saving the appearances.

With the new Netanyahu government, the anti-Palestinian violence (the pogrom in Huwara, the attacks on the Stella Maris Monastery in Haifa, etc.) is no longer even formally condemned by the state. The fate of Itamar Ben-Gvir is the clearest indicator of this shift. Before entering politics, Ben-Gvir was known to have a portrait in his living room of

Israeli-American terrorist Baruch Goldstein, who in 1994 massacred twenty-nine Palestinian Muslim worshipers and wounded 125 others in Hebron, in what became known as the Cave of the Patriarchs massacre. He entered politics by joining the youth movement of the Kach and Kahane Chai party, which was designated as a terrorist organization and outlawed by the Israeli government itself. When he came of age for conscription into the Israel Defense Forces at eighteen, he was barred from service due to his extreme-right political background. And such a person condemned by Israel itself as a racist and terrorist is now the Minister for National Security who should safeguard the rule of law . . .

The State of Israel which likes to present itself as the only democracy in the Middle East now de facto morphed into a "halachic theocratic state (the equivalent to Shari'a law)."[23] This shift is not just a secondary degeneration of the original vision since it indicates a fatal flaw in the original vision itself. (A further twist in this story is that most of today's messianic Zionists are not even really religious: they remain secularists brutally and cynically using religion as an instrument in the struggle for power.) In Lacanian terms, the obscene violence is the surplus-enjoyment which we gain as a reward for our subordination to an ideological edifice, for the sacrifices and renunciations this edifice demands from us. In today's Israel (as in Manipur) this surplus-enjoyment no longer dwells in the obscene underground, it is openly assumed:

> the surplus-enjoyment as (killing Palestinians, burning their homes, evicting them from their homes, confiscating their lands, building settlements, destroying their olive trees, Judaizing Al-Aqsa, etc.) becomes explicitly articulated. While these forms of surplus enjoyment were previously viewed as an exception in official Zionist discourse, they are now considered as the norm.[24]

By designating the Israeli Jews as somehow "degenerate," did we not regress to the worst kind of anti-Semitism? Not at all: the Jews who support the ongoing trend effectively are degenerate *in exactly the same sense as we all are*. By acting as they do on the West Bank, they lose any superior status and become just one among the fundamentalist nation-states. Another name for this degeneracy is ideology: a symbolic edifice sustained by obscene surplus-enjoyment. But why use this provocative term? A reference to the use of the term "degeneracy" in quantum mechanics may be of some help: in quantum mechanics, "degeneracy" refers to the fact that "two or more stationary states of the same quantum-mechanical system may have the same energy even though their wave functions are not the same. In this case the common energy level of the stationary states is degenerate."[25]

> Imagine you're shown two identical objects and then asked to close your eyes. When you open your eyes, you see the same two objects in the same position. How can you determine if they have been swapped back and forth? Intuition and the laws of quantum mechanics agree: If the objects are truly identical, there is no way to tell. But for a special type of anyons (particles that occur in two-dimensional space having characteristics of both fermions and bosons), quantum mechanics allows for something quite different. Anyons are indistinguishable from one another, but some (non-Abelian) anyons have a special property that causes observable differences in the shared quantum state under exchange, making it possible to tell when they have been exchanged, despite being fully indistinguishable from one another.[26]

("Abelian" refers to Niels Abel, a Norwegian mathematician from the early nineteenth century.) It is easy to see how the non-Abelian anyons open a new path for quantum computation: when we swap particles around one another like strings are swapped around one another to create braids, the virtual braid that forms the quantum background of two particles can contain much more information than just two particles which are indistinguishable in their actual presence. But what matters to us here is the fact that the obscene underground of ideology is "degenerated" in a similar way. procedures which are in themselves indistinguishable (ethnic violence, torture, rapes, denial of the human dignity of the "enemy," etc.) are accompanied by a braid of different symbolic narratives. The task of the analysis is thus to recognize the same "energy" – libido, libidinal investment – in Muslim fundamentalism, Zionism, Hinduism, Christian fundamentalism: obvious differences in their narratives should not blind us for this sameness.

Even when a country fights for its survival and is engaged in heroic self-defence, the Cause of freedom is as a rule contaminated by some kind of obscene racist and sexist background which spoils the purity of its struggle. Those of us who stand firmly behind Ukraine are often worried about the fatigue of the West: as the war now drags well into its second year, will not the countries which support Ukraine gradually get fed up by the permanent emergency state and the material sacrifices demanded of them? One should bear in mind that this fatigue is not simply caused by objective of exhaustion and rejection to continue to endure sacrifices: it is also clearly the result of the systematic propaganda spread by the unholy alliance of the extreme Right and the extreme Left. This propaganda operates at three distinguished levels of argumentation: abstract pacifism (we need peace, suffering has to stop at any cost), a "balanced" view of the war (Ukraine and NATO were also provoking Russia and forced it to counter-attack), egotist protection of our own welfare (why give billions to Ukraine, a corrupted country run by oligarchs, when we have more than enough of our own problems – new forms of poverty, etc.). The paradox of this mixture is that what presents itself as a principled stance – peace at any price – is a mask for the worst ethnic egotism and ignorance of the other's suffering: are we aware that, although Ukraine defended its independence, it has already lost close to half of its population (ten million emigrated to the West, Ukrainians in the occupied part are exposed to brutal russification).

However, a much more serious case is that of Ukraine itself where signs of fatigue are gradually multiplying. It is already close to a miracle that the majority retains their will to fight after a year and a half of fierce battles, with no ending in sight. But here also fatigue is not just objective: it is fed by the serious ideological and political mistakes by the Ukrainians themselves. What the Ukrainians can and should do is clear – the main medicine against the war fatigue is *justice in Ukraine*: no privileges for the oligarchs and other higher strata. Is there anything more demoralizing than to see ordinary Ukrainians fight while many of the rich emigrated and organized for their sons to be exempted from military service? A good sign pointing in this direction was that, on July 25 2023, Zelensky

> has warned government officials and lawmakers that 'personal enrichment' and 'betrayal' will not be tolerated, after the arrest of a military recruitment chief on embezzlement charges and an MP accused of collaborating with Russia. His comments came after the arrest of Yevhen Borysov, head of the military recruitment office in Odesa, by Ukraine's State Bureau of Investigation (SBI) and

Prosecutor General's Office. The National Agency for the Prevention of Corruption said he had illegally acquired more than $5mn through elaborate business schemes.[27]

It was discovered that, after the beginning of the war, Borysov discreetly bought a series of luxury properties in France and Spain . . . And obviously this phenomenon is universal: on August 11 2023, Zelensky announced that the heads of *all* Ukraine's regional military recruitment centres were being dismissed from their jobs amid concerns about corruption.[28] However, while the need for the fight against corruption is obvious, another point is no less important. To avoid collapse in the ongoing war, a truly united front against the common enemy is needed. Lately signs are multiplying of a very worrying phenomenon: many Leftists and non-nationalist liberals in Ukraine are ready to fight against Russia – they volunteered and are now on the frontline. (One of them who likes my work sent me the photo of his machine gun lying on the two Ukrainian translations of my work which he reads in the pause between battles – needless to say this photo made me quite proud.) Since these Leftists resist aggressive conservative nationalism with its crazy counter-productive measures (recall just the prohibition to perform publicly the works of all Russian composers), they are as a rule side-lined by the authorities and often even suspected of Russian sympathies, as if Putin, the hero of the European and US Right, somehow still stands for Socialism . . .

Suffice it to mention the great Ukrainian documentary film-maker Sergei Loznitsa, the internationally-acknowledged author of films like *Maidan* and *Donbass*. Loznitsa now lives in Lithuania and cannot return to Ukraine: he learned that, since he is not yet sixty years old (the limit age for conscription), his passport will be confiscated if he returns home. Other internationally-known artists can travel abroad freely, so we are dealing here with a clear case of revenge by conservative cultural bureaucrats. I know this disgusting strategy from my own past: in Slovenia also, the Nationalist Rightists always castigated secular Leftist opponents of the Communist regime as suspicious masked agents of the old Communists. In the 1970s, I was never allowed to teach and for years was unemployed, while I am now regularly attacked as a "man of the old regime" . . .

Not surprisingly, anti-feminism also enters the scene here. In Ukraine many women also joined the armed forces and fight on the front – some of them are known as excellent snipers. Unfortunately, many of them now "express anger at stigma and treatment by male colleagues and say complaints are being ignored"[29]: they have to fight at two fronts, against the Russian enemy and against harassment from their own masculine colleagues. One should generalize this situation: Ukraine itself is fighting at two fronts: against Russian aggression and for what Ukraine will be after the war. If (hopefully) Ukraine survives, will it be a nationalist fundamentalist country like Poland and Hungary? Will it be a de facto colony of global capitalism, or . . .?

It is totally wrong to claim that all these question will be resolved after the war, and that now it's the time for unconditional unity, not for democratic debates. The problematic measures are those which NOW undermine this unity, weaken Ukraine's defence and put in place social practices which will define how Ukraine will look after the war. So NOW is the time for a non-exclusive unity: only a wide popular front in which there is a place for everyone – from LGBT+ individuals to the Leftists who opposes the Russian aggression – can save Ukraine.

A Leftist Plea for Law and Order

The implications of these paradoxes are clearly discernible in two events which attracted the public attention at the end of June 2023: the failed military coup in Russia and the explosion of violent protests in France. While our media cover both events in detail, what passes unnoticed is a feature they share. Let's begin with the French protests. After a seventeen-year-old boy – identified as Nahel M – was shot dead by a police officer on Tuesday, June 27 2023, chaos exploded in France, with initial protesting descending into looting and arson. Rioters have erected barricades, lit fires and shot fireworks at police, who responded with tear gas, water cannons and stun grenades. However, the events took a much more ominous turn when the police began to act as an autonomous agent, posing a threat even to the government – they said

> they were "at war" with "savage hordes" of rioters and two of the top unions representing officers threatened to revolt unless President Emmanuel Macron stepped in. "Today the police are in combat

because we are at war. Tomorrow we will enter resistance and the government should be aware of this."[30]

These statements announce nothing less than a crack in the state power edifice: in a reaction to the popular protests, the hard-liners in the police threaten to act on their own against the state power. In other words, this threat to act outside the scope of state authority means that the French police announced its intention to act as a vigilante group, again following a trend which is today widespread in the so-called Third World countries. In Haiti, private vigilantes are killing hundreds of suspected gang members because of police inefficiency, giving place to calls from Haiti and abroad for a foreign military intervention to restore minimal civic order:

> Gun-toting gangsters have been robbing, raping and murdering the innocent. Weak or corrupt police and officials have done little, or worse. Now, the people are taking action and a wave of brutal vigilante justice is roiling Haiti, concentrated in this capital of about 1 million. The vigilantes close off neighborhoods. They stone and often chop the limbs of suspected gangsters, behead them and set them afire, sometimes while they are still alive.[31]

We are not yet there in France, but the first step in that direction is taken. (One should note that police acting as a vigilante group is the obverse of police not doing anything, just helplessly observing crimes being committed: in both cases, the police is prevented to act against crime as a legal force, as a state apparatus.) And in Russia they made more than the first step in this direction: the failed Prigozhin coup did not, as expected, reassert the state monopoly over violence; on the contrary, on Friday July 14 2023 the official Kremlin said

> it is considering granting legal status to some of the more than two dozen private military companies active in Russia. Legally, these shadow paramilitary groups do not exist – which allows them to operate parallel to Russia's armed forces, at times doing high-risk "dirty" jobs for the army while giving Moscow a measure of deniability.[32]

We should always bear in mind that the path to this direction was opened by neoliberalism – as some perspicuous observers noticed, perhaps the most dangerous tendency of neoliberalism was privatization of spheres and activities which, in the previous stage of "normal" democratic capitalism, remained an exclusive domain of the state. Let's take what I consider the most obscene case: the privatization of prisons. Since a state has to have a monopoly on physical coercion, the very notion to delegate the running of prisons to a private company which, obviously, does it for profit and not to meet justice, runs against the notion of the rule of law. The same goes for education: there has to be a minimum of education equally imparted to all citizens, "regardless of their power and wealth differentials":

> Because the state declared certain areas off-limits for private contracting – leaving them impervious to calculations of utility – a modicum of dignity could be enjoyed by all citizens, in the workplace and beyond it, regardless of their power and wealth differentials. In subjecting the state to utility and efficiency-maximizing imperatives, neoliberalism once again opens it up to private contracting.[33]

It is only such a universally-shared common space that sustains "a modicum of dignity enjoyed by all citizens" – and this space is under threat today, especially by the vast domains of privatized commons. Although the idea that we are entering a kind of neo-feudalism is problematic, the theorists who advocate it are right to point out that arguably the greatest threat to the common space are today big digital corporations like Google which privatize important aspects of this space – once in it, we move in a privatized feudal space.

The predictable Leftist narrative is here, of course, that the French police is racially biased (Nahel's murder was totally unjustified), French *egalite* is a fake, young immigrants violently protest because they don't see any future ahead, so the way to solve this problem is not more police oppression but a radical change of the French society itself, the elimination of its de facto racism. Subterranean anger was accumulating for long years, and Nahel's death just made it explode openly – violent protests are a desperate reaction to a problem, not the problem, and has to attack the problem at its roots . . .

There is a profound truth in this narrative: already when the first wave of protests exploded in 2015, analyses brought out the thick network of prejudices and exclusions that determine the daily life in immigrant youth; precise and very realist proposals were made on how to ameliorate the situation, but nothing came out of it . . . However, this truth is maybe too profound: while true in an abstract sense, I find it problematic on multiple accounts. The targeting of local buses by the protesters, so crucial in transporting workers from the low-income suburbs on the edge of Paris,[34] indicates two things: the riots aimed at destroying the infrastructure that sustains the daily lives of the ordinary people, and their victims were the poor, not the rich.

Public protests and uprising definitely can play a positive role if they are sustained by an emancipatory vision – suffice it to remember the Maidan event in Ukraine (which was an authentic social explosion, far from a CIA-organized plot) and the ongoing Iranian protests triggered by Kurdish women who refused to wear burka. Even the threats of violent action is sometimes necessary: our media like to mention as the two successful negotiated solutions the rise of the ANC to power in South Africa and the peaceful protests led by Martin Luther King in the US – in both cases, it is obvious that the (relative) victory occurred because the establishment feared the violent resistance (from the more radical wing of ANC as well as of the American Blacks). In short, negotiations succeeded because of this ominous threat . . . This, however, is decidedly NOT the case now in France: if law and order are not promptly restored, the final outcome may well be Marine Le Pen as the new president.

Is there a Russian version of Le Pen? No, since Le Pen is already in power there. It is difficult to miss the comic nature of Prigozhin's march on Moscow. It was over in 36 hours, and a deal was made: Prigozhin avoided legal trial, but has to withdraw his troops from Ukraine and go to Belarus. We don't know enough to say what really happened: was his march really meant as a full attack with the goal to occupy Moscow, or was it an empty threat, a gesture not meant to be fully realized, as Prigozhin himself later vindicated ("We felt that demonstrating what we were going to do was sufficient."[35])? So who is worst here? One cannot but repeat yet again Stalin's answer from the late 1920s to a journalist's question about which deviation is worse, Rightist or Leftist: they are both worst. Prigozhin's brutal excesses do not make Putin a more reasonable agent who tries to contain military extremists. Prigozhin admitted that Ukrainians fight well and that Zelensky is a good leader. He is right in accusing the Russian army and elite of corruption and inefficiency, so no wonder he was cheered in Rostov.

So what is the difference between the two? To find a parallel, we have to reach back to Nazism: Prigozhin versus Putin is like SA versus SS. SA were the brutal "honest" Fascists, so Hitler had to sacrifice them if he wanted to be accepted by the establishment of the army and the big capital. Likewise, Putin has to balance between different factions of his insiders elite – a process which takes place in a non-transparent way, totally outside the public space. The fact that the Russian state needed a private army like Wagner Group is in itself the clear sign of a failed state. Today failed states are not found only in the Third World, from Somalia to Pakistan, with South Africa approaching this abyss. If we measure a failed state by the cracks in the state power edifice, the atmosphere of ideological civil war, and the growing insecurity of public spaces, we should add to the list Russia, France, the US (with downtowns in decay), and with the signs of such a decay in the UK (gangs threatening public spaces in London suburbs . . .). The fact that many sidewalks in front of the expensive stores in the rich San Francisco downtown are covered by lines of the cheap tents in which the homeless dwell tells a lot. Language in its contingency (what Lacan calls *lalangue*) sometimes produces wonders – for example, "kkotjebi" is a North Korean term for homeless people, and in everyday Slovene (borrowing from Serb), this word sounds uncannily close to "ko te jebe" (pronounced "ko te yebe"), which means "who /the hell/ is fucking you," i.e., an aggressive stance of indifference. Homeless people are our "kkotjebi": their numbers are growing all around, up to the downtown San Francisco full of their tents, and in spite of our feigned compassion we don't give a damn for them. In this situation, the Left has to gather the courage to fully assume the slogan of law and order as its own.[36]

One of the most depressing facts in recent history is that the only case of a violent revolutionary crowd invading the seat of power took place on January 6 2021 when Trump's supporters broke into the US Capitol in Washington D.C. They viewed the election as illegitimate, a theft organized by corporate elites (they were right up to a point!). Left-liberals reacted with a mix of fascination and horror. Some of my Leftist friends cried, saying: "WE should be doing something like this!" There was a bit of envy in their condemnation of "ordinary" people breaking into the sacred seat of power, creating a carnival that momentarily suspended our rules for public life. Does this mean that the populist Right stole the Left's resistance to the existing system through a popular attack on the seat of power? Is our only choice between parliamentary elections controlled by corrupted elites or uprisings controlled by populist Right? No wonder Steve Bannon, the ideologist of the new populist Right, openly declares himself as the "Leninist for the twenty-first century": "I'm a Leninist. Lenin . . . wanted to destroy the state, and that's my goal too. I want to bring everything crashing down, and destroy all of today's establishment."[37] And no wonder that, while the populist Right was ecstatic about the violent uprising, the liberal Left was acting like a good old conservative and complained: "Where is the police, where is the National Guard to crush the rebellion?" Although, of course, this is not the true answer, there are moments when it is a necessary one. But the Right got its lesson back: after it penetrated the Congress building, it found there no mysterious centre of power – basically, it found nothing. True power resides elsewhere, in the complex network of state coercion and ideological apparatuses.

Consequently, we shouldn't be afraid to add to the tasks of the Left the care for the safety of the daily life of many ordinary people: there are clear signs of the growing decay of public manners, of youthful gangs terrorizing public places, from bus and train stations to shopping malls. Just to mention this decay is often dismissed as yet another Rightist obsession directed at immigrants, and the standard reaction is that we have to look at the "deeper social roots" of such phenomena (unemployment, racism . . .). However, if we act like this, we are conceding to the enemy an important domain of dissatisfaction that pushes many to the Right. Everyday insecurity hurts the poor much more than the rich who live calmly in their gated communities.

Therein resides the lesson of a very depressing thing that happened to me in July 2023 in London: at a public debate at BBK Summer School, a Black woman from South Africa, an old ANC activist, said that the predominant stance among the poor black majority is now more and more a nostalgia for apartheid – their standard of living was, if anything, a little bit higher than now, and there were safety and security (South Africa was a police state, after all), while today poverty is supplemented by an explosion of violence and insecurity. If a white person were to say this, one would be, of course, immediately accused of racism – but we should nonetheless take the risk and *think* about it. If we don't do it, the new Right will do it for us (as they are already doing it in South Africa).

The long series of cases we listed will undoubtedly be soon supplemented by other, probably even more terrifying, ones. But we have to deal with them again and again because they are fragments which, put together, provide a mosaic of global catastrophe. Here is the last important stone in this mosaic. Everybody who pretends to be a Leftist today has to analyse closely Oliver Anthony's "Rich Men North of Richmond," a working-class protest song which in two days exploded into "the protest song of our generation"[38] with tens of millions of viewers and listeners. The word "authentic" regularly occurs in positive reactions to the song: there are no special effects, it is just a voice and a guitar of a simple worker recorded on a real camera . . . We get here the direct raw voice of those ignored by the big media: poor working men, barely surviving, with no clear prospect for a better life. Here are (most of) the lyrics:

> I've been sellin' my soul, workin' all day / Overtime hours for bullshit pay / So I can sit out here and waste my life away / Drag back home and drown my troubles away // It's a damn shame what the world's gotten to / For people like me and people like you / Wish I could just wake up and it not be true / But it is, oh, it is // Livin' in the new world / With an old soul / These rich men north of Richmond / Lord knows they all just wanna have total control / Wanna know what you think, wanna know what you do / And they don't think you know, but I know that you do / 'Cause your dollar ain't shit and it's taxed to no end / 'Cause of rich men north of Richmond // I wish politicians would look out for miners / And not just minors on an island somewhere / Lord, we got folks in the street, ain't got nothin' to eat / And the obese milkin' welfare // Well, God, if you're 5-foot-3 and you're 300 pounds / Taxes ought not to pay for your bags of fudge rounds / Young men are puttin' themselves six feet in the ground / 'Cause all this damn country does is keep on kickin' them down[39]

There is an obvious truth in these words: yes, millions work while the rich exploit them; yes, big corporations and government agencies exert a frightening power of control over us . . . But the details of the song point towards the disturbing background of this truth – and details matter here. Why "north of Richmond"? Because Richmond was the capital of the Confederacy during the Civil War – a clear hint at where Anthony's political sympathies lie. Why fudge rounds? Because this term has a double meaning: (1)fudgy round chocolate cookies, sandwiched together with chocolate buttercream; (2) when engaged in anal sex, a female loses control of her bowels, leaving a circular imprint around the base of the male's genitalia – again, a hint at the link between the new rich and sexual perversions. Who are the "obese" rich men living comfortably by way of overtaxing ordinary working people? They are at the same time the new corporate elites controlling us and the lazy (racial, sexual . . .) minorities getting fat from the generous donations provided by the welfare state.

One should locate into this series of Rightist low-class protests also *The Sound of Freedom* (Alejandro Monteverde, 2023), a movie based on a true story of a former government agent turned vigilante who embarks on a dangerous mission to rescue hundreds of children from sex traffickers in Latin America. Most of the big liberal media dismissed this surprise low-budget hit (it surpassed at the box office the new *Indiana Jones* and *Mission Impossible* movies) due to the proximity of the director and actor (Jim Caviezel) to QAnon conspiracy theories. It is also weird that, in the film, some children are sold as sex slaves to the FARC movement leaders in Colombia – sex slavery is thus portrayed as a feature which unites the corporate elite of Hollywood and the extreme revolutionary Left . . . But child trafficking and sex slavery *are* a horrible thing, and it is all too easy to leave it to the new populist Right, while the Hollywood mainstream is occupied by the woke projects like the remake of *Snow White* in which Show White is not white, dwarves are not dwarves but "diverse" people, and the ending is not the old one (with the prince awakening Snow White with a kiss) but the empowerment of Snow White who will became a new legitimate ruler . . . The sad thing about *The Sound of Freedom* is that we have a modest movie produced outside of the big Hollywood machine which deals with sex crimes against children from poor Latino families and is a surprising box-office hit, but was *made by Rightists.*

The new wave of Rightist working-class protests and the "protect-the-minorities" corporate liberalism are not simply opposites: what they share is that they both avoid confronting the basic social antagonisms that characterize our era. While the Rightist working-class protests address actual problems that haunt many ordinary workers, they portray the enemy as the "rich," the corporate and state elites, in conjunction with the lazy recipients of the welfare help – the struggle against racism and sexism is thus dismissed as the strategy of the elites to control workers and the productive capital. We get here the old Fascist idea of uniting workers and productive capital against the parasitic extremes of the elites and the lazy welfare-state recipients . . . These protests are a reaction to what is false in today's liberal Left which deftly manipulates the fight against sexism and racism and for the rights of minorities in order to avoid confronting the perverted logic of global capitalism.

A protest may be authentic, but authenticity is not in itself a sign of truth – even a most brutal form of racism and sexism can also be experienced as an authentic feeling. At the end of July 2023, my own country – Slovenia – was for a brief moment in global news: it was hit by floods and landslides, with thousands of homes destroyed and whole towns cut off. The reaction was an unexpected show of solidarity: Slovenes offered too much help and too many volunteers, so that all of it couldn't be used, and even Ukraine sent help . . . Although this show of solidarity was sincere, it was not yet what will be needed in the catastrophes that await us. For the large majority in Slovenia life went on as normal, and the display of solidarity just allowed us to feel good without in any way changing our way of life. For a moment, we acted as if the pursuit of comfortable daily life is not all, our moderate sacrifices made us feel that life gained meaning. The display of solidarity was thus the expression of a desperate wish NOT to confront the depth of our crisis.

Back to Anthony's song, the first simple counter-question of the Left to its words should be: OK, poor working people are exploited – so why doesn't the song mention the standard solution: UNIONIZE? Old working-class protest songs, from "Joe Hill" and Pete Seeger's "Solidarity Forever" to Billy Bragg's "There is Power in a Union" all point in this direction. As for American patriotism, how far is Anthony's song from the great Leftist working-class protest song, Bruce Springsteen's "Born in the U.S.A."! Here are its first lines: "Born down in a dead man's town / The first kick I took was when I hit the ground / You end up like a dog that's been beat too much / Till you spent half your life just covering up" – a similar experience of being downtrodden, but from a totally different political background.

One should not be amazed if Anthony's song will be praised by billionaires from Elon Musk to Donald Trump, the rich man from Mar-a-Lago who, by means of complex legal tricks, for years avoided paying taxes. Warren Buffet, one of the richest men in the world, was shocked to discover that he is paying less taxes than his secretary – no wonder that, when President Obama was accused of irresponsibily introducing "class warfare" into political life, Buffett snapped back: "There's class warfare, all right, but it's my class, the rich class, that's making war, and we're winning."[40] And what we are getting in Anthony's song is the ultimate triumph of the rich in the class warfare: even a downtrodden proletarian struggling for social justice takes their side.

If we really want to cope with this catastrophe, the first step to make is to fully assume a series of insights which, self-evident as they are, we prefer to flout. There will be unimaginable ecological catastrophes, dozens of millions of humans will die. There will be massive movements of populations which will cause additional suffering and deaths. Artificial Intelligence will dominate us in a non-transparent way, its human creators themselves will not grasp what is going on. The large majority of humans will never fully awaken to the crisis, they will again and again invent fictions (even fictions of a catastrophe) that will enable them to go on as usual. In short, we can rely neither on the spontaneous wisdom of the majority nor on the knowledge of scientific experts who will solve our big crises the way they neutralized the threat of AIDS. The political model of liberal democracy is obviously exhausted, and there are two alternate options which imply their own deadlocks. One is the notion of state as a de-politicized machine serving social needs (think of countries like Switzerland or Singapore where a large majority even doesn't know who is their prime or foreign minister) – but if there is a lesson to be learned from the last decade, it is that the repressed political dimension returns with a vengeance in the guise of the new Rightist populisms. Then there is the so-called (by some) Asiatic model of a benevolent dictatorship which enforces a basic homogeneity and serves the interests of the majority better than a state power exposed to political conflicts (Singapore again, even China) . . . In short, there is no future for us (if, by future, we understand a further progress in human history within the coordinates determined by our past).

Does this mean that all of humanity is caught in a weird death drive, involuntarily sliding towards self-obliteration? This conclusion is to be avoided for two reasons. First, what we are dealing with is not a collective psychic phenomenon but a social process grounded in the predominant mode of production. Second, in a crucial dialectical unity, the Freudian notion of death drive does not designate a morbid thrust towards self-obliteration but almost its opposite, libido as something that insists beyond the cycle of life and death. Death drive is Freud's name for immortality, for undeadness. Therein resides the gist of the Hegelian notion of "tarrying with the negative" which Lacan rendered in his idea of the deep connection between death drive and creative sublimation: in order for (symbolic) creation to take place, the death drive (the Hegelian self-relating absolute negativity) has to accomplish its work of, precisely, emptying the place and thus making it ready for creation.[41] The Christian name for this emptying is the death of God on the Cross which condemns us, humans, to freedom deprived of any guarantee in the big Other, and the creative act grounded in this harsh freedom is the Holy Ghost, the first figure of what, among other names, later was known as the Communist Party.

The inference that imposes itself is evident: in contrast to the "evident" truths of the critics of Freud, it is only today that the time of psychoanalysis has arrived. The memorial service is a little bit too hasty, commemorating a patient who still has a long life ahead – psychoanalysis may be dead, but it is a monstrous living dead which cannot be disposed of. This undeadness does not only characterize the fate of the psychoanalytic theory, it is also its key feature. How this undeadness penetrates and sustains political struggle is perhaps best rendered by *Twelve*, a 1918 poem by Aleksandr Blok, one of the great Russian poets of the twentieth century who considered it his best work.

With its mood-creating sounds, polyphonic rhythms and harsh, slangy language, the long (around 1,000 verses) poem promptly alienated Blok from a mass of his admirers – accusations ranged from appallingly bad taste to servility before the new Bolshevik authorities and betraying his former ideals. But even the opposite side (most Bolsheviks) scorned Blok's mysticism and asceticism and especially the mention of Christ (some Soviet reprints even replaced "Christ" by "sun"!). The poem describes the march of twelve Red Guards (likened to the Twelve Apostles) through the streets of revolutionary Petrograd in the snowy winter of 1918, with a fierce winter blizzard raging around them. The Twelve are not idealized, their mood as conveyed by the poem oscillates from base and even sadistic aggression towards everything perceived bourgeois and counter-revolutionary, to strict discipline and sense of revolutionary duty.[42] In the (most controversial) last stanza of the poem, a figure of Jesus Christ is seen in the snowstorm, heading the march of the Twelve as the invisible and undead thirteenth passenger, we might say:

. . . And so they keep a martial pace, / Behind them follows the hungry dog, / Ahead of them — with bloody banner, / Unseen within the blizzard's swirl, / Safe from any bullet's harm, / With gentle step, above the storm, / In the scattered, pearl-like snow, / Crowned with a wreath of roses white, / Ahead of them — goes Jesus Christ.[43]

(An alternate translation of the last lines: "Soft-footed in the blizzard's swirl, / Invulnerable where bullets sliced — / Crowned with a crown of snowflake pearl, / In a wreath of white rose, / Ahead of them Christ Jesus goes."[44]) John Ellison's description of its social impact is worth quoting:

The poem first appeared in early March 1918 in a Bolshevik newspaper. Jack Lindsay wrote in his introduction to his own translation that it had 'an immediate and vast effect. Phrases from it were endlessly repeated; hoardings and banners all over Russia bore extracts'. It became 'the folklore of the revolutionary street'. In November 1918 *The Twelve* was published in its own right in Petrograd, adorned with Yuri Annenkov's drawings. Forsyth states simply that it 'became accepted as the essential expression of the Revolution, not only in Russia, where readers were either excited or disgusted by it, but also abroad'.[45]

Unfortunately, Blok was quickly disappointed by the Bolshevik Revolution, and his last work before his early death in 1921 was a patriotic poem "Scythians" which advocates a kind of "pan-Mongolism," a clear precursor to today's Eurasianism: Russia should mediate between East and West, but also politically between the Reds and the Whites. Already in its style, "Scythians" returns to more traditional poetic language with no common vulgar sounds and expressions, and no crazy rhythmic cuts – with none of what makes *Twelve* so unique. In *Twelve*, we get a unique series of overlapping of the opposites: the poem praises the October Revolution, but it is as far as possible from the usual revolutionary pathetic, full of vulgar low-class language and course gestures. Christ at the head of the group which patrols the Petrograd hell of natural and public chaos – let us not forget that their goal is to prevent social chaos, i.e., to maintain the new law and order. This is an authentic image of the theologico-political short-circuit, an image of what Christian Atheism means as a political practice. Christ is not their leader, he is just a virtual shadow whose presence signals that the twelve are not just a group of individuals pursuing their particular interests but a group of comrades acting on behalf of a Cause. There is no promise or image of heavenly bliss in this image, it is just a group of comrades acting out of utter emergency, without any assurance of what the final outcome will be – maybe they will be liquidated by the enemy, or they will simply perish in the blizzard. Even if they are not aware of it, they *act* in their utter dedication as if Christ is at their head. Even in our "developed" West, we recently encountered such groups which were inspecting locked-down areas for the victims of the pandemic, or looking for abandoned survivors of flooding and heat waves, or – why not – patrolling an area and searching for Russian mines on the Ukrainian front. And the list goes on: a group of artists engaged in a collective project, a group of programmers working on an algorithm that may help in our struggle for the environment . . . Without thinking about it, they were and are just doing their duty.

The subjective stance of the members of such a group was as far as possible from Politically Correct concerns and suspicions, they were totally foreign to the collective spirit that motivated the January 6 Trumpian mob which attacked the Congress building (a mob just performing a media spectacle), they left behind any traces of liberal individualism. They were in hell, with no God to protect them, and Christ was there.

NOTES

Introduction

1 This is the problem Juergen Habermas struggles with in his two thick volumes *Auch eine Geschichte der Philosophie* (Frankfurt: Suhrkamp 2019) which offers a detailed historical genealogy of postmetaphysical thought from the perspective of the relationship between faith and knowledge: the origin of (his own) universalist and proceduralist position resides in the path where the theological reflection was indispensable, which is why religious discourse can still provide a valid contribution in a secular context. The book was criticized for its Eurocentrism, since it focuses on the Judeo-Christian tradition; while I don't see this feature as a limitation, I consider my position simultaneously more atheist and more religious than that of Habermas: Habermas seems to describe precisely the passage from actual religious belief to its survival as an idea(l) that should regulate our lives.

2 See Adorno / Gehlen: Ist die Soziologie eine Wissenschaft vom Menschen? – YouTube.

3 In the past decades, I've dealt with the topic of Christian atheism in three books which propose a materialist reading of Christianity: *The Fragile Absolute* (London: Verso Books 2000), *On Belief* (London: Routledge 2001), *The Puppet and the Dwarf* (Cambridge: MIT Press 2003), as well as in *The Monstrosity of Christ* (a dialogue with John Millbank, Cambridge: MIT Press 2011). These four books form a quartet in which a certain line of thought is brought to the end; with *Christian Atheism*, I make a new beginning and move to a different focus (the link between the transcendental parallax and the ontological incompleteness of reality), which is why I ignore the first quartet.

4 All Milner quotes are from Jean-Claude Milner, "On Some Paradoxes of Social Analysis," *Crisis & Critique* Volume 10, issue 1 (2023), p. 243–5.

5 See Remi Adekoya's outstanding *It's Not About Whiteness, It's About Wealth* (London: Constable 2023). Among the black studies which problematize the woke stereotypes, Adekoya's book is one of the rare

which correctly grounds "racist prejudices" in wealth differences (drawing attention to the different notions of "corruption" in the allegedly "egalitarian" West and in Africa), and warns against the ambiguity of the "feminization" of power in the developed West (which can also serve to render invisible new forms of colonization).

6 Utah primary schools ban Bible for 'vulgarity and violence' – BBC News.

7 See https://www.thecut.com/2018/10/tarana-burke-me-too-founder-movement-has-lost-its-way.html.

8 What would the young Slavoj Žižek think of the old Slavoj Žižek? – Mark Carrigan.

9 This already happened to me in India more than a decade ago: in a public debate, I praised Ambedkar, a critic of Gandhi, for his egalitarianism and rejection of the caste system, and I was told that the caste system is a key part of Indian tradition that eludes the Western egalitarian notion of emancipation.

10 (DOC) Pacifist Pluralism versus Militant Truth: Christianity at the Service of Revolution in the work of Slavoj Žižek | Haralambos Ventis – Academia.edu.

11 Rising antisemitism focus at European Jewish Association conference – JNS.org.

12 Intersectionality – Wikipedia.

13 https://www.spiegel.de/politik/deutschland/michael-wolffsohn-und-michael-naumann-im-streitgespraech-wer-antisemit-ist-bestimmt-der-jude-a-00000000-0002-0001-0000-000174544040.

14 Downloaded from Roger Hayward Undecidable Monument – Impossible trident – Wikipedia_files.

15 See europeapatient.com.

16 The hard right and climate catastrophe are intimately linked (msn.com). We get here a nice case of metaphoric displacement: flood as the result of global warming is repressed and replaced by the "flood" of immigrants.

17 Op. cit.

18 Op. cit.

19 See Churchill, Hitler and the Unnecessary War – Wikipedia.

20 No, Capitalism Isn't Democratic (msn.com).

21 Personal communication.

Chapter 1

1 Jure Simoniti, personal communication.

2 https://monoskop.org/images/f/Lacan_Jacques_Television_A_Challenge_ to_the_Psychoanalytic_Establishment.

3 A case of the so-called "Spanish Flu" provides a case of how truth can be disclosed by a lie. It killed around 20 million people at the end of the First World War, but its name is a misnomer: because of censorship, only Spanish newspapers reported on it (Spain was neutral during the First World War), although it did not affect Spain. However, if one knew this fact, one gets the truth about the conditions of censorship in the society of that time: although millions must have talked about it, it was "cancelled" from the public space.

4 I quote from the manuscript generously made available to me by the authors.

5 Since I've already elaborated how I relate to Johnston's transcendental materialism in my *Freedom* book, I'll focus here on Chiesa's agnostic atheism.

6 The oscillation immanent to Hegel's work is the one between his creative works (*Phenomenology*, *Logic*) and his university manuals (*Encyclopaedia*, *Philosophy of Right*) written as a report on already-acquired knowledge. However, it would be all too fast to read this oscillation as the one between truer authentic creative thought and the "dogmatic" recapitulation of a dogma.

7 Frank B. Wilderson III, *Red, White, and Black*, Durham: Duke University Press 2010.

8 Wilderson, p. 65–6.

9 Op. cit. p. 30–1.

10 Op. cit. p. 30.

11 Op. cit. p. 9.

12 Op. cit. p. 9.

13 Op. cit. p. 11.

14 Op. cit. p. 14

15 Op. cit. p. 16

16 Op. cit. p. 12.

17 Op. cit. p. 66.

18 In her "Desire" (unpublished manuscript).

19 Hegel's Philosophy of History (marxists.org).

20 Roberto Bolaño, *Last Evenings on Earth*, New York: New Directions 2006, p. 102. I owe this reference to Maria Aristodemou.

21 See Ted Lasso – Wikipedia.

22 Jean-Daniel Causse, *Lacan et le christianisme*, Paris: Campagne Prem 2018, p. 162.

23 Adrian Johnston, quoted from Chiesa/Johnston, *God Is Undead* (manuscript).

24 Jacques Lacan, *Le Seminaire XVI: D'un autre a l'Autre*, Paris: Editions du Seuil 2006, p. 253.

25 Lacan, *The Seminar of Jacques Lacan. Book XXIII*, p. 116.

26 ** Enjoy Your Forgiveness **. I owe this reference to Martti Paloheimo, New York.

27 Israel should 'erase' Palestinian village, minister says after settler rampage (nbcnews.com).

28 Tennessee Republican calls for lynching-style hangings in state executions (msn.com).

29 See Public drag performances restricted in Tennessee – ABC News (go.com).

30 See mannoni_i_know_very_well.pdf (warwick.ac.uk).

31 Alenka Zupančič, "Perverzni obrat utajitve" ("The Perverse Reversal of Disavowal"), *Problemi* 7–8 2022, Ljubljana.

32 Adrian Johnston, quoted from Chiesa/Johnston, *God Is Undead* (manuscript).

33 Johnston, op. cit.

34 Adrian Johnston, quoted from Chiesa/Johnston, *God Is Undead* (manuscript).

35 Snow White and Cinderella under attack from woke sensitivity readers | Books | Entertainment | Express.co.uk.

36 Chiesa, op. cit.

37 Chiesa, op. cit.

38 Chiesa, op. cit.

39 Chiesa, op. cit.

40 Chiesa, op. cit.

41 Le Séminaire de Jacques Lacan, Livre XV, session of February 21, 1968 (quoted from File:Seminaire 15.pdf – No Subject – Encyclopedia of Psychoanalysis – Encyclopedia of Lacanian Psychoanalysis).

42 The Night They Drove Old Dixie Down – Wikipedia.

43 I resume here my reading of the film from Chapter 8 of my *Disparities*, London: Bloomsbury Press 2016.

44 Lacan, *The Seminar of Jacques Lacan. Book X: Anxiety*, Cambridge: Polity Press 2016, p. 309.

45 Chiesa, op. cit.

46 Chiesa, op. cit.

47 Chiesa, op. cit.

48 Chiesa, op. cit.

49 G.W.F. Hegel, *Phenomenology of Spirit*, Oxford: Oxford University Press 1977, p. 21.

50 Hegel, op. cit., p. 103.

51 Why more people are seeking out "ego death" via psychedelic drugs. Salon.com.

52 There are also echoes of *The Prisoners* in Olivia Wilde's *Don't Worry Darling* (2022).

Chapter 2

1 Nagarjuna, ecophilosophy, & the practice of liberation (uvm.edu), and Nagarjuna, ecophilosophy, pt. 2 (uvm.edu).

2 See "On Being None With Nature: Nagarjuna and the Ecology of Emptiness". John Clark – Academia.edu.

3 Ivakhiv, op. cit.

4 Op. cit.

5 Clark, op. cit., p. 28.

6 Ivakhiv, op. cit.

7 Op. cit.

8 Zizek's Western Buddhism (Redux). And Now For Something Completely Different (wordpress.com).

9 Incidentally, I DID read Suzuki, not only in my youth (when he was a key point of reference of the hippie movement) but also later, when I learned that, in the 1930s and early 1940s, he fully supported the Japanese war against China and elaborated how a Zen training can make individuals much better soldiers.

10 Ivakhiv, op. cit.

11 Op. cit.

12 See *The Seminar of Jacques Lacan, Book II: The Ego in Freud's Theory and in the Technique of Psychoanalysis*, New York: Norton 1991, p. 48.

13 Quoted from Reproduction of Honey Bees (honeymell.com).

14 Lorenzo Chiesa and Adrian Johnston, *God Is Undead: Psychoanalysis Between Agnosticism and Atheism*, manuscript (manuscript). Quotes within the quote are from *The Seminar of Jacques Lacan. Book X: Anxiety*, Cambridge: Polity Press 2016, p. 226.

15 Buddhist_Economics.pdf (urbandharma.org).

16 Buddhist economics – Wikipedia.

17 Ethnic cleansing in the kingdom of happiness – Foreign Policy.

18 Inspirational Quotes About Happiness From Dalai Lama – Lifehack.

19 Relational Dharma: a Modern Paradigm of Transformation—A Liberating Model of Intersubjectivity – DocsLib.

20 Op. cit.

21 Op. cit.

22 Op. cit.

23 Bodhisattva – Wikipedia.

24 Ivakhiv, op. cit.

25 G.W.F. Hegel, "Jenaer Realphilosophie," in *Frühe politische Systeme*, Frankfurt: Ullstein 1974, p. 204; translation quoted from Donald Phillip Verene, *Hegel's Recollection*, Albany: Suny Press 1985, pp. 7–8.

26 G.W.F. Hegel, *Phenomenology of Spirit*, Oxford: Oxford University Press 1977, p. 19.

27 Karen Ng, *Hegel's Concept of Life*, Oxford: Oxford University Press 2020.

28 Jensen Suther — Back to Life? The Persistence of Hegel's Idealism (A Response to Karen Ng, Hegel's Concept of Life: Self-Consciousness, Freedom, Logic) (boundary 2).

29 Jordan Gray: Don't tell me what a woman is, based entirely on what she is not. The Independent.

30 Shamelessly copied from Wikipedia.

31 This is why the idea that Jesus was a Buddhist monk totally misses the logic of Christian sacrifice – see Jesus was a Buddhist Monk BBC Documentary – YouTube.

32 Jean-Daniel Causse, *Lacan et le christianisme*, Paris: Campagne Prem 2018, p. 162.

33 I condense here my reading of Tarkovsky from "Thing From Inner Space," *Angelaki* , Volume 4, Issue 3 (1999).

34 Soren Kierkegaard, *Works of Love*, London: Harper Books 1962, p. 355.

35 Soren Kierkegaard, *Training in Christianity*, Princeton: Princeton University Press 1972, p. 121.

36 Soren Kierkegaard, *Journals and Papers*, Bloomington: Indiana University Press 1970, entry 1608.

37 See Charles Maurice de Talleyrand-Périgord – Wikipedia.

38 See Thomas Metzinger, *Being No One: The Self-Model Theory of Subjectivity*, Cambridge (Ma): The MIT Press 2003.

39 Op. cit., p. 627.

40 Op. cit., p. 566.

41 Available online at http://thinkexist.com/quotes/neilgaiman.

42 Such jokes which unexpectedly take an asexual turn are much more effective than the usual "dirty" ones – here is another case. In the middle of freezing winter, a beautiful and recently widowed young woman desperately knocks on the door of a lone cabin where an old man lives alone. He lets her in after she explains that her car broke down nearby. She asks him for some hot tea, which he gives her. Then she asks for some warm dry clothes, which she also gets. Finally, she tells him: "You know what my dead husband did to me in such a situation? We both undressed and lied down together, so that I got properly warmed up . . ." The old man explodes back: "Now you ask too much! I did everything you asked me for, but I am not ready to go out to your husband's grave, dig his body out, warm it up and bring it to you!"

43 Roberto de la Puente, "Einverstanden mit Ruinen (Agree With Ruins)," paperblog, originally published December 11, 2012, https://de.paperblog.com/einverstanden-mit-ruinen-472883/

44 I am resuming here a line of thinking which is developed in detail in my philosophical books, especially *Less Than Nothing* and *Sex and the Failed Absolute*.

45 See Michel Foucault, *The History of Sexuality*, Vol. I, Harmondsworth: Penguin Books 1981.

46 Private conversation.

47 I condense here the line of argumentation from the Chapter 11 of my *Less Than Nothing*, London: Verso Books 2012.

Chapter 3

1 My gratitude to Robinson Erhardt who went through this chapter and suggested many changes to make it better.

2 I am well aware the some interpretations of quantum mechanics (like the Many Worlds interpretation) don't need the notion of collapse of the wave function. In this chapter I am concerned mainly with interpretations that retain wave function collapse and are not deterministic, since I consider the notion of collapse of the wave the crucial contribution of quantum physics to a new ontology.

3 I presuppose that everybody knows the storyline of *Casablanca*.

4 See Rick On Theater: 'Everybody Comes To Rick's'.

5 I am well aware that only certain interpretations of quantum mechanics (mostly those linked to Copenhagen orthodoxy) interpret "observer" as consciousness, and that many scientists try to explain the collapse of a wave function without an observer: they claim that observers play no role, and measurement can be better understood as mechanical intervention rather some more metaphysically charged idea of observation. (Decoherence is often mentioned here, although there is controversy as to whether it really solves the measurement problem.) My view is that one cannot translate observation into an objective process, so that the enigma remains.

6 See Lee Smolin, *Einstein's Unfinished Revolution*, London: Penguin Books 2019.

7 In quantum mechanics, complementarity means that objects have certain pairs of complementary properties (like position and momentum) which cannot all be observed or measured simultaneously. An example of such a pair is position and momentum. According to Niels Bohr (who introduced this notion), setting up an experiment to measure one quantity of a pair excludes the possibility of measuring the other, yet understanding both experiments is necessary to characterize the object under study.

8 But is this really Rovelli's position? What about his idea – we'll deal with it later – that "time is an effect of our overlooking of the physical microstates of things. Time is information we don't have. / Time is our ignorance."(Carlo Rovelli, *Reality Is Not What It Seems*, London: Penguin Books 2017, p. 222–3)

9 As a Hegelian I should note here that, although, in his late philosophy of nature, Hegel gives priority to space over time (time emerges out of the self-relating negation of space), in his earlier Jena-philosophy Hegel's position is more ambiguous.

10 Stephen Hawking and Leonard Mlodinow, *The Grand Design*, New York: Bantam 2010, p. 5.

11 Three scientists share Nobel Prize in Physics for work in quantum mechanics– YouTube.

12 In quantum mechanics, hidden-variable theories refer to proposals to provide explanations of quantum phenomena through the introduction of (possibly unobservable) hypothetical entities. The best-known case is that of Einstein according to whom, since universe is a deterministic whole, quantum indeterminacy means that quantum mechanics is an incomplete theory – it ignores yet unknown features which would explain reality in fully deterministic terms.

13 For a simple but concise report on this critical wave, see Adam Becker, *What Is Real?*, London: John Murray 2018.

14 See Counterfactual definiteness – Wikipedia.

15 See entropy-24-01380.pdf.

16 Again, I am well aware that to cover this gap is part of the purpose of the Many-Worlds interpretation, as the observer and measuring system are construed as part of the system – but I think the price to be paid for this solution is too high.

17 Quoted from Laplace (gsu.edu).

18 What does Bell's inequality mean, in layman's terms? – Quora.

19 Quantum Mechanics: What is an explanation of Bell's Theorem in plain language? – Quora

20 Is the limitation of such "knowledge in the real" not clearly discernible in the confusions caused by global warming? We often get high temperatures already in February, and then another cold wave takes place in late March or April. Nature (whose "knowledge" tells it that warm weather comes with Spring) "misreads" the hot February as the beginning of Spring and begins to come into flower, but the new cold wave then destroys the premature blooming and disturbs the entire reproductive cycle.

21 See his interview in So sieht Quantenphysiker Anton Zeilinger die Welt | Sternstunde Religion | SRF Kultur – YouTube.

22 Niels Bohr – It is wrong to think that the task of physics. . . (brainyquote. com).

23 Heisenberg's Physics and Philosophy (marxists.org).

24 Alenka Zupančič, *Let Them Rot. Antigone's Parallax*, New York: Fordham University Press 2023, p. 57.

25 Alenka Zupančič, op.cit., ibid.

26 Schrödinger equation – Wikipedia

27 I owe this idea to Sean Carroll who deployed it in a debate with me recorded on July 21 2023 on Robinson Erhard's Apple Podcast.

28 Furthermore, in many-worlds view, there is no interaction between different worlds, they exist without mutual contacts (in contrast to symbolic superpositions). Is this the ultimate fact or is it possible to think that the reality in which we live is somehow inherently linked to its superposed variants?

29 The situation vaguely recalls Spinoza's substance with an infinite number of attributes of which we (humans) know only two, extension and thought – we know absolutely nothing about other attributes, they play no role in our understanding of reality, we just have to presuppose them for purely logical reasons.

30 Letter to Max Born (1926), published in The Born-Einstein Letters, Walker and Company, New York 1971.

31 Remark made by Einstein during his visit to Princeton University, May 1921, quoted from Albert Einstein Quotes III (notable-quotes.com)

32 Quoted from Lorenzo Chiesa's contribution to *God Is Undead*.

33 See "Yad'lun!" with Jacques-Alain Miller (2011) – YouTube.

34 Brian Greene, *The Elegant Universe*, New York: Norton 1999, p. 116–19.

35 Lacan, Seminar XII, lesson of 3 February 1965 (quoted from File:Seminaire 12.pdf – No Subject – Encyclopedia of Psychoanalysis – Encyclopedia of Lacanian Psychoanalysis).

36 Quantum physicists now performed the first measurement of time reflection: they have managed to reverse time on a quantum level, and even to showcase how time reflections happen. We cannot but wait and see what will follow . . . See Physicists perform first measurement of 'time reflection' in microwaves – Physics World.

37 Jean-Pierre Dupuy, *The War That Must Not Occur*, Redwood City: Stanford University Press 2023 (quoted from the manuscript).

38 Being and Becoming in Modern Physics (Stanford Encyclopedia of Philosophy).

39 The illusion of time (nature.com).

40 See Carlo Rovelli, *Reality Is Not What It Seems* (all non-accredited numbers in brackets refer to the pages of this book).

41 See Hanns Eisler – Komponist (1898 – 1962) – Dokumentation 1992 – YouTube.

42 See Roberto Mangabeira Unger and Lee Smolin, *The Singular Universe and the Reality of Time: A Proposal in Natural Philosophy,* Cambridge: Cambridge University Press 2014.

43 Roberto Mangabeira Unger, *The Self Awakened,* Cambridge: Harvard University Press 2007, p. 57.

44 Castoriadis, Cornelius | Internet Encyclopedia of Philosophy (utm.edu).

45 Terrifying close-up of an ant's face gives horror movie monsters a run for their money (msn.com)

46 Lorenzo Chiesa and Adrian Johnston, *God Is Undead* (unpublished manuscript).

47 The "classic" is here Fritjof Capra's *The Tao of Physics: An Exploration of the Parallels Between Modern Physics and Eastern Mysticism* (1975). For a recent popular version, see Nobel Prize 2022 – Universe is not real | Where quantum physics meets Vedanta – YouTube, where the author claims that modern quantum physics demonstrates what already the ancient Vedanta knew: (1) the world is not real; (2) observer brings the world into existence.

48 See So sieht Quantenphysiker Anton Zeilinger die Welt | Sternstunde Religion | SRF Kultur – YouTube.

49 Byung-Chul Han, *Non-things*, Cambridge: Polity Press 2022.

50 See Sweet – Co-Co – Disco 11.09.1971 (OFFICIAL) – YouTube.

51 Grass Mud Horse – Wikipedia.

52 See Häagen-Dazs – Wikipedia.

Chapter 4

1 For a more systematic elaboration of the notion of parallax, see my *Parallax View*, Cambridge: MIT Press 2006.

2 See Alenka Zupančič, *Let Them Rot. Antigone's Parallax*, New York: Fordham University Press 2023. Numbers in brackets refer to the pages of this book.

3 My own translation.

4 Quoted from Immanuel Kant, "Perpetual Peace," available at http://www.mtholyoke.edu/acad/intrel/kant/kant1.htm.

5 Kant, op. cit.

6 See Robert B. Pippin, *Hollywood Westerns and American Myth*, New Haven: Yale University Press 2012.

7 Ernest Gellner, *Plough, Sword, and Book: The Structure of Human History*, Chicago: University of Chicago Press 1988, p. 239.

8 See Father Rupnik accused of psychological and physical violence. The silence of the Jesuits | Silere non possum, and in Slovene Rupnik se je pri "trojčku" skliceval na sveto trojico – OBALAplus.

9 For a closer analysis of this dimension, see Gary Hills, *Papal Sin*, New York: Doubleday 2000.

10 Jean-Pierre Dupuy, *The War That Must Not Occur*, Redwood City: Stanford University Press 2023 (quoted from the manuscript).

11 See Julian Assange loses latest attempt to appeal against extradition to the US | CNN.

12 Putin: Drone attack 'terrorist act' | Watch (msn.com).

13 Belarusian President Alexander Lukashenko offers nuclear weapons to nations willing 'to join the Union State of Russia and Belarus' | CNN.

14 Quoted from Hildegard Knef Sings 'Mackie Messer' in German (thoughtco.com).

15 See "World's Deadliest Wars Go Unreported": Journalist Anjan Sundaram | Democracy Now!.

16 Trump calls for the termination of the Constitution in Truth Social post | CNN Politics.

17 Incidentally, a group of Russian opponents of Putin now organized a military unit of volunteers to fights for Ukraine, and, with a wonderful irony, they called themselves Mozart Group – one can only hope they will bomb Russian army soldiers with chocolate-filled Mozart balls (*Mozart Kugeln*) . . .

18 Russia to scrap punishments for crimes in occupied Ukraine if 'in interest of Russian Federation' (msn.com).

19 Quoted from Temelj za mir mora biti, da bosta obe strani odšli domov – Delo.

20 Troubles aside, Xi says China on 'right side of history' – ABC News (go. com).

21 Quoted from Banning free speech in the name of inclusivity and diversity is the Fringe's sickest joke (msn.com).

22 ectolife: the world's first artificial womb facility (designboom.com).

23 Ibid.

24 Saddam Husseins final speech [Historical Speeches TV] – YouTube.

25 Jesus' earthly dad, St. Joseph – often overlooked – is honored by Father's Day in many Catholic nations (udayton.edu).

26 We should also mention the three versions of *Dead On Arrival* where the plot is as it were turned around: a guy appears at a police station to report a murder and, when asked who is the victim, answers: "Myself." He was poisoned and has 24 hours to discover his own murderer.

27 Shamelessly compressed from The Double (2011 film) – Wikipedia.

28 Understanding "The Man Who Was Thursday" by G. K. Chesterton. (everymancommentary.com).

29 Chesterton, G.K., "A Defense of Detective Stories," in H. Haycraft, ed., *The Art of the Mystery Story*, New York: The Universal Library 1946, p. 6.

30 See Rene Girard, *Sacrifice,* Ann Arbor: University of Michigan Press 2011.

31 As for the violent dark side of Buddhism, see Brian Victoria, *Zen War Stories*, London: Routledge 2003, as well as *Buddhist Warfare*, ed. by Michael Jerryson, Oxford: Oxford University Press 2010.

32 Tatiana Troyanos – Wikipedia.

33 I deal more in detail with this aspect of monstrosity in the Chapter I.2 of my *The Parallax View*, London: Verso Books 2006.

34 Dominick Hoens and Ed Pluth, "The *sinthome*: A New Way of Writing an Old Problem?", in Luke Thurston, editor, *Re-Inventing the Symptom*, New York: Other Press 2002, p. 8–9. I again resume here my argumentation from the Chapter I.2 of my *The Parallax View*.

35 I resume here a more detailed argumentation from my *On Belief* (London: Routledge 2001),

36 Why Shiv Did THAT In Succession's Series Finale (screenrant.com).

37 See Der Teufelstritt (The Devil's Footprint) – Munich, Germany – Atlas Obscura.

38 See Zhao Tingyang, *All under Heaven*, Los Angeles: University of California Press 2023.

39 Resumed from Zhao Tingyang on Democracy – Reading the China Dream.

40 Tianxia: All Under Heaven – NOEMA (noemamag.com).

41 Zhao Tingyang, op. cit., p. xiii/xiv.

42 Exclusive-Bill Gates in China to meet President Xi on Friday – sources (msn. com).

43 The New Tianxia System: Towards a World of Coexistence? (europeanguanxi.com).

44 Resumed from Zhao Tingyang on Democracy – Reading the China Dream.

45 Quoted from Zhao Tingyang on Democracy – Reading the China Dream.

46 See One Divides into Two – Wikipedia.

47 Zhao Tingyang, op. cit., p. xv.

Chapter 5

1 I follow here Boris Groys's reading of Soloviev: Wisdom as the Feminine World Principle: Vladimir Soloviev's Sophiology – Journal #124 February 2022 – e-flux.

2 Quoted from Russian Cosmism and Putin's spiritual eugenics – Philosophy for Life.

3 Op. cit.

4 Available on Russian Nuclear Eschatology: Pathologies on the Ruins of Modernity – The Philosophical Salon.

5 Quoted from Orlando Figes, *Natasha's Dance*, London: Allen Lane 2001, p. 447.

6 Te Paa Daniel to Baccalaureates: 'We offer ourselves as signs of God in the world' – Church Divinity School of the Pacific (cdsp.edu).

7 See Yuval Noah Harari, *Homo Deus. A Brief History of Tomorrow*, London: Harvill Secker 2016, p. 305. Numbers in brackets in this chapter refer to the pages of this book.

8 Israeli firm involved in 'destablising democracies and disrupting elections' operates in India: The New Indian Express.

9 New, Creepy Porn App Lets You Paste Anyone's Face on the Star's Body (newsweek.com)

10 A horrifying new AI app swaps women into porn videos with a click | MIT Technology Review.

11 Voice Cloning App | Make your Voice Sound like Anyone.

12 See 'I Want to Break Free' (Queen) Performed In North Korea – YouTube.

13 See North Korean Military Choir Did Not Perform Queen's 'I Want To Break Free', Viral Video Is Edited – Newschecker.

14 Alarmed by AI chatbots, universities start revamping how they teach | eKathimerini.com.

15 Microsoft is looking for ways to rein in Bing AI chatbot after troubling responses | CNN Business.

16 The stupidity of AI | Artificial intelligence (AI) | The Guardian.

17 Op. cit.

18 Eat Up: Take a Look at These Hilarious Restaurant Signs and Get Your Fill of Laughter – Herald Weekly.

19 Personal communication.

20 Quoted from http://www.hf.uio.no/ikos/english/research/projects/tls/publications/Kleist%5B1%5D.pdf.

21 ŽIŽEK, "Artificial Idiocy", March 23 2023 : CriticalTheory (reddit.com).

22 Quoted from #stitch with @themindhub #foryou #fyp #leftist #zizek #race #racism # #vb TikTok.

23 Let's ignore here the rare cases where, in a very specific context, not only the n word may be used by a non-black person without hurting any black person but, even more importantly, where NOT using this word but implying it subtly with expressions associated to it can be almost more hurtful. Plus, incidentally, it's the same with the expression "God help me!" – if, at that point, god were to appear and really intervene on my behalf, I would be totally shocked.

24 https://sci-highs.com/artificial-idiocy-responds-to-zizek/.

25 See http://www.robert-pfaller.com/20-years-of-interpassivity.

26 Rowan Williams, *Dostoyevsky*, London: Continuum 2008, p. 8.

27 I owe this idea to Manca Renko, Ljubljana.

28 ChatGPT: A New Unconscious? (sublationmag.com).

29 Tibetans Explain What 'Suck My Tongue' Means. It's Not What You Think. (vice.com).

30 Is romance dead? – In the future we'll outsource sex – Žižek.uk (zizek.uk).

31 See Robert Pfaller, *Zwei Enthüllungen über die Scham*, Frankfurt: Fischer Verlag 2022.

32 Essex-Westford School District is changing gender language within their health units (wcax.com).

33 See Yuval Noah Harari, op. cit.

34 AI makes non-invasive mind-reading possible by turning thoughts into text | Artificial intelligence (AI) | The Guardian.

35 In this last sub-chapter, I am just providing a condensed version of the more detailed argumentation from my *Hegel in a Wired Brain* (London: Bloomsbury Academics 2020).

36 Elon Musk And Tech Leaders Call For AI 'Pause' Over Risks To Humanity (forbes.com).

37 Bernie Sanders, Elon Musk and White House seeking my help, says 'godfather of AI' | Artificial intelligence (AI) | The Guardian.

38 Hegel against the machines – New Statesman.

39 Op. cit.

40 Nassim Nicholas Taleb, *Antifragile*, London: Penguin Books 2012.

41 One should also dismiss the view of China as a closed "totalitarian" country – among other things, we still have there a surprising moment of authentic democracy at the local level, especially in the countryside where villages are allowed to freely elect representatives which will advocate their interests at a higher level official body. Another crucial fact is that these primary level freely elected representatives are mostly women. Of course, from that level upwards, democracy ends, candidates for higher positions have to be vetted by the authorities.

42 See Is China a fascist state? | openDemocracy.

43 Can pornography be healthy? If it follows six rules, perhaps | Australian lifestyle | The Guardian.

Chapter 6

1 Rowan Williams, *Dostoyevsky*, London: Continuum 2008, p. 8.

2 Paraphrased from Brecht's Poem In Praise of Communism | MLToday.

3 Maximilien Robespierre, *Virtue and Terror*, London: Verso Books 2007, p. 129.

4 See Yanis Varoufakis, *Technofeudalism. What Killed Capitalism* (quotes from the manuscript).

5 See Yanis Varoufakis, *Another Now. Dispatches from an Alternative Present*, London: The Bodley Head 2020. Numbers in brackets refer to the pages of this book. In what follows I rely on Chapter 3 of my *Surplus-Enjoyment*, London: Bloomsbury 2022.

6 See Jean-Pierre Dupuy, *Avions-nous oublie le mal? Penser la politique après le 11 septembre*, Paris: Bayard 2002.

7 See John Rawls, *A Theory of Justice*, Cambridge (Ma): Harvard University Press 1971 (revised edition 1999).

8 See Friedrich Hayek, *The Road to Serfdom*, Chicago: University of Chicago Press 1994.

9 See Fredric Jameson et al., *American Utopia*, London: Verso Books 2016,

10 Jean-Pierre Dupuy, *The War That Must Not Occur*, Redwood City: Stanford University Press 2023 (quoted from the manuscript).

11 Louis Antoine de Saint-Just, "Rapport sur les factions de l'étranger," in *Œuvres complètes*, Paris: Gallimard 2004, p. 695.

12 Martin Heidegger, *Being and Truth*, Bloomington: Indiana University Press 2010, p. 73.

13 In his *Heidegger in Ruins*, New Haven: Yale University Press 2023.

14 Quoted from Ian Kershaw, *Hitler. 1936–45: Nemesis*, Harmondsworth: Penguin Books 2001, p. 604–5.

15 Heinrich Himmler's speech at Posen (alphahistory.com).

16 See Odilo Globocnik – Wikipedia.

17 See Parsley massacre – Wikipedia. The name for the massacre came from the shibboleth that Trujillo had his soldiers apply to determine whether or not those living on the border were native Afro-Dominicans or immigrant Afro-Haitians. Dominican soldiers would hold up a sprig of parsley to someone and ask what it was. How the person pronounced the Spanish word for parsley (*perejil*) determined their fate: if they could pronounce it the Spanish way the soldiers considered them Dominican and let them live, but if they pronounced it the French or Creole way they considered them Haitian and executed them.

18 Quoted from Bukharin: The Great Humanist Revolutionary – Mainstream Weekly.

19 "On Modes of Exchange: Interview with Kojin Karatani," *Crisis&Critique* Volume 10, issue 1 (2023).

20 Quoted from Sportpalast speech – Wikipedia.

21 One should note here the ultimate irony that occurs in the last one-hour radio-speech by Goebbels about the state of the war on February 28 1945 (see Goebbels Speech about the State of the War – 28 February 1945 – YouTube). While fully acknowledging the hopelessness of the situation, his main argument that Germany still has the chance to win is the comparison with the United Kingdom and Soviet Union earlier in the war: in 1940, England was also on the brink of capitulation, heavily bombed and standing alone in Europe, but it persisted and fought back; the same goes for the Soviet Union where, at the end of 1941, Leningrad was cut off and Moscow almost encircled, but they mobilized all their forces and pushed Germans back – so if the enemies could do it, why not Germany with a much stronger military spirit?

22 J. Arch Getty and Oleg V. Naumov, *The Road to Terror. Stalin and the Self-Destruction of the Bolsheviks, 1932–39*, New Haven and London: Yale University Press 1999, p. 300.

23 J. Arch Getty and Oleg V. Naumov, op. cit., p, 370.

24 Professor fired for showing art class image of Muhammad with his face visible (something not unusual in the history of Islamic art). Students and university go wild with crazy allegations of "Islamophobia" – Why Evolution Is True.

25 Cambridge don in trans row after boycotting gender-critical speaker (msn. com).

26 The Menu (2022 film) – Wikipedia.

27 See Transgender rapist Isla Bryson moved to men's prison – BBC News.

28 See Ernesto Laclau and Chantal Mouffe, *Hegemony and Socialist Strategy*, London: Verso Books 2001.

29 See Janet Afary and Kevil B. Anderson, *Foucault and the Iranian Revolution*, Chicago: Chicago University Press 2010.

30 Uganda MPs revive hardline anti-LGBTQ bill, calling homosexuality a 'cancer' | Global development | The Guardian.

31 Quoted from Zupančič, "Desire" (manuscript).

32 Resumed from The Mathematical Danger of Democratic Voting – YouTube.

33 Marx and Engels, *Collected Works*, vol. 47, Moscow: Progress Publishers 1995, p. 234.

34 Colin Jones, *The Fall of Robespierre*, Oxford: Oxford University Press 2021, p. 456.

35 Op. cit., p. 53.

36 Op. cit., p. 59.

37 https://www.wired.com/story/game-of-thrones-a-battle-of-reality-versus-fantasy/.

Conclusion

1 Theodor W. Adorno, *Minima Moralia: Reflections from Damaged Life*, London: Verso Books 2020.

2 Antonia Hofstätter, "J'Accuse," available online at J'accuse | Krisic | Journal for Contemporary Philosophy.

3 NHS faces crackdown on giving puberty blockers to children as Tavistock clinic is shut down (telegraph.co.uk). Appeal court overturns UK puberty blockers ruling for under-16s | Transgender | The Guardian

4 Refusing to fund a spouse or partner's gender transition could be domestic abuse, says CPS (msn.com).

5 Michel Foucault, *Confessions of the Flesh*, New York: Pantheon Books 2021, p. 42.

6 See Adrian Johnston's monumental *Infinite Greed* (manuscript).

7 Karl Marx, *Capital*, Volume I, New York: International Publishers 1967, p. 163.

8 Quoted from Marx, Das Kapital Buch 1 (1890) | Online Library of Liberty (libertyfund.org).

9 See Kojin Karatani's *Transcritique. On Kant and Marx*, Cambridge (Ma): MIT Press 2003.

10 Karl Marx, "A Contribution to the Critique of Hegel's Philosophy of Law: Introduction," in *Collected Works*, Vol. 3, New York: International Publishers 1970, p. 175.

11 See Cock and Ball Crushers – Lovegasm.

12 Op. cit.

13 Mladen Dolar quoted from: Freud, Slovenia, and the Origins of Right-Wing Populism – Notes – e-flux.

14 Quoted from Paul Roazen, *Edoardo Weiss: The House that Freud Built*, New York: Routledge 2005, p. 98.

15 Quoted from EN(d)JOY! The Super-Ego & Its Relation to Enjoyment (dbs. ie).

16 I developed the logic of the superego much more in detail in Chapter III of my *Surplus-Enjoyment*, London: Bloomsbury Press 2022.

17 Jacques Lacan, *Ethics of Psychoanalysis*, New York: Norton 1997, p. 310.

18 I developed these distinctions in my *How to Read Lacan*, London: Granta 2006.

19 *The Complete Letters of Sigmund Freud to Wilhelm Fliess 1887–1904*, Cambridge (Ma): Belknap Press 1985), p. 309.

20 Op. cit.

21 See Dolar, op. cit.

22 Manipur violence: What is happening and why – BBC News.

23 Jamil Khader, Huwwara and Stella Maris: The Truth about Judicial Overhaul, Israeli Protests – Palestine Chronicle.

24 Jamil Khader, op. cit.

25 Degeneracy | Article about Degeneracy by The Free Dictionary.

26 The world's first braiding of non-Abelian anyons – Google Research Blog (googleblog.com).

27 https://www.ft.com/content/4efba087-3fea-4caf-810c-b3cc4fead0.

28 Ukraine to fire all regional military recruitment chiefs – Zelenskiy (msn.com).

29 'Fighting two enemies': Ukraine's female soldiers decry harassment | Ukraine | The Guardian.

30 Quoted from Paris police prep for 'war' against 'hordes' of rioters as cops with shields line streets (msn.com).

31 Vigilantes in Haiti strike back at gangsters with brutal street justice | AP News.

32 Private Russian military companies are multiplying – and so are the Kremlin's problems (msn.com).

33 Evgeny Morozov, Critique of Techno Feudal Reason, NLR 133 134, January April 2022.pdf, p. 97.

34 A monument to French rage: buses torched in riots over police killing | France | The Guardian.

35 Prigozhin says he turned march on Moscow around to avoid Russian bloodshed | CNN.

36 A decade ago, I was accused by an ex-Trotskyte of being a "Left fascist" (see Alan Johnson, "Is Slavoj Zizek a Left-Fascist?", *The Telegraph*, January 1 2013). Now I can set the record straight: no, I am a Rightist Communist.

37 Quoted from https://www.versobooks.com/blogs/3577-the-rise-of-the-leninist-right.

38 This Is The Protest Song Of Our Generation – YouTube.

39 Oliver Anthony – Rich Men North Of Richmond Lyrics | AZLyrics.com.

40 Quoted in Ben Stein, "In class warfare, guess which class is winning," *New York Times*, November 26 2006.

41 I've dealt with this notion in detail in my *Less Than Nothing*, London: Verso Books 2013.

42 The Twelve (poem) – Wikipedia.

43 Alexander Blok. Twelve. Translated by Maria Carlson (ruverses.com).

44 Alexander Blok. The Twelve. Translated by Jon Stallworthy and Peter France (ruverses.com).

45 Black night, white snow: Alexander Blok's The Twelve (culturematters.org.uk).

INDEX